ONCE UPON A
TIME
IN
LIVERPOOL

Jim Elliott

Published by: MiddleView

an imprint of
Avid Publications, Garth Boulevard,
Bebington, Wirral, Merseyside.
CH63 SLS.
Tel / Fax (44) 0151 645 2047
e-mail: info@Middleview.co.uk.
www. AvidPublications.co.uk

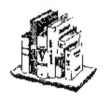

© James Elliott 2006.
Edited by William David Roberts MA
Typsetting © Middleview / Avid Publications

ISBN 1 902964 0 6 3

Other books and DVDs / Videos from MiddleView and AVID are detailed
at the rear of this book.

These can be obtained direct from AVID on:
Tel / Fax (44) 0151 645 2047
or e-mail to : info@Middleview.co.uk

My Mother and Hughie

In memory of my dear son
Jonathan James
who died tragically aged 29 years on
the 29th November 2001.

This story is dedicated to all the
people I ever knew, past and present.

'It's Liverpool Jim! Just as I knew it'

Billy Butler - BBC Radio Merseyside

THE AUTHOR

Jim Elliott was born in the Scotland Road area of Liverpool.

He worked for the NCR company for many years before setting up his own business equipment company, E.C.R Ltd, with offices in Liverpool and Manchester, selling cash registers and employing 12 staff.

He has also owned two betting shops in his chequered life, served as a local counciller as well as sitting on various boards of Govenors.

He is currently enjoying his retirement and happilly married to his wife June, living in the Maghull area of the city of his birth.

Chapter 1

The year was 1943. I was seven years old and it was late at night. The siren warned us of another air raid. A loud hailer was informing everybody to go to the shelter right away. My Mam collected me and our Alec from our bed carrying Mary, our baby sister, in her arms. Once outside our house we were ushered to the nearest Anderson air raid shelter, one of the huge concrete bunkers situated in every street. Inside the shelter people were crowded together sitting on long wooden benches. Normally the women would knit or tend to the young children but this evening the bombing seemed particularly bad, then the lights went out. In the total darkness, children started to cry and Mothers could be heard trying to comfort them.

After what seemed hours, an eerie silence descended over the shelter. The bombing had stopped but it was still pitch black. Suddenly the doors were thrown open, torches appeared and there were voices. We were ushered outside. Fires were raging everywhere. We were taken to the "Conny Onny" rooms (Conservative assembly rooms) in Netherfield Road and given blankets and tea. The next day we were told our house in Arkwright Street had been completely destroyed.

My recollections of the war include seeing huge barrage balloons suspended over Liverpool as far as the eye could see, of gas masks and how everything seemed to taste of soot, of listening to the sirens warning us of another air raid. And the time when my Mam took us children to Jerome's the photographer's in London Road, to have our portrait taken for our Dad in the Army. I remember the Home Guard climbing over walls in training, in preparation for an invasion, and standing on the steps of my friend Bobby Howard's house, watching an aerial dog fight taking place in the sky, before our anxious mothers took us indoors. I remember Bobby's father coming home from sea and tasting peanut butter, bananas and tangerines for the first time. When the sirens sounded we were sometimes taken to the air raid shelter just outside our house, but more often than not the whole family hid beneath the stairs, and to a boy of seven it seemed to be one huge game. When the all clear sounded, people swarmed back onto the streets for news and to see what damage had been caused by the bombs and gangs of youngsters would roam the streets in search of shrapnel. I've often wondered since how we managed to survive those raids. None of our immediate friends was evacuated, although whole streets between

Netherfield Road and Great Homer Street were flattened by the bombing. Nearly 4000 people were killed on Merseyside in the blitz, and a memorial stone in Anfield cemetery commemorates the fact. There are also plaques in Bootle and the Jewish cemetery in Stalmine Road, Walton.

One day my Mam collected me from Penrhyn Street School and soon after we arrived home, there was a knock on the door, and a stranger was invited in.

This was the first time I met Hughie Smith. My Mam was still married to my Dad at the time.

Being the eldest child I can still recall the confusion of having another man in the house and being told, "This is Hughie - a friend of your Ma's." I never did find out exactly where they met. Both my Dad and Hughie were serving in the Army, my Dad being overseas.

We now lived in Robsart Street, Everton, off Netherfield Road, a predominantly Protestant area - and Hughie, I later discovered, was a Catholic from the "Bull Ring". Hughie eventually married my Mam and they had two more children. It was natural that at first I should resent Hughie's presence in our house and I must admit I was a very difficult child but I can honestly say that Hughie never raised his hand to me in all his life, and as I grew older I came to respect him, although at times I thought I hated him.

After the war ended my Dad also remarried and moved to the south end of Liverpool. While the war was on, I never really got to know my Dad and it wasn't until many years later, when I had completed my own Army service, that I really got to know him well and we became more like good friends than father and son. I used to meet him and his wife in Yate's Wine Lodge in town each Saturday evening for a few "whites". Lunatic soup as it was known. Occasionally we would go for a Chinese meal before I went off with my friends to one of the many clubs in town.

My friends all liked my Dad and always addressed him as Mr Elliott. Prior to this of course, I was only a youngster when my parents separated and in those days "Divorce" wasn't as acceptable as it is today. To overcome my embarrassment, I used to say to all my friends, "I'm luckier than you, because I have two Ma's and two Da's" but deep down I felt very vulnerable and I know Alec did too. It also made my brother and me very independent and protective of our family, and at times quite stupidly stubborn, refusing to accept charity from anyone.

I recall an occasion when I visited a friend's aunt and she offered us tea and biscuits. I said "No thank you," and sat there whilst everybody else ate, all the time wanting to eat also, but my pride wouldn't allow me. The poor lady of the house kept saying, "Are you quite sure you won't have some?" Returning home with my friend, I had to pretend that I had already eaten before I left home.

Times were very hard and people did not have much money but everybody seemed to have an immense pride in themselves. My mother worked extremely hard, like most other mothers in similar circumstances. She used to leave our house very early in the morning, having been woken up by the "Knocker upper".

(For those who do not know what a "Knocker upper" was, it was an elderly person, usually retired, who carried a large pole and for a small fee, knocked at bedroom windows at specific times to wake people for work.)

All the houses in our neighbourhood were Victorian back - to - back, one storey high and the back doors faced the back doors of the next street with an entry separating them. The houses consisted of two rooms downstairs and two rooms upstairs, with five or six stone steps leading to the front door, which was almost never locked.

If the door was locked, the key could be found hanging from a piece of string inside the letter box. Entering, you would travel along the "lobby" to the first room which was the "parlour", the best room in the house, and never used, no matter how overcrowded the house might be. We had no carpets, the floors of the lobby, kitchen and parlour being covered in oilcloth. Elsewhere was bare wood.

The parlour held our finest possessions and was intended for visitors, or the doctor when we were sick. (Ma would have arranged a bed on the settee).

Along the "lobby" past the stairs lay the kitchen. This was the main room, what today would be called the living room, and every activity took place there, eating, bathing, washing and ironing. The kitchen had an open fire, from which the bricks were taken each evening and wrapped in cloth to warm the beds. We also had an oven from which the hot plate would be removed to warm the bed. On the hob stood a large kettle for continual hot water. (One of the weekly tasks for the girls, was to black lead the hearth and to scrub the steps with a piece of sandstone obtained from the "olla.") (waste ground)

Inside the kettle was an "olly", which prevented the sediment in the water sticking to the kettle. Unknown to our Mam, we often borrowed the "olly" to play marbles with other children in the street.

In the centre of the kitchen was a table and four wooden chairs, and a sofa against the wall facing the window, which overlooked the back yard.There was also a sideboard with a picture of my Mam's mother hanging above it. Suspended from the ceiling above the fireplace hung the clothes maiden, and on the wall was our only means of illumination, a single gas light. One of my jobs was to run to Jack Brown's shop to buy the mantle, that enabled the gas light to work.

Our one cold water tap, was in a small cubicle leading off from the kitchen. From here a flight of stone steps led down to the back yard and our outside toilet.

Because of the war, everything was in short supply. Each family was issued with a ration book which allowed you to purchase particular items of food, such as cheese, bacon and eggs depending on the size of your family. When that was gone you had to do without. Sweets were practically unheard of. I recall our staple diet at that time was porridge, bread pudding, fish and chips and blind scouse, a stew with no meat.

Our one item of luxury was the wireless, and provided the accumulator was charged, we were able to listen to all the current programmes every evening, whilst our Mam knitted clothes. One of the younger children would help my Mam, by having the wool wrapped around their outstretched arms, while she wound it into a ball.

Sometimes the cellars beneath the houses were occupied by families, but not in our case. We had two bedrooms, one for our parents and the other for us three children. Later there would be two editions to the family, so it was boys in one bed and girls in the other. Old overcoats and patchwork quilts our Mam had made kept us warm.

However, we were much better off than some families in our street who lived in the court's. Can you imagine 60 people crowded together in a court with only three communal taps and toilets outside in the centre of the "court"?

It seemed all the women did extra work to feed their families. In the early hours of the morning, dozens of them could be heard leaving their homes, their heels clicking along the empty pavements as they hurried off to clean city offices or to the better-off people in the suburbs. Just a few women remained at home and took in washing and ironing.

Our Mam had to walk about two miles to Soho street to clean Caplans the tobacconist's, before returning home to take us to school and the nursery. (Mr Caplan later became Lord Mayor of Liverpool.)

IN LIVERPOOL

Often on her way home from work, Mam would buy off- cuts of chamois leather from a factory in Islington, and in the evenings she would stitch them together into larger pieces on her Singer sewing machine. (This machine is still used by my sister Mary, who inherited it on our Mother's death.)

When my Mam had sewn enough leathers, she would place them in a large basket, and take me or Alec with her by tramcar to Childwall or Woolton, where she sold them door to door. The brother who was left at home had to take care of our younger sister Mary and this happened throughout our formative years.

I imagine we must have looked like a couple of gypsies, but no doubt this helped to sell the "chammy" leathers. We didn't worry what people thought because nobody knew us in that area. It was quite a thrill on returning home, to watch our Mam counting pennies in rows on the kitchen table, to see how much money we had taken. I cannot recall seeing anybody begging in those days but people did all kinds of odd jobs to make ends meet.

Towards the end of the war, I recall my uncle Alec calling to our house. He was on leave from the Army. To me he was a huge man and like my father was a sergeant in the Kings Regiment. He brought me a present of a model aeroplane with the roundels of the Royal Air Force on its wings and suspended it from the ceiling for me.

Apparently my Dad had been wounded. Unable to come to our house, he was on leave convalescing at the Great Western Hotel in Lime Street, facing St George's Hall.

(This beautiful building, unfortunately, lay empty for many years, until John Moores university re-opened it in 1997 for student accommodation.)

My uncle took me to see my Dad. The Hotel was then occupied by the Army and my Dad soon appeared, dressed in the blue uniform, white shirt and red tie of the wounded.

Our meeting was strained to say the least. I hardly knew my Dad and was frightened he might start asking me about Hughie.

After spending some time with my Dad, I was taken back home to my Mum, carrying a stuffed squirrel in a glass case which my father had given me. I later exchanged this for some American comics. This was the last time I ever saw my uncle Alec. He never married and spent most of his life in the Army. Followed by work for the M.O.D. Many years later, my Dad told me he visited Uncle Alec in South Wales, when he lay dying in hospital. My Dad's other brother Uncle Andrew moved to Blackpool for his health immediately after the war with his family, and my wife and I, with my father and his wife

Eileen, visited them there many years later.

Occasionally my grandfather on my mother's side would visit our house and have a meal with us. (My grandmother had died giving birth to my mother). My Mam and her elder sister Margaret had been raised by their Aunt Ginny. My other grandparents on my fathers side were dead and we children never knew them. My mother often spoke with affection of her Aunt Ginny who was a spinster but took on the role of mother to the two girls to prevent them going into care.

My grandad always seemed to be telling us children off, and I remember one occasion very well, when he chased me up the bedroom stairs swinging his belt because of something I had failed to do. My Mam told me Grandad was a strict disciplinarian and both daughters were terrified of him. On my mother's wedding day he refused to allow her into the local pub with my father for a celebration drink. She was aged nineteen at the time.

I discovered many years later that Grandad had died in the Unique Men's Hostel at 45 Shaw Street, Liverpool, in 1944. His body was taken to my Aunt Margaret's house in Back Prince Edwin Street, prior to burial. As a mark of respect, both sisters sat in the room where grandad lay. My mother was very nervous and told me later that the coffin sometimes squeaked, on hearing this, they would both run from the room. My aunt would plead with my mother to stay with her, by offering her some cigarettes. My grandfather was finally buried in a "pauper's" unmarked communal grave at Anfield cemetery.

I also discovered he had served with the King's Regiment in India, and had contracted malaria out there. Such a sad way to die after having served your King and country.

Just before the war ended, when I was nine, I distinctly remember my Mam calling my name in the early hours of the morning. She was obviously in great pain and told me to fetch the midwife from an address at the bottom of Arkwright Street where the houses hadn't been bombed. I dressed hurriedly and in the darkness ran through the entry connecting the streets. It took me nearly fifteen minutes.

I knocked hard on the door crying, "Me Ma's sick and she needs help". After a few moments the midwife appeared, and was soon able to determine where I lived. She left ahead of me on her bicycle. I followed running quickly behind her.

Back home I found my Mam lying on the settee in the kitchen, crying. There was blood everywhere, and the midwife announced that I now had a new baby sister! I was then sent back to bed with my brother and sister.

The following day my Aunt Margaret was in attendance, getting us ready for school and cooking our meals. She told me my Mam had been taken to hospital by ambulance and that Mrs Howard who lived nearby had gone with her.

I never did see my baby sister, who sadly lived for only a short time. My Mam discussed this with us all much later and told us she had been christened Patricia.

Soon after that event, Alec and Mary were asleep on the settee in the kitchen, when my Dad appeared at the front door in his Army uniform and extremely drunk. He insisted on coming into the house. My Mam allowed him in to prevent a scene "at the front door". He staggered along the lobby into the kitchen, a wad of money protruding from his top pocket.

She made him a meal and he sat at the table, all the time talking about Hughie Smith. Soon he fell asleep without tasting the food, his head bent forward on the plate slobbering. My Mam and I smiled at each other and were tempted to help ourselves to his money but we were too frightened he would discover it missing.

He then awoke some time afterwards and became very abusive, picking up his plate of food and smashing it against a mirror on the wall above the settee, scattering the contents and broken glass over Alec and Mary who by this time had woken up. They started to cry. He grabbed hold of my mother and shouting insults began to strike her about the head. She began screaming for help. I tried to separate them but to no avail. Mam shouted "Jimmy fetch auntie Maggie". I ran from the house and through the jigger (entry) to aunt Margaret's house, a few streets away.

Returning home quickly with auntie Margaret, we discovered my Dad had left the house and my Mam was in the process of attending to the children, and cleaning broken pieces of glass from the settee. Auntie Margaret comforted my Mam who was sobbing.

The next day Mam packed a few items of clothing in a bag and took us children to stay with her aunt Peggy and uncle Billy who lived in the south end of Liverpool. Whilst we children stayed with her relatives, she spent the next few days visiting various people in town returning later in the day. I was delighted to find they had chickens in the back yard and spent most of my time there attending to them. Apparently my Mam was making arrangements with court officials, to prevent my Dad visiting our house again.

Soon afterwards we returned home to Robsart Street. Alec and Mary had by this time become ill, contracting pneumonia brought on by shock, I was told. They were taken to Myrtle Street childrens hospital, were they had adjoining beds. Mary was discharged first and had to be "sneaked" out of hospital to prevent Alec seeing her, he was kept in a little longer with suspected meningitis. Fortunately he also recovered and soon came home.

Another time I remember well, when climbing on the back walls of houses, with other boys my age. We used to run along the top of the walls of the entry to each other's houses. On this occasion I had stood on a loose brick and fallen with a loud crash, masonry and all into somebody's backyard. I tried to stand up but was unable to, a sharp pain ran up my leg, I looked at my leg, it was all misshapen. (I found out later I had broken my leg). Crying with pain, I shouted to my friends, "fetch me Mam".

I cannot recall much after that. I was taken to the Liverpool Royal Infirmary, and after being examined by a doctor, my leg was put in plaster. How I arrived at the hospital, or how I got home later, I cannot remember but I do remember some weeks later, my Mam carrying me to the tram stop at the top of our street, to take me back to hospital to have the plaster removed.

I then spent a period of time at a convalescent hospital in Frodsham, a small town in Cheshire, which seemed like a million miles from Liverpool, and yet my Mam came to visit me quite regularly. Goodness knows how long it took her to arrive there and return back home. Even today, it would take you the best part of an hour to drive there by car.

At that time she would have had to travel by tram to the Pier Head, then take a ferry boat to Birkenhead, then a bus to Chester, from where she would have had to change once again to go to Frodsham. She was only a tiny woman and extremely pretty with long black hair and immense inner strength.

On another occasion I distinctly remember. I had been reading in bed by candle light, (I have always been an avid reader). This time I had apparently fallen asleep.

The next thing I recall, was being woken up by the sound of my dog Rex barking. He always slept at the side of my bed. There was smoke everywhere and a strong smell of burning. The lighted candle had completely melted the wax and the flame had started a fire which was burning the curtains and woodwork next to the window. I jumped out of bed shouting for my Mam, who was downstairs in the kitchen, to come quickly. Hearing my call for help she hurried up the stairs to our bedroom, and seeing the dense smoke, instructed me to go next door to fetch Mr Guy, our next door neighbour, while she ushered my sleepy eyed brother and sister from their beds.

The last thing I witnessed before running next door, was my Mam throwing the "po" contents over the flames. This utensil was kept under the bed for us children to use when we needed to go to the toilet. Without this, it would mean having to use the toilet in the backyard, and in winter time it would invariably be freezing cold. Mr Guy soon came to our rescue and put out the fire. Afterwards my Mam said, "Rex probably saved our lives".

After the war ended I remember all the street parties that took place, the decorations and bunting in everyone's windows, the banners hanging from washing lines hung across the street, welcoming home all the men who had been away to fight in the war. The pubs were packed to overflowing. Everybody appeared to be so happy, dressed in their Sunday best. Children wore paper hats made from newspaper and waved union jack flags. There was lots of dancing in the streets, complete strangers would hold hands to dance the hokey cokey. We children seemed to have been forgotten, nobody told us to go to bed. They were good times.

Up to this period, there was an absence of men in our life. Our "real" dad was prevented from coming to the house, and Hughie was seen only very occasionally.

Alas, what should have been a happy period for our family at that time, sadly was not. Our Mam was once again expecting a baby, and the neighbours in our immediate vicinity all knew of my parents marital difficulties.

On this particular occasion I was accompanying my Mother on a message along Sanderson Street, when we approached a number of women approximately my mam's age, sitting on the front steps of a house "janglin" (talking together). Suddenly as we drew near, one of the women leapt to her feet and stood directly in front of us, preventing us from passing, and with her hands on her hips started to accuse my Mam of adultery.

We stood still unable to pass. My Mam made no reply but looked obviously upset. The next thing I knew, two more women jumped up from where they were sitting and like a pack of wolves attacking their prey, pounced on my mam. Taking hold of her hair, they pulled her to the ground, and screaming insults, struck her about the body with their fists. My Mam fought back bravely but it was no use, she being heavily pregnant and too many of them. I stood there for a moment helpless, then tried to pull the women away from her, at the same time crying, "leave me Mam alone". The fighting soon stopped and my mam struggled to her feet. Taking me by my hand we hurried home. The shouted insults following us.

Reaching home my Mam wearily sat in a chair completely exhausted and leaning her head in her arms, began to cry. I was so confused. I said "don't cry Mam I'll get you a drink " I then went to the tap and returned with a cup of water. Standing by her side stroking her hair with one hand, and a cup of water in the other, I vowed to myself that I would never forgive the women for what they had done to her, and at that moment I really hated them.

Because of my age, I did not know at the time, that an altercation of this kind, could quite easily have made my Mother miscarry, but she was really tough, and a few weeks later, there was an addition to the family. Our sister Margaret was born. Another mouth to feed.

Ironically, one of the women who had attacked my Mam that day, later gave birth to a child out of wedlock. The father was an American serviceman, but not before I, unknown to anybody else had broken her windows with my catapult.

How times have changed. Much later when I was older and found myself in the presence of these women. I could not help thinking of the time, when they assaulted my Mother.

Throughout the divorce proceedings and for a long time afterwards, our family was often visited by the welfare department of Liverpool City Council. I think it was a council official who arranged for us children to get "free" meals at school. Our Mam was always very nervous of officials, and would hide anything of value from them. For example, the sewing machine. She would instruct us to help clean the house, "cause the man from the sheltered homes was comin". She was frightened, that the authorities would take us children into care, if they thought we where not being looked after properly.

Hughie had now been demobbed from the Army and had returned to live with us. He had got a job with the City Council, 'emptying bins. (These were huge metal containers which fitted into a recess of each persons back yard, and had to be carried up the narrow entry to the refuse vehicle to be emptied) To prevent any embarrassment, it was decided that Hughie would use the rear door of our house, until the neighbour's got used to him living here.

He took on the mantel of 'fatherhood' very seriously and seemed to be very proud of his new family, taking us everywhere with him.

I remember him taking us all to town soon after the war, to see the crashed German bombers and anti aircraft guns on display at St George's Plateau. It was so exciting for us youngsters to climb over them and imagine the planes once again flying over Liverpool and being shot down.

I also remember, the many times we visited the Shakespeare theatre in Fraser Street, to see the shows. Hughie would have a whispered conversation with the man on the door, and the next thing we knew we would be ushered up to the 'Gods', the highest part of the circle, without paying.

Once safely inside the theatre, 'cocoa powder' in paper bags or 'toffee apples' would mysteriously appear. The toffee apples had a stick protruding from them, and had been dipped in a sweet tasting substance and left to go hard.

One of the shows we most enjoyed seeing was "The Army game", a comedy, with an all male cast, some of the cast dressed as women, although we children could not tell the difference at the time.

Unfortunately this lovely theatre is no longer there, one day it caught fire and burnt to the ground.

Returning home one time from one of our nights out at the "Shakey". I became very embarrassed. Hughie had taken us to Lyon's cafe in Lime Street, and sat us down at a table. He then waited his turn in the queue carrying two trays, one on top of the other. Hughie filled the tray with various items of food, and called to me Mam. "Mary, take hold of the tray". He then passed the tray to her over the handrail. My Mam innocently took hold of the tray and distributed the food amongst us and we began to eat. He then continued in the queue filling the second tray with cups of tea and soft drinks for us children. Returning to the table he smiled at my Mam and said. "I only paid for the drinks". Hearing this, my Mam became very flustered and nearly fell from her chair with fright. Telling us to finish our meal as quickly as possible, we hurried from the cafe, expecting at any moment to be approached by the manager.

Chapter Two

Very often on the way home from the "Shakey". Hughie would call at "Sampson and Barlow's" the chicken house, in London Road, to buy a bag of chicken wings, or maybe a fish and chip shop to purchase what seemed to me huge amounts of food, then we would return home and feast like kings before retiring to bed. Our visit to the "shakey" was one of the highlights of the week for us children.

Our first Christmas together was great fun. For weeks leading up to Christmas, our Mam when shopping at Paddy's market in Great Homer Street, would buy extra items of food and toys to put in our stockings.

She then hid them on the top shelf of the cupboard in the parlour. Unknown to her I knew of this and when she was out, I would climb up to the shelf to see what she had bought. It was like Alladin's cave to me, seeing packets of biscuits, Christmas cake and odd tins of fruit.

Meanwhile our Dad had purchased a three wheel bicycle for Alec and a most peculiar doll for Mary, which had two heads, one black and one white, and by turning the doll upside down, the dress fell over one head to reveal the other. There was also a rocking duck not unlike a rocking horse but not as large, a pair of boxing gloves, some lead soldiers and an assortment of games .

He had sent these gifts to our house via a mutual friend. Since the break up of the marriage, there had been more fighting and rows with my Mother. (He was prevented from coming to the house himself, because of a court order forbidding him.)

Occasionally when playing out, I would see my Dad standing at the top of the street waiting for me, sometimes I would be informed by a friend knocking at the door. " Yer dad wants yer". When this happened I would run up to Netherfield Road to meet him, and be given money to share with my brother and sister. I was still very nervous in his presence.

A few days before Christmas, Hughie and my Mam went dancing to the Grafton Ballroom. I was left in charge of the children, and anxiously waiting for them to return home, bringing with them the usual packets of crisps, and fish and chips. But this time they also had with them a huge Christmas tree. Goodness knows where they got it from at that late hour, but after eating our food we spent the next hour decorating it.

Christmas Eve, we youngsters were all very excited anticipating what presents we might receive?.

Hughie was saying. "Father Christmas would be coming that evening if we were good"! (My Mam would wink at me and I would smile back knowingly).

After washing our hands and face in the warm water prepared for us and brushing our teeth with salt and water, (toothpaste was unknown to us) we went to bed.

I hardly slept that night. I listened to every noise, trying to guess what was happening in the kitchen downstairs.

Finally the morning arrived and we children raced down stairs to see what presents had been provided for us. Finding a carton with my name on, I opened it. I had oranges, tangerines, sweets and nuts, yes, the boxing gloves were for me.

After carefully inspecting each others gifts, we took our presents upstairs to show them to Hughie and our Mam, they were still in bed. Torn paper lay abandoned everywhere.

Climbing on the bed, I asked my Mam to tie the laces on my boxing gloves and began to spar with her. She was laughing. Suddenly without warning, I swung out with my fist and struck her hard on the nose, her head jerked back hitting the headboard with a loud bang. Her nose began to bleed. Blood running down her face onto her night dress.

Seeing the blood, Hughie hurried downstairs to fetch a wet flannel. Realising what I had done, I put my arm around her shoulder and said. "I'm sorry Ma", all notions of sparring now gone from my mind. Holding her head back to stop the flow of blood. she replied. "It's okay, it was an accident", moments later we all ended up laughing about it. That's how I remember our first Christmas together.

Sometime after that period, (although he was strictly forbidden to do so), my Dad visited the house. As usual when he came to the house he was drunk, it was late at night and Hughie was home. My Dad without any warning, ran into the house and attacked Hughie who was relaxing in a chair. After a short scuffle Hughie managed to flee out of the back door. That night, he stayed at his mothers house. It was very upsetting for us children to witness all this. (I believe my Dad served a month in Walton prison because of this).

One day Hughie came home with some day old chicks, I was thrilled to bits. I immediately took charge of them and kept them in a large cardboard box near the fire. A few days later, one of the chicks was accidentally stood on in the dark and killed. I was heartbroken. I cried that night, but was assured another one would be bought to replace it.

Sure enough the next day Hughie returned home with more chicks. We now had six all together.

Soon they grew so big we could no longer keep them in the house. Hughie built a pen for them in the back yard, and each day we children would feed them scraps from the table. One day Mary was feeding the chickens when my Mam happened to look out of the rear window.

She screamed out loud, and ran to the back door, Mary had been feeding a huge rat thinking it was a cat.

One day arriving home from school, I discovered one of the chickens had disappeared. They were quite large now and the cockerel sometimes chased you. He was the one that was missing. I climbed on the back wall and running along the top, began looking in neighbours yards thinking he might have strayed there. After about twenty minutes I couldn't find him, so I returned home.

Dinner was served later that evening and to my dismay it was chicken. My Mam then told me, that Hughie had killed the cockerel. "That's why people keep chickens" she explained. I ran to the bin and looked at all the feathers laying inside. Once again I was heartbroken. I refused to eat my dinner, and for some time afterwards, I would not speak to Hughie.

There was another time, when I refused to speak to him. One evening my Mam had just finished washing my hair. She remarked. "Your hair is getting long, you'll have to go to the barbers". Hughie, hearing this said. "I'll cut his hair later, before he goes to bed!". Consequently I was sat in a chair. A towel placed around my shoulders was tucked into the top of my shirt.

Hughie then placed a large tin basin on my head. I protested, but he insisted "that's how you cut a straight line". I was facing the wall unable to see what was happening behind my back. Hughie then proceeded to cut my hair with the scissors.

After what seemed ages sitting with the basin on my head, Hughie removed it and instructed my Mam to "fetch me razor and brush, so I can to finish the job". Bending my head forward he lathered the back of my neck and above my ears with soap, before carefully shaving me. Finally my neck was dried, my hair dampened and combed, and the towel removed from my shirt.

I was asked to "stand up and turn round for everyone to see". I stood up and turned round to face everyone, I looked at my mother enquiringly to see what response there was, she smiled back reassuringly. Suddenly the remainder of the family burst out laughing. I said "what's wrong"? and asked for a mirror. A mirror was produced from off the wall in the back kitchen, and when I looked at my reflection, I burst out crying. I looked like one of the Three Stooges, (comic characters seen at the cinema).

Eventually I calmed down enough for my mother to finish cutting my hair, but for many days, I would not speak to Hughie.

A great change now occurred in our lives. For weeks Manweb had been digging up the road and laying cables for electricity to peoples houses, people spoke of nothing less, now it was our turn. At the flick of a switch you had immediate light.

For me it meant no more looking for things in the dark with lighted paper, or running to Jack Browns shop for gas mantles.

I think it was soon after we got electricity, that I brought a cat home with me. It was raining heavily. I was running through the entry on my way home from school, when I saw in front of me a heavily pregnant cat. It was soaking wet and crying. I stopped and picked it up and stroked it's back gently.

The cat purred it's delight and seemed to thank me by cuddling closer. The rain was still pouring down. I put the cat under my coat and holding it firmly against the warmth of my body, hurried home with my new found friend.

Arriving home, my Mam tried to persuade me to take the cat back to where I had found it, by saying. "The cat probably lives where I had picked it up, and it wasn't lost at all". I would not listen and begged her to keep the cat, until finally she agreed. A short time after the cat gave birth to a litter of kittens on my trousers. The evening before I had undressed in front of the fire, and as usual I had placed my trousers on the settee before going to bed that night.

When the kitten's were old enough to feed themselves, they were given away to our neighbours .

Quite often, we children would be invited to a party at Lee Jones's,(The League of Welldoers) which was over the bridge in Scotland Road.

(There was no bridge in Scotland Road! this was an expression which separated the Catholic community from the Protestant community.)

The League of Welldoers is a benevolent society which took an interest in the welfare of the children of the area, and was renowned for its hospitality, and the cocoa and rock cakes which they served to you. Many years before they provided soup kitchens and clothing for the poor and unemployed. The premises are situated in Limekiln Lane, on the opposite side of Scotland

Road to where we lived.

(Whilst in the neighbourhood quite recently, I stopped my car to look at the building once again. I then spoke to a man approximately my own age who happened to be passing at the time. I mentioned to him "the wonderful times me and my family had spent there many years ago", we chatted together for a few more minutes exchanging stories.

Suddenly his facial expression changed and lowering his voice, he informed me that "the area had now gone down the nick".

"Look at the facilities the kids have now", indicating the floodlight football pitch with a sweep of his arm, You can't win. They (meaning today's children) are too selfish. Did you know, he continued, one kid fell over on the football pitch the other day and scraped his knee.

I believe he's suing the club for damages, and if your parking your car round here, be careful he warned, or else you could have it broken into". It's sad how times have changed.

I remember one time when we received an invitation to visit "Lee Jones's. Hughie said he would take us there. We left by the back door and followed him down the entry in single file until we reached Great Homer Street. After crossing the road safely, Hughie lifted Alec onto his shoulders, and we walked the remainder of the way up Penryhn Street to Scotland Road.

Holding on tightly to each other, Hughie guided us carefully through the traffic. (There being no pedestrian crossings then). The traffic consisted of trams, lorries, bicycles, and lots of horse and carts. Scotland Road was extremely busy, being the main arterial road to north Liverpool and the Lancashire towns.

I cannot recall how we obtained our invitations?, perhaps it was through the school, but there was always lots of children present from both communities, and from the moment we arrived, we were made to feel welcome and entertained by all the staff.

At interval time we were given our cups of cocoa and a slice of rock cake, and before leaving, a small gift to take home with us.

Returning home we passed by my school, Penryhn Street, which I believe was the only school in Liverpool which had a playground on it's roof. From this vantage point you could see the ships on the river Mersey and also the Catholic children in the playground at St Anthony's School.

I read somewhere, that All Soul's Church, Collingwood Street, built in 1872, at a cost of £4,970, was paid for by local Protestants, to serve as a mortuary and chapel for the local Catholics to bring their dead, prior to burial.

IN LIVERPOOL

The Protestant community apparently were distressed at the overcrowded housing conditions of local Catholics, who had to keep their dead at home until burial. All Soul's church was closed in 1968 and this facility was transferred to St Anthony's Church in Scotland Road.

Who would have thought that was possible, in the confrontational periods of the fifties. When crowds of people of each religion verbally abused each other, whilst celebrating their own particular special day, the 17th March and the 12th July respectfully.

Each year, the Orange Lodge would parade on the 12th of July, when thousands of people would celebrate the battle of the Boyne, which took place in 1690 in Ireland. It was there that Prince William of Orange defeated the Catholics.

When I was a child, many of the walls in the courts, leading off the streets of Netherfield Road and Great Homer Street, had huge portraits painted on them of King Billy riding a white horse and waving a sword.

The 12th of July was always an exciting period for everybody in our neighbourhood, It was an unofficial holiday. All the men would take a day off work and we children would be kept off school.

The lodges would assemble on street corners along Netherfield Road, all dressed in different uniforms. Each lodge would have a name, a person dressed as "King Billy" and a band. They would form up in lodge order and march to Exchange Street Station to take the train to Southport.

On arrival at Southport everyone would spend the day celebrating the occasion in their own particular way, before returning home to Liverpool. The children to the fairground or the beach, the grown ups to the pubs.

En-route to and from Exchange Street station, the lodges would have to pass by the Bullring (St Andrews Gardens) and Soho Street. Both of which were occupied by the Catholic community, who would sometimes act more Irish than the Irish. Although most of them had never seen Ireland.

Occasionally, there would be trouble between the communities. Sometimes caused by one lodge member I knew, named Tosh Marsden.

Tosh would lead the Ivy Lodge and march along Netherfield road, waving his pace stick to the beat of the band. On reaching the crowd of watching Catholics, he would signal with his pace stick to mark time. The lodge now stood still would then begin to play a different tune and the following words would be sung.

"Bobby, bobby, don't take me, take that bastard behind the tree, he belongs to Popery, and I belong to King Billy"

Now deliberately enraged the Catholics would shout obscenities and surge forward as if to retaliate, but be held back by a line of policemen. After a minute or two Tosh would throw his pace stick in the air, and on catching it, the band would swagger forward on their way.

It was not unknown for some Catholic women to lift their skirts, when the lodges were passing, to display the green Knickers they wore. Sometimes bricks and pepper would be thrown at the lodge. (Hence the expression "pepper thrower", to identify a Catholic). But on the whole there was more shouting than actual violence

Another member of the lodge Mr Pemberton, was renowned for always having a knuckle duster on his fist, which he hid with a bandage. This was to disguise detection by the police. He would smile knowingly when asked about it and reply. "In case of trouble".

There is a recorded instance during the blitz, with tons of bombs raining down, of a man who ran into the George Wise Protestant club in Netherfield Road, to rescue a portrait of the King and Queen, to prevent it from being damaged. (That's patriotism for you).

Although I thoroughly enjoyed "seeing the lodges" each 12th of July, I cannot recall being a member, although my brother and sisters were.

The 12th of July is still celebrated to a lesser extent even today, but with the clearance of the slum dwellings in the 1960's. Whole communities where split up and rehoused in the new towns, on the outskirts of Liverpool.

When rebuilding took place on the old slum areas of Netherfield Road, huge tower blocks were erected and Catholics as well as Protestants were encouraged to live there.

One of the tower blocks was actually named "The Braddocks" after a famous Liverpool Catholic Member of Parliament, Bessie Braddock, and her husband Jack.

Now thirty years later the tower blocks are being "knocked down" and the whole area is being turned into one huge park.

In those days Penryhn Street school was on the perimeter of the Protestant area, the east side of Scotland Road, although small numbers of Catholics also lived there. Notably, Jimmy Melia and Bobby Campbell, both professional footballer's who attended St Anthony's school.

The view from the school roof was quite panoramic and when out playing you might occasionally see your Mam waving to you, while doing her shopping in Great Homer Street.

Penryhn Street School, and the adjacent St Anthony's School, have now been demolished. Some days before demolition, I met an old school friend Billy Myers, who told me he had the contract to remove some of the fixtures and fittings. We both felt rather sad and reminisced about the old days. before parting I asked him to get me a souvenir of the school.

A few days later, Billy returned and presented me with a 5ft solid oak banister. "This he told me, "led to the playground on the roof".

I can now boast, to being the proud owner of one school handrail.

Writing now as I am of the school. I think of all the times when as a child over fifty years ago, I must have held this rail when going to the roof to play. all the memories come flooding back. Where are you now, Mr Greenwood? my school teacher, who played cricket for Lancashire.!

Mr Greenwood tried ever so hard to persuade us children that cricket was a far superior game to play than football.

In the 1940's Scotland Road, Great Homer Street and Netherfield Road were densely populated areas, with hundreds of small shops and a pub on every corner. Saturday afternoon was everybody's favourite day. No school and no work for the grownups.

In those days, we children invented our own games. lots of boys made steering carts from bits of old wood and pram wheels. Quite often we would kick a ball between goal-posts chalked on the side of a brick wall. Other times we would place empty tin cans on tram lines, and wait for the tram to run over them, squashing them flat. From the flattened can we would make "hatchets" for the younger children to use when playing cowboys and indians. Some children would tie a rope to a lamp-post to make a swing. The girls would tuck their dresses inside their knickers and somersault against the wall, or play hop scotch, or skip with a rope.

Sometimes boys and girls would play "rounders" together. (Known as base-ball in America).

The older children would often be members of the local youth clubs in the area, namely the Victoria Settlement in Netherfield Road or the Rydal Youth Centre in Great Homer Street. There you could dance to records until 9pm at night.

About this time I became infected with warts. my hands were completely covered in them. I was so embarrassed. I would often over-hear other children talking about me, saying, " Don't play with him, you can catch his warts yer know". I tried everything to remove them. I took a box of matches from home and wet the sulphur on the match with my tongue, to rub on my warts. I even attended the clinic in Plumpton Street, but it was no good.

Finally, one day in desperation, when everybody was out. I decided to borrow one of Hughie's razor blades and cut the warts off. I persevered until they were all removed. Surprisingly there was very little blood. When my Mother found out, she was so angry, and told me how stupid I had been, and how I could have harmed myself. Soon afterwards all the warts completely disappeared. I don't know whether it was because of what I had done, or the treatment from the clinic but I do know I felt much better.

Occasionally the "Fair" would arrive and occupy a piece of waste land were the bombed houses had once stood.

The music could be heard playing from quite a long way off and the sky above the fairground would be brightly lit up.

The "Fair" would attract people from far and wide, young and old. Parents with small children and strange gangs of youths, Catholic and Protestant, eyeing each other suspiciously in case of trouble, but confident in the knowledge that they were with their friends.

Sometimes fights did break out, mostly to impress the girls who would be in attendance, but I cannot recall any serious injuries being done to anyone. For a few pennies, you could enjoy the different rides, or try your hand at winning a prize on the stalls.

When we had spent our money, my friends and I would wander round the fair listening to the music. It was mainly American records. I can still remember one particular song being played over and over again. "Wheel of fortune", sung by Kay Star. The men manning the fair where gypsies I was told.

The "Fair" usually occupied the site for two weeks. Then the workmen would be seen dismantling all the equipment. Everything would be loaded on to huge lorries to go elsewhere. For the period of time it was there, you could escape from your usual routine and make new friends. Television and computer games were unheard of then.

At the corner of Robsart Street and Netherfield Road stands a public house named the "Stingo". The proprietor at the time was a man named Roy, a southerner with a strange London accent.

Apparently he had recently been demobbed from the Royal Air Force, and for some unknown reason had decided to manage the pub. Roy always looked very smart in appearance but what was most unusual about him, was that he had a pet monkey, which he chained to a post in the pub. The monkey would sit on the counter in the public bar. It was very tame and some of the regulars who worked at Bibby's mill, would bring home peanuts which they fed to it.

Once we youngsters found out there was a monkey in the pub, we would climb on the window, or open the door slightly, trying to see inside, Until we became such a nuisance to everyone, they chased us away.

My Mam and Hughie used to frequent this pub quite a lot. My Mam would go for the last hour when the young children had gone to bed. It was less than fifty yards from our house, so she could pop back quite often to see how the children where doing.

In the summer time, lots of youngsters could be seen waiting in the doorway of public house's, for their parents, who occasionally "looked out" to hand their siblings crisps or lemonade.

The interior of the pubs always looked very inviting and would be thick with cigarette smoke. The sound of an accordion or piano would sometimes be heard in the back ground. They held a strange fascination for us youngsters.

Everybody appeared to be having so much fun. We youngsters looked forward to the time when we would be old enough to go in ourselves.

Each weekend. At lunchtime when the pubs had closed. Large groups of men would gather together to gamble outside some of the pubs.

These gatherings were called 'crap school's'. The men would play, pitch and toss, cards, or dice for money. The nearest "school" to our house was through the opening in Conway Street, outside a pub named the Gordon Arms. Lookout's would be posted to look for policemen. In those days the police where very strict on gambling, and went to great lengths to arrest people. The police often disguising themselves as ordinary working men to outwit the look-outs.

Sometimes on being "raided" by the police, the men gambling would scatter and run in every direction, often running through the front door of a persons house, and out through the back door to prevent capture. This seemed to be accepted by everyone. Quite often men would be arrested and escorted to the police station in "black Marias" which had been discreetly hidden from sight. On witnessing these raids, we children would run to where the 'crap school' had been, to see if any money had been left abandoned.

A favourite pastime of many youngsters would be to visit the site of a "crap school", after the gambling had finished for the day. They would have with them a broom- handle with a piece of soap attached to the end. They would peer down the grids or cellars in the immediate vicinity where the gambling had taken place, looking for money. If any money was found, they would lower the broom-handle down the grid and press the soap on to the coins. The broom handle would then be gently raised and the money retrieved from it, and shared out between the participants. Quite often, we children would walk the length and breath of Greaty and Neddy Road, looking down grids for money.

On other occasions we would collect cigarette ends from the gutters in the streets, and I remember on more than one occasion, mixing horse manure with the tobacco, before selling it to the older boys who smoked. The older boys could be found standing each evening outside Jack Pickles paper shop, or Maggies chippy in Netherfield Road.

One summers day I was sitting at our front door, when a man and woman came into view walking towards me up the street. They had obviously been drinking and looked under the influence of alcohol. Suddenly "Jagger" our newspaper man appeared selling his papers. Shouting, "Echo, Express", advertising the local newspapers for sale. (Jagger advertised and sold newspapers throughout the Everton area each day in all kinds of weather.) I called out to me Mam. "Ma, Jagger's here"? I was then given some money and instructed to fetch the evening paper. By this time the man and women had practically reached our house, they also wanted a newspaper.

I stood behind them waiting to be served, the man put his hand in his pocket and extracted some coins to pay for the paper.

Unknown to the man, a ten shilling note fell from his pocket and began to blow in the wind down the street, I ran after it and picked it up.

I ran back to the man who was quite oblivious to what had happened, and said, "hey Mister, this is yours", and handed him the ten shilling note, explaining what I had done.

He was delighted and remarked how honest I was. He said, "don't go yet"! and once again put his hand in his pocket obviously looking for some loose change, The woman tugged at his sleeve and said. "Forget it. lets go for a drink".

The man insisted on rewarding me and gave me a sixpenny piece. I was delighted. I ran back to our house and told everyone what had happened. Afterwards I would say to my friends, "I found a ten bob note yer know, but I gave it back"! I had never held a ten shilling note before. It's strange how these small incidents stick in your mind.

Chapter Three

When one became older, you where allowed to visit "Paddys Market" in Great Homer Street with your friends. If you went very early you would see dozen's of horse and carts lined up being unloaded. The stalls would be laid out like one great big jumble sale, selling everything you could possibly think of. The noise would be indistinguishable from anything you had ever heard before, a cacophony of different sounds, and the air would be filled with the smell of all the produce on view. Flowers, vegetables, clothes, lino, shoes, furniture, leather, wax and spices. Mix this together with the teeming mass of thousands of human beings talking and milling about, and it will give you some idea of what it was like.

Paddy's market was renowned throughout the world. You could buy almost anything there. Dozens of ships would be berthed along the seven miles of Liverpool's docks, their crews all anxious to visit the market. You could easily identify the foreign seamen. They would be wearing three or four coats all at once, in glorious sunshine, and a number of hats balanced on their heads, having just purchased them to take back home to Africa, or other faraway places. (These coloured seaman where endearingly known as 'Johnnies').

At 5pm when the market was due to close. If you had not managed to get yourself "a job", you and your friends would collect as many empty discarded wooden boxes that you could carry, to take home for the fire, or for a pigeon, or chicken coop in your back yard. I can still recall some of those boxes in various positions in our house, our Mam having put tablecloths over them to look like pieces of furniture.

One day our Mam took me and Alec to Paddy's market to buy him a coat for school. After spending some time rummaging amongst the different stalls, she picked up a coat and asked Alec to "try it on".

Alec put the coat on, and after inspecting it, began to complain, saying "he didn't like it, cause it was a girls coat". He continued, "the buttons are on the wrong side".

My Mam smilingly replied. "It fits you okay, doesn't it Jim"? looking at me for agreement. She continued, "it will be alright when I've altered the buttons" but Alec would not agree, and eventually she gave in to his pleading. She then took us to Ginny's cafe for lunch. (The cafe was situated directly across the road from fleming's dungaree shop in Scotland Road).

Finding an empty table we sat down and Mam ordered three college puddings covered in custard.

(This was a treat we looked forward to whenever we went to the market with her.)

After finishing our meal, Mam said, "We'll go to town and look at the shops there" Catching one of the many trams that ran along Scotland Road, we alighted at the entrance to the Mersey tunnel.

Walking up William Brown Street. Our Mam paused for a moment and said. "I stood here in 1935 with your auntie Maggie, when they opened the Mersey tunnel" and proudly pointing to our surroundings continued. "That's St Johns gardens over there, and those statues are of famous people". " Now beginning to walk again she indicated with a sweep of her arm. These buildings on our left, are the Museum, the Picton reading rooms and the Hornby library". She ended by saying, "The end building is the Walker art gallery and the two statues at the entrance are of Michael Angelo and Raphael." Alec and I listened intently to all this and thought. Isn't our Mam clever. Reaching the top of the hill we rested for a moment on the steps of the Wellington Monument, and watched children play in the Steble fountain.

Now captivated by what she was saying our Mam continued. "Years ago people who made their fortune here, donated buildings to the city and they were named after them" "This is an example of that and is one of the loveliest streets in Liverpool.

(When ever I am in the vicinity, I agree, this is probably one of the finest views of any civic building's anywhere in the country. If the reader find themselves in the area, just pause for a moment, and look about you. You will see the entrance to the Mersey tunnel and Dale Street, gently sloping away before you. On your left is the famous St Georges hall, the cenotaph and the various statues facing the North Western Hotel in Lime Street. I will always remember Mother telling us all about them).

Crossing Monument place, we continued to our destination, TJ Hughes department store in London Road.

Inside the store Mam made some small purchases, before crossing the road to visit Collier's, another large store. Colliers took cheques which allowed you to purchase goods on the weekly. (credit/tic) by exchanging the cheque your Mother had received from the club man for clothes.

Once inside the shop, Mam asked Alec to try on an assortment of coats, before deciding which one to buy, she also bought some items of clothing, for other members of the family.

I was always fascinated when in Collier's store, watching the completed transactions being catapulted in a steel box, along a wire to the cashiers office, which was situated high above the counter's.

When ever in town, our Mam would always made a point of buying "Salt Fish" from the fish market. This was for Sunday Lunch. To get to the market she would take us through the narrow St John's Lane. On Saturday's hundreds of people would gather here to buy the dozens of caged birds and pet animals on view.

("Salt Fish" was and is still to a lesser extent, a Liverpool delicacy, and consisted of a piece of haddock (I think) covered in salt, and usually sold hard like a rock. Before you can eat it, it would have to be "steeped" in cold water overnight to soften, and have the salt removed. The following day after a few more changes of water, it would be boiled in a pan for about twenty minutes until cooked.)

At Sunday lunch, our Mam would share it out amongst the family. If you were fortunate enough to have margarine to spread on it as well,together with a cup of Schofield's lemonade, it was a feast fit for a king.

Even today when out shopping, my wife occasionally brings me home, salt fish, pigs feet or tripe to eat. She knows I enjoy it so much. Although I am the only one in our household who will eat any of it.

I cannot emphasise too much, just how poor people were in those days. Money lending was rife, and one lady in particular Lizzie Breen, helped a great many people in distress, and to my knowledge she did not charge a great deal of interest, if any at all. Her husband was a seafarer, away at sea most of the time, the Breens had a large family, and I went to school with two of the sons.

All our weekly shopping took place in Greaty, but a couple of doors from our house was a shop named "Ben's, which opened until 10pm and was on the corner of Sanderson Street and Robsart Street. (There was a shop in Great Homer Street, which stayed open until 1am and was known by everyone as the "One o'clock shop")

All our local purchases took place at Ben's. The advantage of Ben's was that it was open until late and quite near to were we lived. But more importantly was the fact that you could obtain "tick" there. Each time you made a purchase your name and amount would be written in a book, to be paid for at the end of the week when Hughie got paid.

On the ceiling of the shop was a painting of a boy standing near a cow, and a sign saying, "Ah Bisto for the gravy."

Alec told me he used to stare up at this painting, when handing in a note asking for groceries on tick, he felt too ashamed to look the shopkeeper in the eye. At Ben's you could also get ten shillings deducted from your next bill, when you redeemed the coupons your Ma had collected from drinking Mantunna Tea.

Ben's shop was owned initially by my friends mother, Mrs Shannon. One day Billy informed me that "He would be moving soon to another house, because his Mam had sold the shop". Apparently in a fit of depression, she had mentioned to Mr Parry in the "Stingo" pub one evening. "If she could find somebody to buy the shop she would sell it right away".

I believe Mr Parry who had recently been demobbed from the Royal Navy left the pub immediately, and returned soon afterwards with enough money to buy the shop. The deal was concluded that night in the pub.

The shop then remained in the Parry's possession for many years until demolition, but was always known as Ben's.

Most parents I knew belonged to a club, which enabled you to take out a loan. The loan would be given to you in the form of a "cheque" which could be redeemed for clothing at specific stores throughout the town, in our case this would be "Sturla's" in Great Homer Street or like I mentioned earlier Colliers, in London Road. Thereafter a representative of the store, known as the clubman, would call to your house each week to collect an agreed amount of money off the loan. To be seen wearing a new item of clothing would invariably invite the comment from other children in the street. "Has your Ma had a new cheque from Sturla's?".

I believe in those days, Sturla's department store would only employ people of the Protestant faith, and yet fifty percent of their business must have come from the Catholic's in the area. How stupid can you get.

Occasionally your parents would be invited to apply for Police clothes. This was a fund set up by the local constabulary to help children in need, the clothing could be obtained from Rose Hill police station but to my knowledge our family never took advantage of this facility, although I knew of some family's that did. A joke at the time, when asked. "Have you had any police clothes"? The reply would be. "No the boots are too big".

As we grew older, to supplement the family's income, me and Alec would scavenge wood from the bombed houses, to chop up and sell to people for their fires. We would also go to Paddy's Market on a Saturday morning and offer to carry rolls of "oil cloth" for people who had just bought it for their home.

Sometimes you might get a job helping to push a handcart to some one's house, and hope they gave you some money for doing so. Other times, we would go to the fruit market in Great Nelson Street very early in the morning, before other kids got there, to collect potatoes, carrots etc, which had fallen from the lorries and fruit carts whilst being unloaded. Occasionally the men working on the vehicles would give you some vegetables. But more often than not you would steal them if nobody was looking.

Taking our spoils home with us, Our Mam, would say." I hope you didn't steal these"? We would reply. "No Ma the man gave them to us honest". Haven't had this assurance from us , she would prepare the vegetables and cook a large pan of scouse. Having made the scouse, she would put some in a dish and ask one of us children to take it to Mrs Needham, an elderly lady who lived by herself in one of the cellars in Beatrice Street. We scousers (Liverpudlians) are the only people I know who are named after a meal. What we did as children was not unusual, because all our neighbours did exactly the same,

Unfortunately soon afterwards, one of our school pals, I believe his surname was Nelson, was accidentally killed collecting similar items of food, by a vehicle reversing over him.

The whole school was shocked, everyone was ordered to attend the assembly hall and Prayers were said for him. On the day of the funeral, each class were led outside to watch the cortege pass the school. The streets were crowded with people, many crying, paying there last respects.

After that, at each morning assembly, the headmaster would warn everybody of the dangers of going to the fruit market to collect food.

Obviously people didn't have television in those days, and some of the happiest moments I remember as a child, was visiting the many cinemas in our area. The Popular, The Tivoli, The Lytton, The Roscommon, and the Homer. Most children belonged to the Saturday morning club, and were given a badge to wear. Our local cinema was the Popular in Netherfield Road, and each Friday evening, Our Mam, would give us our pocket money to attend the matinee the following day. Then on Saturday morning, we would join hundreds of other youngsters and form a queue outside the picture house.

When the doors were thrown open, you would hurry forward to buy your ticket from the cashier and enter the cinema proper. The inside of the cinema would be brightly illuminated.

After handing your ticket to the ticket collector you would be directed to your seat by one of the usherettes. It would be absolute bedlam and the noise deafening. Children would be running everywhere looking for their friends. Suddenly the safety curtain would rise and the lights would start to dim. The noise would immediately stop and every one would sit down in their seat and look towards the stage. The room would go completely dark, and the screen would be lit up by a beam of light from the projectionist's room situated behind you. Then the words of the Saturday club song would appear on the screen, and a tiny ball would bounce over each word as we all sang the words.

Immediately afterwards we would be shown a short comedy, featuring Popeye or Donald Duck. Then the big picture would start, and the likes of Tarzan or Roy Rogers with his famous horse Trigger, and his assistant Tonto, would endeavour to rescue some poor damsel in distress. The big picture would end with the Goodies always beating the baddies.

Finally a trailer would be shown, which would end with the hero facing certain death, only to be continued the following week.

Soon afterwards the exit doors would be thrown open by the attendants, and the sunlight would come streaming in. We youngsters would be ushered out onto the street, many smacking their backsides as if on a horse, still in the world of make believe.

When you were older your parents would allow you to attend the cinemas in the evenings, but you had to be accompanied by an adult. Many youngsters would wait outside the cinema until a grown up came along, then ask, "Can yer take me in please?", if the adult said "yes", you would hand them your money and the adult would purchase the ticket for you. On entering the cinema you would part company with the adult, and sit with your friends who had hopefully been admitted previously. This is certainly something that would not be considered today!.

Very often me and a number of my friends, would wait outside the cinema and count how much money we had. We would gather in a group and empty our pockets. The contents of each persons pocket would be placed in a pile and counted, to see if we had enough money to buy a ticket. Some boys would run home and ask their mother could they take the empty bottles back to the shop, and keep the money?. Sometimes we would still not have enough. Then we would ask grownups entering the cinema. "Could you lend us a penny, for the pictures please?". When we had collected enough money, we would gather together again and each of us would choose heads or tails. A coin would be spun and the loser would stand to one side. This would continue until everybody was eliminated, and we finally had a winner.

The winner of the 'Toss up' would receive the money which had been placed in a neat pile.

Not everybody liked winning, for it was now the winner's job, to get taken into the cinema by an adult. Once inside the cinema, he would separate from the grown up and sit as near as possible to the emergency exit.

Inside the cinema, it would be absolutely pitch black, the 'winner' now had to get used to the dark and look to see were the attendant was. If the coast was clear and the attendant was far enough away, he would creep up to the exit door and release the emergency bar securing the lock. This was usually very simple. For safety reasons the slightest pressure from inside the door, released the lock. Meanwhile the rest of our gang would be waiting outside the door, ready to rush in as quickly as possible when the door opened.

I often took part in these 'tarpaulin musters', (a navy term) it was great fun if you did not get caught. If you got caught, you would be escorted back outside the cinema by the attendant, but not before having received a slap at the back of the head, and the message booming in your ear. "I'll remember you, the next time you come here."

The films being shown at the cinema would be changed twice a week and they were always well attended. Roscommon Street had two cinemas, the Tivoli and the Roscommon.

The Tivvy was known as the local flea pit and the attendants used to walk down the aisles, spraying insecticide in the interval.

Whereas the Rossy was much posher. Before the film began, you would be entertained by a team of dancer's, accompanied by an organist, who would appear on stage, as if by magic, from a lift in the floor.

The organist would play until the film was shown, then disappear once again into the floor. Alongside the Rossy was a house with a blue plaque on the wall, which read.

Sir Herbert Morton Stanley GCB. Explorer-1841-1904. Finder of Doctor Livingstone who lived at this address, 22 Roscommon Street, 1858 - 1859.

Looking at the plaque as a child. I imagined Stanley cutting his way through dense jungle in Africa with a machete, to rescue Livingstone, who had been taken prisoner by the natives. And to think he lived in this house!. I thought to myself. But unfortunately this was not the case, when I read the story much later of how they actually met.

(Visiting the area recently, I noticed the plaque now appears to be missing. It would be nice if Liverpool City Council took it upon themselves to restore all the missing plaques of 'famous' people, who had contributed something or had an association with Liverpool. Particularly now that Liverpool wishes to attract tourists to the city).

Our other local cinema, was the Homer in Great Homer Street. This cinema was mentioned in broadcasts in the war by William Joyce, better known as Lord Haw Haw. He even spoke of Mary Blun who sold fruit from a basket outside the cinema. I distinctly remember this lady, she was ever so tiny and if my memory serves me correct, she was the mother of a boy, who if still alive today would be now in his fifties.

I also remember Capaldi's the Italian ice cream shop in Great Homer Street. Known locally as Leo's, having its windows broken at the commencement of the war with Italy.

Lord Haw Haw, in his broadcasts to Britain would often claim that well known places in Liverpool had been destroyed by German planes. I once heard him mention that the Caradoc pub on the dock road had received a direct hit by a bomb. I believe before the war he lived for a period of time in Liverpool. William Joyce an Irishman was hanged for high treason after the war, in Wandsworth Jail.

Chapter Four

At the age of 11 I was transferred to Roscommon Street Secondary Modern School. Me and my former classmates had now been 'streamed' into 'A' 'B' and 'C' classes, except for one or two college puds who had gone to the Collegiate College in Shaw street. The Collegiate is a beautiful building built in 1840 and designed by Harvey Lonsdale Elmes, the architect who designed St Georges Hall in Lime street. (The Collegiate had lain empty for many years and is currently being converted into apartments).

At Rossy, I was chosen to go into class 'B'. The teacher being named Mr Critchley. Mr Ford had class 'C' and Mr Thompson had class 'A'. Each class was named after a famous character from the past, namely, Howard, Livingstone, Shaftsbury and Wilberforce our class was named Shaftsbury. We were encouraged by our teacher's "to have a pride in your house" and compete with each other, on the sports field, in boxing matches and various other tasks.

Our class often took this quite literally as you will see.

I remember Mr Critchley with great affection, he made a lasting impression on me in more ways than one. He was a very caring person who would often bring items of clothing into school, wrapped in newspaper. When school finished for the day, he would discreetly take one of his pupils aside, and present them with a parcel.

He was very careful not to embarrass anyone. Although we all knew what the parcels contained.

One day I was sat in my seat near the front of the class. Mr Critchley must have noticed how badly I needed shoes. My feet were showing through the bottom of the soles.

The next day when school let out, Mr Critchley asked me to stay behind a few minutes and offered me a new pair of shoes. My initial reaction was one of embarrassment then to refuse, but he persuaded me to accept them, by saying. "Nobody would know." Although I knew differently.

Returning home with the parcel I told my Mam what had happened. After listening carefully to what I had to say, she asked me to "try them on". I don't know how he had managed to find my correct size but they fitted perfectly.

She then found some writing paper and a pen, and wrote a letter for me to take to school the next day, thanking him for his generosity. She remarked

"You'll have to wear them to school now, to show him how much we appreciate it". I wore the shoes from that day on, and nobody   mentioned a word about them.

Because of overcrowding, at Roscommon Street school, (each class had about 50 pupils). 'Our year', had to spend a great deal of time at All Saints School. This was a Catholic School in Great Nelson Street approximately 250 yards from Roscommon Street. All Saints was apparently surplus to requirements by the Catholic Church at the time.

I remember when our class first entered All Saints. Me and my mates looked everywhere for statues and any evidence of Catholics having been there. The school was situated next to the fruit market. It was like mana from heaven for us youngsters, we could now look for "fades" (damaged fruit which had been thrown in the tip.) And at lunchtimes collect all kinds of things from the market. This was immediately after the war and rationing was still taking place.

At the end of each school day, dozens of us youngsters would rush to the tip to see what we could find, and like soldier ants on the march, carry all manner of fruit and vegetables away with us.

When you arrived home with all you could carry, you would proudly present them to your Mam, who would gratefully take them from you, and after inspecting them, cut off all the bad bits, before washing and preparing the good parts for a meal.

Besides helping to feed the family it also saved a lot of money.

Roscommon Street School was divided between boys and girls. Each section having its own Headmaster and Headmistress.

One day on my way to school, I stopped at the stables located at the top of "Rossy". I don't know what I expected to see. I had been told, the animals there were from the circus, that was performing that week at the Empire theatre in town. Climbing to the top of the wall, I sat astride it to get a 'better look' but was seen by one of the men working there, who walked towards me and shouted. "Get off that bloody wall" Quickly dropping to my tummy I lowered myself down the wall, I hung by my fingertips before dropping the remaining 3ft to the ground, but in my haste to escape, I tore the seat of my "kecks" (trousers). This happened quite often.

Thinking no more of it I continued on my way to school. I thought to myself. "I'll tell my mates I saw all kinds of elephants when I climbed the wall of the stables". Suddenly I was woken from my thoughts by the sound of laughter behind me, I turned to see a number of girls, also on their way to school, laughing at seeing my backside visible through the rip in my trousers.

Like many of my friends at that time. I never wore any underpants.

I felt embarrassed, and could feel myself blushing. I stopped walking, and leaning my back against the wall, pretended to tie my shoelace. The girls passed by still giggling amongst themselves.

I must have been the last person in school that day and the last person out, not even playing at play time. When school ended. I hesitated until everybody had gone ahead of me, which was unusual. I was usually the first out the door. Outside the school, I looked to see if any girls were about before running home as fast as I could, to have a patch sewn on my trousers by my Mam.

One day the school was invited to enter a writing competition organised by the RSPCA. When our class was informed, Mr Critchley knowing my fondness for animals, took me to one side and suggested, "You should have a try". I hesitated at first but agreed to do so when other boys in the class agreed.

I distinctly remember Mr Critchley encouraging us to write. He would say. "You can beat that lot from class A and class B".

When we had finished writing our stories, he collected them from us and having read them, advised us to change one or two items before finally submitting them to the competition.

Some time later at assembly, the headmaster called out my name and informed the whole school. "That I was the successful candidate from Roscommon Street, and that my story was judged to be the best". I was asked to stand alongside him on the platform. I climbed the steps and replied "thank you Sir" before returning to my class.

I thought no more about it until a few weeks later, when I was told my story, with winning entries from other schools in Liverpool, were presented to a panel of judges. I was informed that I had won the competition, and that the winning prize was a token worth one guinea £1.1.0 (which could be exchanged for food at any co-operative shop), together with a book entitled, "Mr Midshipman Easy" by Captain Frederick Marryat.

The prize was to be presented at the town hall by the Lord Mayor of Liverpool and officials from the RSPCA the following week. I was told that there would be lots of children present who had also won prizes.

Unfortunately for me, I did not have any decent clothes to wear for the occasion, my own clothes were full of patches, and my Mam didn't have enough money to buy any new ones for me.

She went to the Town Hall by herself, and made an excuse on receiving my prize, "that I was sick and unable to attend that day".

The guinea was certainly welcome in our house. There was a Co-op shop in Greaty and my Mam often did her shopping there. For every purchase you made you received dividend stamps, which could be redeemed against your next purchase. later I went with my Mam to the Co-op to spend the token I had won, and became very embarrassed at her telling everybody how I had won it.

I cherished my book Mr Midshipman Easy for many years. One day our next door neighbour, Cissie Cavern a girl approximately my own age asked if she could borrow it, in exchange for the loan of some American comics. I cannot remember her ever returning it to me, but I no longer have it any more. Strangely enough the same writing competition was won by my brother Alec, when he was at Roscommon Street School, and by his daughter Tracy, many years later.

My teacher Mr Critchley, was a very kind man, but low behold you if you misbehaved. On one occasion he was talking to the class and asked the question, who am I? meaning himself, the teacher.

I shouted out in reply "tatty head", because of his curly hair. The class all started laughing. He was furious, I was called out to the front of the class and given three strokes of the cane, for my disrespect.

I quite often received the cane because of my bad behaviour. He was a splendid teacher and we all respected him very much. He paid a great deal of attention to educating each one of us. At that time the classes were very large unlike today. In those days you also had the same teacher for the whole of the time spent at school. I remember another occasion, when Mr Critchley caught a number of boys smoking in the toilet. I was amongst them, they were my friends.

I insisted I was not smoking, but Mr Critchley would not believe me.

I have never smoked cigarettes even to this day, but non the less, to teach us all a lesson, we were marched back to the classroom, and caned in front of the remainder of the class. When you did something wrong, you were ordered to come out in front of the class to be punished, depending on the severity of the offence. You would be instructed to hold out your hand, and the teacher would strike you a series of blows across the palm of your hand with the cane. After receiving their punishment, lots of boys would bunch their hands together into a fist, and blow in them to try and relieve the pain.

IN LIVERPOOL

Most children had a great deal of respect for their teacher but we knew, if we broke the rules we would end up "getting the stick".

Looking back, the punishment my friends and I received, and believe me it was very often, appeared to do us no harm at all, in fact, contrary to what people say, I believe it did a great deal of good. Since then of course, corporal punishment has been dispensed with in schools, and in my opinion, to the detriment of school discipline.

On another occasion, me and a number of my school pals "sagged school", (took the day off without permission) and went to Stanley Park. On the way to the park I called home to collect my dog Rex, knowing full well my Mam and Hughie would be out at work. (I had decided I would forge my Mam's signature on a note for school, stating, that I had been ill.)

Arriving at the park, me and my friend's, who had also brought their dog's with them, threw sticks in the lake, and instructed the dog's to fetch them, but my dog would not budge an inch. I was disappointed, and thought my dog ought to go in the water, at least that way he would have a good wash. I picked him up and walked to a small bridge which spanned the lake. I then leaned over the bridge and dropped him in the water. He sank like a stone and emerged seconds later struggling.

He appeared to be in difficulties. Perhaps it was the shock of dropping him in the water from the bridge, perhaps it was his age, I don't know, but I ran to the side and jumped in the water myself. Wading up to my armpits, I grabbed my dog and pulled him clear and carried him to the side. Once on dry land he very quickly recovered. I was so sorry for what I had done and hugged and kissed him. I then realised I was soaked to the skin, I had not been in the park long, and now had to walk two or three miles back home. My friend's laughed and kept making fun of me all the way home, and everybody we passed looked at me in my wet condition.

Arriving home, I climbed up the steps and opened the front door. My Mam was home now and heard me, and came along the lobby to meet me. On seeing the condition I was in, she shouted out. "what's happened to you"?, I explained to her that I had fallen in the lake in the park. I didn't mention the dog, although he was also wringing wet. My mam made a grab for me but I ran up the stairs to the bedroom before she could catch me. She shouted up the stairs, "take those wet clothes off yer, before yer catch yer death of cold". as an afterthought she shouted. "That's what you get for staying off school, I'll tell the school board,(truant officer) about you when

I see him".

I was too frightened of my mam at that time, to go downstairs to get undressed in front of the fire, but soap, towel, and a bowl of hot water was brought up for me, with a change of clothing. Later, "I was asked to come downstairs for something to eat".

One day the local 'school board' Mr Jones, did come to our house. I wondered what I had done wrong, until I heard him ask me Mam. "Would James like to to spend a week of the Summer holidays, with my wife and I at our home"?. He informed my Mam that "he lived over the water".

Mr and Mrs Jones' she discovered, had no children of their own.

My Mam called my name, and when I appeared she asked. "Would you like to go on holiday with Mr and Mrs Jones"? I thought about it for a second or two, and without saying a word nodded my head in agreement, more in awe than anything else. she then turned to Mr Jones and smiled, indicating her permission.

A few days later I was duly collected from our house by Mr Jones and taken to Birkenhead on the ferry. From Birkenhead we took the bus to Moreton were he lived. I wasn't exactly a stranger to the 'ferries.' We as a family, like hundreds of other people from Liverpool, often went to New Brighton or Moreton in the school holidays.

I cannot remember exactly how old I was, but I do remember being met at the front door of this beautiful house by Mrs Jones. I had not seen anything like this in my life before. It was near the beach and the sand seemed to come almost up to the front door.

Mrs Jones took my Army rucksack from me on entering the house. She then asked. "Would you like to go to the bathroom"? I replied "Yes please". I looked about me. The house was carpeted throughout. Mr Jones escorted me upstairs and took me to a room with a bath and a toilet, I noticed a toilet holder on the wall, and folded towels on a rail. I just stood there and didn't know what to do. I thought to myself, these people must be really posh. I had never seen anything like this before. Back home our toilet was in the back yard and we used torn newspaper in the toilet, and our bath was on a nail in the yard. I just stood there staring, not knowing what to do. Mr Jones broke the silence by saying. "do you want to wash your hands before you eat"? I nodded my head. So that's what they meant.

At dinner that evening the table appeared to be groaning under the weight of food, I had never seen so much food all at once. The cutlery was laid out on a lovely decorated lace tablecloth, and the plates were part of a beautiful dinner service.

There was fruit in bowls and flowers in vases, and nobody was sick. I sat there quite shy unable to comprehend it all. After a short period of time and with encouragement from both Mr and Mrs Jones, I started to enjoy my meal. Throughout the meal I began to take small portions of food from my plate, and without looking, I dropped them under the table where I was sitting.

After watching me doing this a few times, Mr Jones looked at his wife, then with a half smile on his face asked. "why are you dropping food under the table James"?. I replied. "It's for the dog, Sir!", Mr Jones still smiling replied, "but we do not have a dog James"! I looked at Mr Jones then at Mrs Jones. I could feel my face going red, I didn't know what to say, I thought everybody had a dog.

To save me from any further embarrassment, Mrs Jones coughed and suggested we finish our meal. Soon afterwards she stood up from the table and disappeared into the kitchen, returning moments later carrying a tray, on which stood three large dishes of ice cream. I soon forgot all about my embarrassment. Apparently at home, I always fed tit bits to my dog at mealtimes.

I was given my own room beautifully decorated, with real blankets and sheets. No coats on the bed like we had at home, each morning I was woken up with a cup of tea and a biscuit.

After using the bathroom, I would hurry down stairs for breakfast. Quite often I would see Mr or Mrs Jones lighting the gas cooker, with a lighter which resembled a gun.

Then after breakfast, we would visit different places of interest. One day they took me to a shop and bought some clothes for me.

I spent a very memorable week in the Jones's company, they took me everywhere with them.

On the final day of my holiday, I packed all my belongings in my haversack, and was preparing to leave. When Mr Jones suddenly asked. "James do you have anything that doesn't belong to you".?

I replied "No! Sir", He then said, "Are you sure?" I then went red and put my hand in my trouser pocket, and produced the lighter, which they used to light the gas cooker with.

How I thought I could ever get away with taking their lighter, I don't know, and what a way to repay someone's kindness. They were a lovely couple, and extremely kind. They had bought a foot ball for me to take home with me, and Mrs Jones had packed a small parcel of food for me to give to my Mam.

Mr Jones escorted me home later that afternoon. On arriving home, I ran up the steps ahead of him along the lobby, calling out. "Ma I'm home". My Mam then appeared from the kitchen smiling, wiping her hands on her pinny, obviously very pleased to see me. She called out. "Come in Mr Jones. I hope he hasn't been any trouble for yer"? Mr Jones entered the kitchen. I could see just by glancing quickly around, that my Mam had been busy tidying up. The grate sparkled from thousands of tiny stars, having been cleaned with zebo. There was no longer any washing hanging above the fire place, and the oil cloth on the floor had been scrubbed clean.

Mr Jones declined the offer of a cup of tea, "explaining that he would be returning home straight away". He told my Mam "that I had been a very good boy". He went on to say, "He and his wife had both enjoyed my company very much". My Mam "thanked him for all he had done for me, and asked him to thank Mrs Jones also". They spoke quietly together for a few more minutes, before Mr Jones made his apologies about returning home. He bade everyone goodnight and departed.

After Mr Jones had left I became the centre of attention. I explained to my Mam and Hughie who had by this time entered the house, all the things I had seen and done that week, (deliberately omitting the episode of the lighter).

My Mam then insisted, "before I went to bed that evening. I was to sit down and write a letter of thank's, to the Jones's for the lovely time I had spent at their home". The Jones's were a real Christian couple. I can recall this memory like it was only yesterday. I still blush thinking about how I had tried to steal their gas lighter.

I think it was Mr Jones who arranged for me to go on holiday to Whitchurch in Shropshire, sometime later that year.

 On arrival in Whitchurch, I discovered we would be staying in a large country mansion situated in it's own grounds. The house overlooked a huge lake and was surrounded by beautiful countryside as far as the eye could see. The air smelled so fresh and I imagined the thick smog we were used to seeing in Liverpool, were never seen here. There were approximately 30 youngsters in our group, from various parts of Liverpool. Many from the ethnic communities. This was the first time I had been in close proximity with someone of another race. I was fascinated listening to a Chinese boy talking just like me, with a Liverpool accent, although at that time I did not know what an accent was.

The lake had a boathouse, and in the boathouse was a rowing boat. Protruding from the bank into the lake, was a landing stage, and tied to the landing stage was a large raft made from oil drums. Presumably the raft had been made by previous occupants of the house.

Naturally me and some of the boys from the Scotty Road area, had to sail on the raft. It was great fun pushing ourselves out with long poles, into deep water. I did not even consider the danger, even though I could not swim very well at the time.

Our's was a mixed group, boys and girls. After a day or two getting to know everybody, me and another boy from Rossy school named Ronnie Wilson, became quite friendly with two of the girls, they were sisters. They were also Catholic and came from the Soho Street area of Liverpool. Ronnie and I spent most of our free time in their company. At the end of the two week holiday, we sat together for our return journey home to Liverpool. It was on the return journey that we agreed to meet again. We exchanged addresses with each other and arranged to visit the girls the following week.

The following week Ronnie and I set off to visit the girl's home. It wasn't too far from were we lived. We walked along Netherfield Road passing Anne Fowler's memorial home for women, and turned right at Prince Ruperts Castle into Everton Brow, which led to Soho Street and the Catholic area. We soon found the address without too much difficulty, stopping outside the house, we hesitated for a moment, before plucking up enough courage to knock at the door. We stood there wondering what kind of reception we would receive. Soon the door was opened by a man whom we discovered a few moments later was the girls Father.

After nervously identifying ourselves. He invited us into the house by saying. "Come in I've heard all about you". We were pleasantly surprised to find that we did not have to bless ourselves before entering the house, like I'd seen a priest do at the pictures. The girls parents made us very welcome and invited us to sit down. I nudged my mate, there was a picture of the Pope on the wall. The girl's Mother prepared some refreshments for us. We sat talking for quite some time, expecting at any minute to be questioned about our religion, but nobody mentioned anything about it, they where just like ourselves.

Returning home later that night, me and my mate had lots to talk about. Some weeks later at our request, the girls took us to visit their local church St Francis Xavier's in Salisbury street, we wanted to see what it looked like inside. Being rather late, nobody was about. It didn't look no different to St Georges Church in Netherfield Road.

After that the girls came to visit our house and met Hughie and me Mam. We remained good friends for a long time afterwards. I know it changed my attitude towards the Catholic religion. If only both communities in Northern Ireland could learn to live peacefully together?. Wouldn't it be wonderful.

The holiday in Shropshire was great, in fact another world as far as I was concerned. There, we were able to mix with children of a different colour and religion. I would certainly recommend it for youngsters in similar circumstances. I know me and my companions certainly benefited a great deal from our stay there.

At least once a week me Mam would have to go to the wash house to do the big wash. This was a facility provided by Liverpool City Council. The wash house was situated next to Tommy Routledge the cobbler, in Netherfield Road. There, for a small fee, you would be provided with a stall and a "dolly" to do your washing in, and an unlimited amount of hot water. It enabled your Ma to do the laundry, which would normally be impossible, with us only having a cold water tap at home.

Quite often I would be required to go to the wash house and wait in the queue for "our turn". I would arrive at the wash house and ask the women already seated there. "Who's Last"? and when one of the women replied "me"! I would sit alongside her keeping me Mam's place in the queue until she arrived, very conscious of sometimes being the only boy there.

I would also have to help carry the washing home when she'd finished.(These chore's ceased when my two sisters became older). Occasionally, I would be required to help wring the washing out on the mangle in the back yard. this piece of equipment was huge and consisted of two wooden rollers mounted on a cast iron base. You would have to put the washing through the rollers and turn the handle to squeeze the water from it. I hated that job. I remember the mangle falling forward on me one time when I tried to climb on it, to get on the back wall, luckily I escaped without any serious injury.

Incidentally, Liverpool City Council was the first in the world to introduce Public wash house facilities. This was due to the insistence of a lady named kitty Wilkinson who lived at that time in Liverpool.

Kitty Wilkinson was renowned for her work with the poor of Liverpool, and demanded 'washing facilities', to combat the spread of disease that was rife at the time. The first 'wash house' opened in 1840 at Upper Frederick Street

IN LIVERPOOL

in the south end of Liverpool.

I had now acquired a set of darts from somewhere. I used to throw them at a target painted on the toilet door in the back-yard. I recall one day it was raining and I was indoors, My Mam and Hughie had gone out somewhere. I was beginning to get bored, I then noticed my Grand-Mother's picture hanging on the wall. She was sitting on a chair her hair in a bun on the top of her head, dressed completely in black, which was the fashion in those days. The glass had been broken in the frame for a long time and had never been replaced. I decided that this picture would make a perfect target, so I began to throw the darts at it.

After a short period of time Grand-Ma's face started to disintegrate, and I suddenly realised what I had done. I was going to be in serious trouble when my Mam returned home. I then called out to my younger brother Alec who was playing elsewhere in the house, inviting him to join me in throwing darts at the picture. I knew full well that when my Mam came home, I could blame him aswell. I then took the picture down from the wall and hid it behind the sofa, instructing Alec, "not to tell me Mam, or else I will kill yer". When my Mam returned home, she soon discovered the photograph of her mother was missing, from it's usual prominent position on the wall. She then asked me. "Jimmy, where's the picture gone from the wall"?. I tried to blame Alec but my Mam realised it was me. I ran from the house with me Mam in hot pursuit. It was the only thing she had to remind her of her Mother and I had destroyed it. I then spent the next hour or so in a shop doorway sheltering from the rain, until I eventually decided it was safe to return home, and sneak upstairs to the bedroom.

Later that evening, Hughie brought me some tea and toast to eat in bed, and for the next few days I kept well away from me Ma.

I had mentioned earlier that in "our year" at school I was in class "B", each class had their own particular teacher, our teacher being named Mr Critchely. Mr Ford had class "C" and Mr Thompson had class "A". Each class being named after a famous person from the past.

Our class was Shaftsbury, we were encouraged to have a lots of pride in our house, and to compete with the other classes, mainly on the sports field and in various other tasks. Our class took this quite literally.

Due to overcrowding, our year at secondary school as previously mentioned meant we had to be accommodated at "All Souls School". All Souls was situated in Great Nelson Street, approximately 250 yards from Roscommon Street along Great Homer Street.

Each lunchtime we all had to return to "Rossy" for our free dinners, there being no facilities at All Souls for meals. It also meant some boys being chosen as milk monitors and having to return to "Rossy" each day to collect the milk.

In those days, every person of school age, was given a pint of free milk each day. On the Monday morning of each week, the teacher's at All Souls school, would ask for volunteers to collect the milk from Roscommon Street school. Immediately all hands would shoot up in the air, with the cry of. "Me! Sir, Me! Sir."

Being chosen 'Milk Monitor' and going back to 'Rossy' was quite an honour. The job would last all week. Not only did you escape from school for a short period of time, but it enabled you if you hurried, to take some extra bottles of milk from the crates of the other classrooms, before they took some from yours.

On returning to All Souls School carrying the crates of milk, me and my companion would detour slightly and cross the 'Olla' to the bombed houses to hide the extra milk we had taken. On being dismissed from school at the end of the school period, in those days it was 4pm, we would hurry back to our hiding speck to collect the milk we had hidden to take home with us. Fortunately for everybody concerned, there was always lots of extra milk left over, in case of breakages.

On one occasion me and my friend named Jimmy McConn, (we sat next to each other in class), had been chosen that week to be milk monitors. This particular day, it was raining rather heavily and we were returning as quickly as possible with the milk to All Saints school, when we happened to witness a most distressing sight.

A horse pulling a loaded cart from Paddy's market, had slipped on the wet cobble stones in Great Homer Street and had broken its leg.

It lay on the ground and kept trying to stand up but was unable to, it's leg was all twisted and bent, it seemed to be crying out in pain and the Carter seemed equally distressed. He was comforting the horse and shouting for somebody to call a vet.

Eventually after what seemed ages, a veterinary surgeon arrived and decided that the poor horse would have to be 'put down'. A policeman had also arrived by this time, and told the gathering crowd to move back. The vet then took a gun from his case, and pointing it at the horses head, pulled the trigger, a shot rang out. The horse collapsed as if felled by an axe. It was all over in a minute. By this time another team of horses had arrived and the dead horse was winched onto a flat trailer and driven away.

I have already mentioned that me and my immediate friends, had been streamed into 'B' class, not quite good enough for 'A' class apparently, but much superior than 'C' class, who we thought were absolute morons.

C class, was a class of its own, with lots of characters. (I know the Pioneer Corp appreciated them, when they were called up for National Service). Their teacher Mr Ford, would have been out of place anywhere else. He was a huge rotund man, going slightly bald, and wore spectacles. When you caught sight of him, he always appeared to have one hand in his trouser pocket scratching his private parts. On meeting a pupil in the corridor, he would bellow. "Come here boy, you filthy arab." He also had this strange habit of sucking his teeth when questioning you, on what you were doing.

Mr Ford always gave us youngsters the impression of being a ladies man. At break time when the tea lady brought his cup of tea, and whilst we children drank our milk, he would escort her back to the door. He would then open the door for her whilst she pushed out her tea trolley, she would thank him, and he would smile back at her, then close the door gently behind her. After she had departed, he would wait a few seconds, then re-open the door very quietly and peep out into the corridor in her direction, presumably to admire her backside, he would then re-appear with a huge grin on his face. Having witnessed this we children would giggle quietly amongst ourselves.

He had some strange habits. One of them was stirring his tea with his comb. Another one was to squeeze the palms of his hands together and expel the air trapped inside, making a loud noise. You could identify members of "C" class, by seeing them all trying to copy this action in the playground.

The boys in his class were forever playing tricks on him. They would hide rotten vegetables in his desk, and remove the chalk from the blackboard.

I remember one occasion, when one of his pupils caught a large 'bluebottle' and placed it in an inkwell. When Mr Ford passed quite near this particular boys desk, examining their work. The boy took the poor drowning creature covered in ink, and gently placed it on his coat.

Unknown to Mr Ford the 'bluebottle' began to climb up the sleeve of his coat, leaving a long trailing ink stain.

I expect when he discovered the stain much later on, he knew it would be one of his pupils, but to my knowledge the culprit was never discovered.

I know for a fact. On the slightest pretext, when things went wrong, Mr Ford would often cane everyone in his class. This was in the believe, that the offender would be punished, and the other pupils would prevent anything like that happening again in the future. Whenever this occurred, pupils could be heard crying out, what's this for Sir? I ain't dun nuthin wrong.

Mr Ford, enjoyed a love/hate relationship with his pupils, they in turn were fiercely loyal to him.

Almost everybody at school had pet pigeons, and quite often at lunchtime a group of us would skip dinner, and go to 'Silcocks' corn mill, down at the docks. Once there we would pinch corn to feed our 'micks'. Then we would hurry back to school with our pockets bulging with corn. On one particular occasion 'Harry Beau' (Henry Charles) one of my friends from 'C' class, caught a squeaker, (a young pigeon). Returning to school that day he sneaked it into class and put it in his desk, intending to take it home later. By this time all the class knew he had a baby pigeon, and were whispering amongst themselves and looking in 'Harry Beau's' direction.

Consequently after a few minutes had passed, Mr Ford realised something was wrong. He shouted, "Charles! What have you got there?" and 'Harry Beau' replied, "Nuthin Sir!" With that Mr Ford hurried to 'Harry Beaus' desk and flung the lid open, you can imagine what happened next.

The captured pigeon immediately took flight, and the whole classroom was in turmoil, everybody trying to catch the poor pigeon flying around the class. Eventually it was caught and on Mr Ford's instructions,it was released from the window. Not only did 'Harry Beau' receive six of the best that day, He also had to stay behind and clean up the pigeon droppings from inside his desk.

When the four o'clock bell rang that day, to indicate the end of lessons, and the class dismissed. There was a mad stampede outside by the pupils, to see if the baby pigeon could be re-captured. Fortunately for the pigeon it was nowhere to be seen.

One day I was playing in the school playground, with another boy from my class, named Frankie Redfern. Frankie suddenly decided to stop playing and leaning his back against the railings, entwined the railings with his arms. On the spur of the moment, and without any warning, I grabbed hold off his arm, trapping him. Then for some unknown reason, I pulled his arm towards me through the rail. There was a loud crack and a cry of pain from frankie. I immediately let go of his arm, too late. Frankie's arm had been pulled out of it's socket dislocating his shoulder. I was so ashamed by what I had done and said to Frank, I'm sorry Frank, punch me in the face to pay me back, I wont do anythin honest! Poor Frankie didn't take me up on my offer, he was in too much pain. The teacher on duty in the playground heard the cry for help and ran over to investigate. Frank explained between groans that he had fallen over and hurt his shoulder. After a brief examination by the teacher, He was rushed to hospital.

Because of that, all our friends thought he was real tough, for not snitchin on me to the teacher.

Frankie had to stay off school for quite some time, and when he eventually returned, he still had his arm in a sling for a long time afterwards.

I appreciated the fact, that he had not told the teacher on me, for which no doubt I would have received the cane, so I gave him my penknife as a way of saying thank you. Although I must admit, I was more frightened of him telling his Mam what really happened. His Mother was a lovely woman and when I used to visit his house, before the accident, she always made me very welcome. I also remember they had a blue budgerigar in a cage in the kitchen.

Later in life, when I used to visit my own Mother, and sometimes take her for a glass of 'Mackies' to The Spion Kop pub in St Domingo Road. Quite often I would meet Frankie Redfern there. He still lives in the area, with a family of his own now. We would spend time talking of old friends, and of our school days together, and of that particular incident. (Sorry frank)

The nicknames we youngsters gave to each other at school were quite funny, and even later in life we were still often known by them. for example. Here are some of the names we gave to each other. 'Yankee Cuttress' 'Lasher Welsh'. 'Joey Bredo,' 'Angel Face,' 'Bocca Nelson,' 'Chunky Ellis,' 'Burno,' 'Billy Boy,' 'Spam Lewis,' 'Docker Naden,' 'Macker' and 'Toby' 'Egg-head' and finally but not least my own nickname 'Elly O Tezz'. It seemed quite natural many years later, on meeting your old school friends to address each other by our nicknames.

A number of years ago, (I had reason, to express my family's sympathy to 'Docker Naden' and his wife, who's daughter had just died tragically in a plane crash at Manchester Airport.)

I remember another occasion very well, when Mr Ford had reason to admonish another friend of mine, named Joey Bretherton, for something he had done. He remarked to Joey. How anybody with such an "angel face" could cause so much trouble I don't know. Thereafter Joey was always known as "Angel Face".

Mr Thompson the teacher in charge of 'A' class had a reputation as a no nonsense teacher. Apparently he would give his pupils a lesson to do and then appear to sit reading a newspaper, but in reality he was watching them through small holes in the print.

He was known on occasion to throw his wooden chalk eraser, or his ruler at you if he caught you talking, and cuffs behind the ear were a way of life in his class. He also had a catapult in his desk that he had confiscated from one of his pupils, and he used it quite often to attract a person's attention, by firing paper pellets at them.

The art teacher's name was Mrs Maudie Kray, she was an elderly spinster lady who unfortunately had to wear a wig. Our class made her life an absolute misery. Although she was obviously much older than us, it was a case of tormenting some one less fortunate than yourself, because of her affliction.

I must confess, I was one of the worst offenders. I must have made her life an absolute hell. Thinking about it, I was so cruel. Oh! If you could only put the clock back and say how sorry you are now.

Much later even my brother Alec had cause to regret the time I spent at 'Rossy'. One day when I was a pupil, I took my penknife and carved my name on a door leading to the playground. Many years later when I had left school, It was discovered by one of the teachers. Despite all his protestations my brother Alec received the cane, for carving his name 'Elliott' on the door.

One day I was on my way home from school with my friends, when I heard shouting. I looked behind me to see what all the noise was about. I then saw a horse, which had escaped from between the shafts of it's cart, galloping towards us. I stood my ground waiting for the horse to come nearer, and when it was almost upon us, I raised both arms hoping it would stop. The horse slowed down but continued to come towards us, everybody scattered in different directions, but I stood my ground, and as the horse passed quite near, I grabbed hold of its reins as it passed by, the horse lifted me off my feet dragging me a short distance before stopping.

Goodness knows how I escaped serious injury, I must have been mad. I could quite easily have been trampled to death. I must have seen too many cowboy films. I stood there trembling like a leaf holding the horse's reins, everybody ran up to me and said how brave I was. The owner eventually arrived, thanked me for what I had done, and took possession of the horse, I was the talk of the school for days afterwards, but when I think of it now, I could have been killed.

My Mam was once again expecting a baby and unable to walk very far. It was now my job each morning when I was going to school, to take my two younger sister's, to the Adam Cliffe day nursery in Everton Road. Alec my brother was old enough to go to school on his own. My Mam would wash and dress the girls and I would then take charge of them. I would hurry them out the back door and up the entry to Sanderson Street and along Neddy Road, hoping none of my mates would see me.

Hurrying along Netherfield Road, we would pass Anne Fowler's, then up the hill past Rupert's Castle, (built in 1787 as a local lock up and depicted on Everton Football club emblem), then past what we youngsters called, the top park, and it's tap shaped like a lion's head sticking from the wall, this was next to the gent's toilet, before arriving at Everton Road, were the nursery was situated.

I remember the nursery had a huge white door, with a brass handle stuck on it. When you walked through the entrance you would immediately be confronted by a large rocking horse, standing in the room. I would usher my sister's inside ahead of me and hand them over to one of the assistants, who would inspect them briefly before sending them into the play area. Sometimes the assistant would remark, is yer Ma still not well? I would mumble a reply before dashing off to school. It was also my job to collect my sisters, when school let out.

This was a task I disliked intensely and thought it was a 'cissy's job'. I would rather have been going to and from school with my mates. I'm sure I must have practically dragged my sisters, by the hand there and back to the nursery, as quickly as possible. So my friends would not see me.

Soon afterwards our Brother John was born but this time it was a difficult birth. John had been born with a twist in his bowels and almost died. He spent a number of weeks in hospital recovering from the operation, and when my Mam finally brought him home, we all gathered round whilst she undressed him, to show us the scar on his stomach.

Hughie had now got a job on the docks, and each morning before he left for work, he would make the fire and prepare the breakfast for us children. He would shout up the stairs, I'm going now, tea's made. The front door would bang as he closed it after him. This would be a signal for us children to get out of bed. My Mam would be attending to John who was still a baby.

One day my friends told me, that a boy from another school had been electrocuted in the bombed 'conny onny rooms'. Apparently he had been removing floor boards with other boys to chop up for firewood, and had touched an electric cable that had been hanging loose from the ceiling. The fire brigade removed his body. Soon afterwards the building was completely demolished.

I mentioned earlier that lots of us children and many grownups kept pigeons. We used to 'race' them against each other. This was called 'catch and run' and was held mainly in the summer holidays. the procedure was for each person entering the race to pay one and six.(eight new pence) We would then select our best 'mick' and meet on the steps of 'Jack Browns' shop in Robsart Street. This was central to where all the pigeon lofts were situated.

Each bird would be placed in a 'tossing basket' in our case a large cardboard box, which had air holes in the side of it. Two people would then be chosen to take the birds on the tram to Aigburth Vale, a district of Liverpool, approximately ten miles from Everton where we lived. The reason two people were chosen, was to prevent any cheating. With a single person, there was always the possibility of that one person releasing his friend's bird first, before the remainder of the birds were released.

The tossing basket would be placed under the stairs on the tram, and on arrival at Aigburth Vale, the basket would be taken to a clear spot, and placed on the ground. Soon afterwards the lid would be opened, and all the different coloured birds would make their escape. Once released, the birds would fly in every direction before joining together in the sky above. they would circle overhead once or twice more getting there bearings, before flying in a flock back to their respective lofts. This is a wonderful spectacle to see.

Back home we youngsters would be anxiously peering into the sky, waiting for our birds to arrive. When the flock was sighted, we would rattle our tins of corn or whistle, for our bird to come to the loft. Sometimes if you had a very tame pigeon, you would hold it aloft, flapping its wings to attract it.

when your bird recognised it was home, it would separate from the flock and land on a 'landing board', before entering the loft through a 'drop in'. The bob wires on the drop in, prevented the bird from leaving the loft once it had entered.

When the bird entered the loft, you would open the door as quick as possible, and grabbing hold of your pigeon, run through the back entry to Jack Brown's shop as fast as you could. The poor bird was pushed into your jumper or pocket, or held in your hand whilst you ran, obviously the first person to present his bird to the judge, won the race. The prize money, was usually in the region of (thirty bob) one pound fifty pence in today's money. with a smaller prize for the bird that came second.

All kinds of tricks imaginable were tried to make your own bird come first.

IN LIVERPOOL

If it was a hen bird you were racing, and she was sitting on eggs, you would have ready an empty egg, from which you would have previously blown the yoke for this particular purpose. You would then put a worm in the egg. Then seal the hole with sticky tape, and place the false egg in the nest. This would be done approximately an hour before the race began.

The worm would continue to move in the egg, and the hen bird would think one of her chicks was about to hatch. She would then be removed from the nest to enter the race, and on release, she would fly back to the nest as quickly as possible.

Another trick, you employed when racing a cock bird, was to remove him from his nest box and put another cock bird in with his hen. He would go berserk trying to re-enter his nest. You would then enter him for the race. Once again, on release you would expect him to separate from the flock and race back to his loft as quickly as possible.

I remember an occasion when one of the contestants tried to cheat. He ran to the checker with a bird of similar looks and colour, to the one he had entered in the race, but was found out by somebody identifying the real bird. We pigeon fanciers visited each other's loft's quite often, and knew each other's micks as well as our own. We would often exchange birds with one another, and if your bird had won a race more than once, everybody wanted to buy one of its young sqeakers. I have already mentioned that most of my school friends had 'micks', this also applied to many grown ups in our neighbourhood. At the conclusion of each race everybody would meet on the steps of Jack Brown's shop. We youngsters would sit there with the men, listening to the conversation of how each persons bird had performed, hanging on to every word.

Occasionally one of us youngsters would win the race, and then all the conversation would be centered around you.

One of the most famous pigeon fanciers in our neighbourhood was a man named Owen Knox, everybody called him "Knoxy". He had a loft on the roof of his house in Robsart Street. One day I was sitting as usual with all the pigeon fanciers on Jack Browns steps, Knoxy's was there with his brother Hughie, another keen pigeon fancier.

I engaged in conversation with knoxy and started to ask him questions about his birds. I remember him saying to me. Would you like to see them? I was thrilled to bits, hardly anybody got invited to see his micks. I immediately replied, yeh please.

The following day I duly arrived outside his house, and stood in the street looking up to the roof, trying to attract his attention. It was no use shouting he was hard of hearing. Finally he looked down and saw me, and threw me his key to open the front door. I climbed the steps, unlocked the door and entered the house. I then walked along the lobby to the flight of stairs leading to the roof. It was an unusual house, probably the tallest in the street. I remember climbing to the top of the stairs and seeing a ladder extending from a trap door in the ceiling, I climbed up inside the attic and finally emerged inside Knoxys loft.

I was completely surrounded by what appeared to be hundred's of pigeon's, of all shapes colours and sizes. After sitting me alongside him, Mr Knox then opened the loft doors and released his birds. The view from the roof was quite panoramic. You could see the Anglican Cathedral in the distance and the clock on the Liver Buildings, whose face I believe is larger than big Ben's.

He then produced a large cane from under his feet, and by waving it in the air, seemed to be able to direct his bird's which ever way he wanted. He told me, that he directed his birds, to other flocks of racing pigeons flying over Liverpool, so both flocks would mingle together, and he could catch the confused birds when they landed.

I actually saw Mr Knox catch some stray birds. He took a tame white fantail pigeon from a small cage alongside him, which immediately perched on his arm, he then fed the hungry bird some corn. Whilst the bird was perched on the palm of his hand, He lowered his arm suddenly, the fantail's wings then flapped open whilst trying to regain it's balance by clinging to his arm. This seemed to indicate to his flock of birds flying in the sky, that feeding time was taking place, and they suddenly dived from the sky to land on his loft, bringing lots of other racing pigeon's with them from other flocks. Mr Knox then throw a handful of corn to the birds, who scrambled madly to be fed, and in the confusion, he captured the stray pigeon's one at a time, which he appeared to identify quite easily. (This appeared to me to be a form of pigeon-napping)

One of my friend's said he even caught one of King George the Sixth's racing pigeons from Windsor, which happened to be flying over Liverpool at the time.

I understood that Mr Knox sold the 'strags' he caught, to a number of Chinese restaurants in town.

I believe that one day, the person who usually delivered the captured pigeons for Mr Knox, to the chinese restaurants, was unable to do so, because he was ill. So another person went in his place.

Unknown to this person, arrangements had been made with the Chinese owner, for the pigeons to be taken to the back door of the restaurant. On this particular occasion the temporary messenger walked through the front door of the crowded restaurant, carrying a basket full of birds straight to the kitchen, and called out to the first chinamen he saw. Here's yer pigeon's yer've ordered.

Knoxy was renowned for his skill in capturing racing birds. He was also resented by many other pigeon fanciers in Liverpool, who blamed him for capturing many of their young birds.

I remember witnessing an occasion when a small crowd of us, where sat on Jack Brown's steps talking about pigeons as usual, when all of a sudden the meeting was interrupted by Mr Nelson who also kept pigeons in Robsart Street. He accused knoxy of capturing one of his young birds earlier that day. Knoxy denied all knowledge of the bird, but promised to look out for it the next time he flew his pigeons. The bird was never seen again.

Although, I must admit, Mr Knox did return a young bird of mine, sometime after that incident.

I mentioned previously, my friends and I would visit the docks, to try and pinch seed to feed our birds, from the corn mills situated there. On the way to the docks we would visit the blackie, a derelict church in Sylvester street on the other side of Scotland Road.

This church had been badly damaged in the bombing during the war, and a pure white pigeon nested there. We would often see it flying into the church steeple when ever we passed. It was a racing pigeon with an identification ring on each foot, it had obviously become lost and had mated with a strag. (a feral pigeon). We youngsters would climb inside the church trying to discover were it was nesting, so we could capture it for our own loft, but you had to be careful, the Blackie was in the Catholic area of Scotland Road, and Fat Harold's gang would fight with us if they saw you.

I later served in the Army with Harold and we became good friends.

The docks at that time where extremely busy. There would be literally, hundreds of horse's and carts, and lorries from all parts of the country, waiting to be called into the dock gates, for loading or unloading. The queues would stretch for miles along the dock road.

Huge crowds of people would be going about their business. I understand twenty thousand docker's worked on the docks at that time. It was an exciting period seeing so many people milling about, but the reason my friend's and I were there, was to get food for our micks, or anything else we could lay our hands on.

My friends and I where particularly interested in the pigeon corn at Silcocks mill. Afterwards we would go to Tate and Lyle's for brown sugar, or Bibby's, for pea-nuts to eat ourselves.

Sometimes the men working in the mills, would allow you to take as much corn as you could carry, that had fallen off the lorries onto the floor. Other times they would chase you away. Then, you would have to sneak back and when they were not looking, help yourself. Sometimes you would have to skip a lorry (jump on the back of it) and without the driver or second man seeing you, rip open the sacks with your penknife, and help yourself to the contents.

At lunchtime, or the end of their shift's. Thousands of women would be seen leaving Tate and Lyle's sugar refiners and Bibby's mill, no doubt heading for home, or the shops, they would be dressed in the regulation blue turban and baggy overalls. The same women would be unrecognisable in the evenings, when they would be going out for the night, to the Grafton ballroom, or the pubs and cinema's in the area.

Quite often when we were scrummaging down the dock road, you would see a steam wagon transferring goods from the ships to Criddle's Mill in Great Homer Street. the steam wagons were quite distinctive, they towed a trailer which had solid rubber wheels. They could not travel very fast, and if you were lucky you might be able to skip a lift on them, from the docks, up Burlington Street to Greaty. The 'Steam Wagons' were three wheeled vehicles driven by steam, with their steering column in the centre of the cab. Sometimes when skipping the steam wagon, you might be unlucky. You may have escaped the notice of the driver and the second man, and be clinging for dear life to the rear of the trailer, quite pleased with yourself, when all of sudden, out of nowhere a policeman would appear.

One policeman in particular, a Sergeant, would sometimes lay in wait for you. He somehow knew that when the wagon started to climb up the steep hill to Scotland Road, there would be youngsters clinging to the back of it. The Sergeant carried a long pace stick, and if you tried to escape by running away, he would throw the stick at you, often entangling your legs making you fall over. If he caught you, you were made to empty your pockets and sent on your way home with a clip behind the ear. Quite often the threat of the Police going to see your parents, or worse still, of going to see the head Master at school, was enough to prevent you jumping on the backs of any more vehicles that day.

Some days we youngsters would just explore the dock area, and if it was warm, go swimming in the canal. other times we would climb onto the roof of the derelict warehouses in Love Lane, looking for birds eggs. In most instances the roofs would be missing, having been blown off in the bombing raids during the war. We would run along the top of the walls twenty or thirty feet above the ground, loose bricks falling as we ran, often because your friends had dared you to do so. Quite oblivious to any danger.

Lots of these buildings had been converted into emergency water supplies, for the fire brigade during the war. The water inside them was dirty and thick with green slime from years of neglect.

If any of us had have fallen from the roof. We would most certainly have been drowned or killed outright. I shudder thinking of how stupid we were. On another occasion me and my friends had escaped the attention of the policeman on the dock gate, and were inside a deserted part of the docks. It was a late summer evening and we had discovered a derelict ship and decided to explore it. I went ahead of my friends and climbed up the ships ladder to the top of the funnel. On reaching the top I tried to 'show off' in front of my friends by letting go with both hands and trying to balance on the edge, but I missed my footing and fell inside the funnel. Fortunately for me I escaped any serious injury, only bruising myself and cutting my ear, but to this day I still bear the scar to remind me.

I recently visited the Pier head, and looking into the mirror of my world, I imagined myself once again as a youngster there. I noticed that wire mesh had been erected around the base of the girders supporting the floating landing stage.

This was another dangerous 'dare' we children did. Running across the girders over the river, which connected the floating landing stage to the Pier Head. The tide comes in here very quickly. I understand at about nine knots, and if you fell into the water, you would be swept out to sea, or die of exposure very quickly indeed.

One day after school, a friend of mine named Tommy frost came to visit me at our house. He asked me, would you like a pet rabbit? He explained that his Mam said he was unable to keep it any longer. I knew my Mam wouldn't let me have another pet, We already had pigeons, two dogs and a cat, but in spite of all that, I returned with Tommy to his house, just to look at it. On seeing this huge jet black, buck rabbit, I immediately fell in love with it. It looked a beautiful animal.

I decided to take it home with me, and hide it in the house. The only place available, was in the loft space under the roof. Consequently I sneaked along the lobby and crept up the stairs without anybody seeing me.

Reaching the top of the stairs, I stuffed the rabbit down the front of my pullover, and being as quiet as I could, started to climb to the loft by extending my arms and feet wide enough, to grip both sides of the two walls. I opened the trap door and climbed inside, it was pitch black. Whatever made me think I could hide an animal here?. 'It will only be fer t'night and then I'll tell me Ma, I thought to myself. Perhaps she will let me keep it'. I then released the rabbit into the loft space and climbed back down the wall. That evening when everybody had retired to bed, in the quiet of the night you could hear the rabbit running around the loft space over our heads. The whole household was awake with the noise, my sisters were crying thinking the house was haunted. My Mam and Hughie soon realised something was wrong and came into our bedroom to ask what the noise was? in the end I confessed to what I had done. It was too late to do anything right then, but I was instructed by my Mam to "give the rabbit back to who ever it belonged to, the next day".

The following day my Mam and Hughie left home to go to work, my Mam's parting words to me before she left was. That rabbit better be gone before I return home this afternoon, or you will know it! Once again I climbed the walls to the loft intending to catch the rabbit and take it back to Tommy. I removed the trap door and climbed inside.

Again it was pitch black, but by leaving the trap door open I could see just a little. After a short period of time, my eyes became accustomed to the dark, and I spotted the rabbit crouched down between the rafters in the roof space. I then approached the rabbit by balancing on the rafters to prevent my foot going through the ceiling. When I was quite near the rabbit, it jumped up, and ran towards the trap door, disappearing into the hole. There was a loud thump as the rabbit hit the landing at the top of the stairs, it must have been all of twenty foot.

I scrambled down from the loft as fast as I could, only to discover the poor rabbit lying motionless at the foot of the stairs, it had killed itself from the fall.

It appeared to have broken it's neck. I picked it up and stroked it, it lay limp in my arms, I was heartbroken and blamed myself completely for the poor animals death.

I sat at the foot of the stairs, and wondered what I ought to do next? I did not want to just put it in the bin like a piece of rubbish. After a few more minutes, I decided to bury it on the waste ground near our house.

I then carefully wrapped the poor animal in newspaper, then proceeded out through our back yard door, and up the entry to the 'olla', where I dug a small hole amongst the rubble and ceremoniously buried the poor creature.

For days afterwards, I was very conscious of the animals death, and would only sleep with my head under the blankets. At night laying in bed, I swear I could still hear the rabbit running about in the loft space, I thought it was haunting me for what I had done to it. One night I even thought it was on the bed and shouted out for my Mam, when she came into the room I told her what I thought was happening. She said it was just my imagination.

It's strange how your mind can play tricks on you.

Chapter Five

One day I was visiting my friend Robbie Brougham's house, and his Mother asked would I like to go with them to the beach that day?. I think it was to Moreton, over the water. I replied yeh I would like to go! Mrs Brougham then instructed me to go home, and "tell ye Ma where your goin".

I immediately ran home and asked my Mam, was it alright if I went to the beach with the Brougham's that afternoon? she replied by saying. I could go with them, "but you must get a good wash first". I washed very quickly and returned to Robbie's house clutching a packet of sandwiches my Mam had made, and some pocket money she had given me.

We then travelled to the 'Pier Head' in a group on the tram, arriving just in time to catch the ferry to the other side of the river. On arrival at Moreton, Robbies Father unpacked the bag he was carrying and pitched a small tent on the beach. Being a hot summer's day, it was decided that we would all bathe in the sea. I had not brought a costume, but Mrs Brougham had brought a spare one, which would fit me, and I could borrow it, she said.

The tent was only small, a bivouac. So we all took turns in changing into our costumes. When it was my turn, I entered the tent and undressed, putting on my borrowed costume.

I inspected myself briefly and noticed I was covered in flea bites. (This was not unusual because most houses were badly infested with vermin, of one type or another) I was embarrassed and did not know what to do. I then decided that I would disguise the 'bites' by rubbing wet sand over them. When I had finished doing what I had to do, I left the tent, joining the other's on the beach. I was told much later, that when I emerged from the tent, I resembled a 'Dalmatian' dog, snow white with black dots all over me. How on earth Mr and Mrs Brougham did not burst out laughing at the sight of me, I don't know. That day, we also discovered a huge dead fish that had been washed up on the beach, similar in size to a sperm whale.

On another occasion when I visited Robbie's house. I was accompanied by a friend of ours named Stevie Ferry. Stephen had apparently been to see the 'Nit Nurse' that day, and she had prescribed an oily substance to put on his hair, to prevent head lice.

On arrival at Robbie's house, we were invited into the parlour, the best room in the house. Sitting down, we started to talk amongst ourselves like youngsters do.

IN LIVERPOOL

Stephen was sitting in a wooden upright chair, with his back to the wall. He had positioned himself, so that he could push himself backwards, balancing the chair on its rear legs, his head touching the wall.

Unfortunately for Stephen, Robbie's Father had recently only just finished decorating the room, and when Stephen stood up to leave, there was a huge black stain on the wallpaper, from the cream on his head. Poor Robbie had some explaining to do that day, but I know his parents were always very understanding.

at that time in the district of Everton, the housing conditions that people had to live in, were very poor, whole streets would be infested with all types of vermin. At school we where regularly visited by a 'Nurse'. Everybody called her the "nit nurse". Nobody knew exactly when she would visit the school. When she arrived, the Teacher would line us up in single file, and instruct us to remove our upper garments. The nurse would then examine us individually.

Sometime after I was born, my Mother had accidentally pieced my flesh with a safety pin, when changing my nappy. Which left a scar. Consequently when ever I was examined by the nurse I was always asked.

How did you receive the scar? I always replied. dunno miss. If any signs of infestation was discovered on examination, you were required to go right away to Plumpton Street clinic, this was in Everton Road, there you would be 'painted' in a blue substance to prevent various infections, the most prevalent at the time being scabies.

Every family I knew, had a 'Steel Comb'. But nobody ever spoke about it. This was to clean your hair of 'Nits and head Lice'. The almost nightly ritual in our house, before your hair was washed with carbolic soap, was for our Mam to spread a large piece of newspaper on the kitchen table. Then taking turns, we children would sit with our heads bent over the paper, to have our hair combed. Our Mam would painstakingly comb our hair with the steel comb until your hair was clean. After combing the newspaper would be littered with head lice that had fallen from the comb.

The paper would then be carefully picked up, and the lice thrown on the fire, soon after popping noises would be heard, as the insects exploded. To many readers this may appear to be rather distasteful but it was absolutely necessary, if you wanted to be clean.

A very common disease at that time was tuberculosis (TB). A cousin of my Mother, named Tommy Best, who was also a close neighbour, suffered from this complaint. We children where told not to play with him in case we caught it. Tommy eventually had to spend some time in a sanatorium, but thankfully he returned home completely cured.

As we became older, our Mam insisted that once a week, we boys had to visit the local 'wash all overs'. (the public baths) this was part of the 'wash house' in Netherfield Road. The baths were very popular, and the procedure was that you 'queued up' on a Saturday morning, to purchase a ticket, the price being twopence. This would enable you to have a proper bath, instead of using the tin bath at home. And if I took my younger brother Alec with me, we could both share the same bath for the price of the one ticket.

I remember an occasion when me and my brother Alec got ourselves a Saturday job, working in a wood yard in Howe Street.

Saturday morning we rose early, and running quickly through the entry arrived at the wood yard for 8am. We were then given the job of counting out pieces of firewood, and tying them with string into bundles, ready for sale.

The proprietor had an electric saw which enabled him to cut long pieces of wood into more manageable pieces. An older boy then chopped the cut wood into smaller pieces, which he threw into a pile near Alec and I.

In this confined space, there was sawdust floating everywhere, and every one working in the yard was absolutely covered in it, ourselves included. At mid day the proprietor called us both to him, and thanked us for the work we had done. He then put his hand in his pocket, withdrew some money, and paid us for our work. He then said. "Yeh can take some sawdust home with yer if yer like, for yer fire". We were both delighted, and Alec and I filled two large sacks to take home with us.

This was ideal for 'backing' the fire, particularly if you had some coal bricks or slack to put on as well, the fire would last all night long.

We proceeded home through the back entry which connects each street, quite pleased with ourselves, carrying our sacks of sawdust on our backs like father Christmas. Grownups stepped aside and looked at us as we passed. Presumably to escape having sawdust brushed on them. We were covered in it, it was in our eyes, our hair and all over our clothes.

Arriving home soon afterwards, we proudly deposited our sacks of sawdust under the stairs in the parlour. We then took the money from our pockets to show our Ma how much we had earned. She was very pleased. She instructed us to go into the back yard, and try and shake the sawdust from our clothes. On re-entering the house, she handed us some money, some towels and a block of carbolic soap and told us to go to the "wash all over's" right away for a bath. Make sure you wash yer hair properly she cried after us, as we left the house.

I remember Alec and I visiting the baths that day, and after using the bath. We stood and watched the water run down the plug hole, it was completely covered in sawdust. The only time I can remember it being dirtier, was when the trams had stopped running in Netherfield Road, and workmen were removing the tram lines. Soon after the workmen had ceased work for the day. Dozens of people emerged from the surrounding buildings carrying crow bars and sacks, and descending on the area like soldier ants, to remove all the 'tar blocks' which had been laid in the road previously for the trams. The following morning, when the men arrived for work. There was not a single 'tar block' to be seen along the whole length and breathe of Netherfield Road.

The 'tar blocks' kept people's fire's going for many days, but they also made you extremely dirty. The tar would be absorbed into your skin and you required really hot water to remove it. I imagine the time that the blocks where stolen, the attendant at the local wash all over's, would have had a very difficult time cleaning the baths after everyone. After I had my bath that day, a ring of 'tar' had collected on the inside of the bath, and no amount of effort on my part could remove it. I sneaked out of the baths when the attendant was preoccupied.

One treat we children particularly enjoyed, was to purchase 'fairy cakes' on tick (credit). My Mam would send one of us children to Mulberry's cake shop at the corner of Opie Street and Netherfield Road, with a note asking for a dozen fairy cakes on trust, until your dad got paid at the weekend.

The cakes would be duly handed over, and Mrs Mulberry would write your name and the price of the goods in a book. At the end of the week your Mother would then 'settle' the bill. I distinctly remember returning home from school one day, and sending my younger brother Alec to the cake shop with a note, purporting to come from me Mam, asking for some fairy cakes on tick, I waited outside the shop.

Alec was served with the cakes and on leaving the shop, I took them from him, to share out amongst my friends, they gathered round, and we ate them in the back entry before returning home.

That was another occasion when I got a good whacking, when my Mam found out what I had done. Discussing this with my sister Mary recently, she informed me, that her and Alec often did the same.

I sometimes had to go with my Mam to the shops, and I recall an occasion when she took me to buy some footwear for school. (We boys wore pumps (plimsols) in the summer, and wellington boots in the winter) It must have been a Saturday morning, because we went straight to Daglish the pawnbrokers, who's shop was at the corner of Luther Street and Great Homer Street. We went to collect Hughies suit. (My Mam did not use the local pawnbrokers named Hodges, in Netherfield Road, because she was ashamed of being seen by any of our neighbour's).

Each Monday morning, Hughie's suit would be 'pawned' for a small amount of money, and each Saturday morning, the suit would be collected for Hughie to wear at the weekend. My Mam's 'nom de plume' was Mary Mint, which was written on the pawn ticket. (My Ma used this name later in life, on betting slips at the bookies.) The money she borrowed for the suit, allowed her to buy some groceries through out the week. (rationing was still in force then)

Using the services of a pawnbroker was normal procedure, and a way of life for almost everybody in our neighbourhood, although it was never openly spoken about.

On this particular occasion my Ma also 'pawned' her wedding ring, and with the money, took me to 'Paddys Market' to buy me a pair of wellington boots. Those wellies were just what I wanted! you could wear socks which had holes in the heels and no one would know, they were great for the rain and you did not need to polish them. You could even tuck the legs of your longies,(long trousers) down them, even trousers which were too short for you. Sometimes yer Ma had to cut pieces off the bottom of the legs, to patch the seat of your pants. There was only one thing wrong with wearing wellington boots. That was, with everyday wear, they left a black mark around your leg where the top of the boot met the flesh, and no amount of scrubbing would remove it.

Once a week, our class was taken to the swimming baths at Borough's Gardens, in Mile End. The baths where known locally as the penny plunge. The entrance fee being a penny. Our teacher Mr Critchley would escort us to the changing rooms, and wait for us outside, before marching us naked in single file to the showers. None of the class had any costumes, We would all be trying to hide our modesty before crowding into the shower. Having showered you where then allowed to enter the pool.

I remember one day when visiting the baths, I got the fright of my life. Some older boys pushed me in the deep end. I thought I was going to drown, before I was finally pulled out by the attendant. I was very nervous of water for a long time after that.

On reflection, when ever our school visited the 'penny plunge', it must have been quite funny being the attendant, To see a pool full of nude, snow white youngsters, all with black rings round their legs, because of the wellington boots they wore.

I loved my wellies, I did everything in them.

Writing as I am now of Wellington boots, my brother Alec informed me of an occasion, when he, and a number of his friends, decided to visit the Grafton Rooms, the ballroom in West Derby Road. He and his friends must have been aged between twelve and thirteen. They had all arranged to meet at the top of our street, Robsie, dressed in their best clothes, before walking to the dance. Alec told me that one of his friends named Frankie Cuttress, arrived wearing his wellington boots, his long trousers covering them. Nobody passed any comment about them. apparently this was not unusual, lots of people went dancing in wellington boots in those days.

None the less, it did not prevent Frankie from enjoying his dancing, nor any of the others dressed like that. That was the way they had been taught to dance, at evening classes in Rossy School. I often wonder, did Mrs Wilf Hamer, the dance band leader at the Grafton ballroom, realise some people wore wellington boots when dancing, to her big band sound?.

I must have been quite a 'joker' when I was young, because I remember an occasion when my friend 'Chunky Ellis' visited our house on his way to school, and I invited him to look at my pigeons. I then persuaded him to enter the loft on some pretense or other, and whilst he was in there, I locked the door. I then told him he would have to clean the loft before I let him out. I then went off to school leaving him locked in the loft. Chunky was shouting for me to let him out. My Mam discovered him there later that morning when she returned home from work, but was unable to release him, because I had the key with me in my trouser pocket. That morning the school roll was called and 'Chunkie' was marked absent. At lunchtime I returned home and released him. Our gang often played tricks on each other like that. Much Later, 'Chunkie' whilst doing his National Service, played in goal for the Army and on being demobbed, he was offered the opportunity of playing in goal for Burnley, but declined to do so because it meant having to live away from home once again.

Roscommon Street School sent many children to Colemendy camp in North Wales. The School was run by Liverpool Education Services and was really an extension of your own school, but in a far nicer environment. For a small payment, you were able to attend the camp for a number of weeks in the year. Our school ran a savings bank facility, to help you save money for your stay there.

Me and my brother Alec decided we would like to go, so we began saving our pocket money. Knowing full well our Mam and Hughie would have difficulty finding enough money for all four of us children to go, we decided to knock on doors in our immediate area, and ask the old people living there, "can we go on any messages to the shops, for yer please" ?.

After a short period of time, we had quite a number of 'customers' who came to depend on us for this service, and from the small amount's of money they gave us, we managed to put it in the savings bank at school.

Each Sunday morning, my Mam would instruct us children, "to put on our best clothes and go and visit Auntie Maggies." Then Alec and I and our two sisters Mary and Margaret would dress in our Sunday best, and visit Aunt Maggie, and Uncle Jimmy. They lived in Upper Beau Street and had five children of their own. (All girls) On arrival, we would knock at the door and march along the lobby. Auntie Maggie would invite us all to sit down. We four youngsters would sit together precariously balanced on the edge of the 'couch', before being offered tea and biscuits. We would be asked questions about my Mam and Hughie, which I always felt embarrassed about because of the divorce. But the real reason we were there, as far as I was concerned was to collect pocket money. As soon as we had received our 'money' from Uncle Jim, this would be an excuse to leave. Arriving home soon afterwards we would change back into our street clothes to play out.

Our Mam always insisted that we children save some of our pocket money for a rainy day. Later in life she had a post office savings book. Each week she would religiously pay the 'clubman' for the insurance, and for any cheques she had on tic. Any money saved from her shopping would go to the post office. On her death in 1990 she had saved more than enough to pay for her funeral.

Eventually the family saved enough money for three of us older children to attend Colomendy Camp. It was fantastic. A school in the middle of a wood, in beautiful countryside, with mountains surrounding it. It had a silence you could listen to. I loved every minute of my time there. Sometimes we would visit Wrexham or Mold with our teacher for a day out. This gave us the opportunity to buy our parent's a present to take home. Other times we went climbing Moel Famau, the mountain alongside the camp.

Those periods at Colomendy Camp made such an impression on me, they will stay with me for ever. They gave me a real love of the countryside. I returned many times afterwards with the school. Even today when driving in North Wales, I often detour to pass that way, and think of the many happy times I spent there.

My brother Alec also enjoyed his times at Colomendy but our sister Mary on arrival, cried to go home, our poor Mam had to come all the way to North Wales to collect her, I believe Mary never went again.

Living as we did in the densely populated slum area's of Everton, it was always a pleasure to visit the countryside. There being no trees whatsoever in our part of Liverpool.

Some of the places we visited by tram in the school holidays where so unlike were we lived, for example, Woolton Woods, with its floral clock and the Cast Iron shore at Aigburth Vale. Other occasions we would visit Lord Derby's estate in Croxteth and climb over the walls to go bird nesting. Part of the estate is now a safari park.

On one of these occasions me and my friends decided to visit Sefton Park in Aigburth. This is Liverpool's largest park, named after the Earl of Sefton, and originally part of Toxteth Park. Apparently when Liverpool obtained its charter from King John in 1207, He required a Royal hunting park on the outskirts of the city from which he used to hunt deer, and wild boar regularly on his visits to the north. Sefton Park was purchased by the city council and opened to the general public in 1872.

The park has had many benefactors in the past. One in particular named George Audley was a bachelor, and like so many people who live in Liverpool he loved his City. One of his many kind deeds just before he died in 1932 was to present to the park, a statue of Eros, with its exquisitely detailed design around the base, similar to the one in Piccadilly Circus, London, together with a Peter Pan statue and pirate ship, once again a replica of the one in Kensington Gardens, London. The park also boasts two large lakes, one a boating lake, and a beautiful conservatory, with wonderful tropical plants growing inside of it. (The Palm House or glass house as we children knew it, is currently being restored)

After spending some time wandering in the park and visiting the aviary, to see and feed the many caged birds, we youngsters visited Otterspool Promenade which was just across the road from the park. We had earlier boarded a number 46 tram in Netherfield Road which took us to the terminus at Penny Lane. From Penny lane we boarded a number 4W tram to take us to Sefton Park. One boy in our company named Bernie Swan, decided to 'skip the tram' taking us there, by clinging to the back of the tram, to save paying the fare. He was notorious for jumping on the back of moving vehicles.

When we realised what Bernie was going to do, we all ran upstairs on the tram, to look out the rear window to watch him. Bernie clung to the bumper bar for quite a long time before being discovered by the conductor and jumping off. I expect he would 'skip' another tram to take him home.

On another occasion I remember, a crowd of us boys travelled by bus from Everton Valley to Lydiate to go pea picking. Arriving at Lydiate, We walked to the farm that required helpers that day. On being hired, we then spent the remainder of the day working in the farmers fields, stopping only at lunchtime to eat the sarnies our Mother's had given us. It was late afternoon and we had finished work for the day. We were getting ready to return home, when all of a sudden, I saw a baby rabbit at the edge of the field and chased after it.

The rabbit ran under a gate leading into the farm yard. To head it off, I climbed over a wall surrounding the farm, and without looking, jumped to the other side but instead of meeting the rabbit as I had expected, I had jumped into a pig sty, landing amongst the pigs, and falling down in their excrement as I landed. I climbed out very quickly indeed, more frightened of the pigs than anything else. I was covered in pig muck and stunk to high heaven.

Everyone laughed at me, I had to clean myself up in the Liverpool to Leeds canal, which runs through Lydiate, before I was allowed to travel home with them on the bus.

Other times our gang would travel to Wales on bikes, going through the Mersey tunnel. At that time cyclists could travel free of charge. Our bikes would be made from frames we had found in the local corporation tip in St Domingo Road, and 'done up', often without mudguards or brakes, but you could overcome this problem by putting your foot on the wheel to stop.

One of my friends named Yankee Cuttress, had a part time job as a delivery boy, working for Irwins the grocers in Great Homer Street. His boss allowed him to take the cycle home at weekends. Yank rode a 'sit up and beg bike' which had large handle bars, a huge basket on the front, and a sign on the frame advertising the grocer's name.

I remember, we decided to visit Wales on our bikes and stay the weekend. We arranged to meet at the side of Ben's shop in Sanderson Street. Eventually everyone arrived carrying what ever was needed for our overnight stay, each of us on our 'made up bikes', some with drop handlebars, others riding the sit up and beg type. Yankee arrived riding his firms bike.

There was about ten of us altogether in our group. I imagine we must have looked quite a site.

We set of for Wales, freewheeling most of the way to the Tunnel which was all downhill. Entering the tunnel we pedaled to the other side shouting to each other en route, our voices echoing off the tunnel walls.

Arriving on the Birkenhead side of the river we made our way to Wales, arriving there approximately three hours later. It was getting dark, none of us had any lights on our bikes. Travelling down a country lane we found what we thought was a suitable field, and quickly pitched the tent someone had brought with them. We then huddled together inside. In the dark we had not noticed that the field was full of stubble, the farmer must have recently cut the hay and it was like sleeping on a plank of nails.

Having spent a most uncomfortable night, we awoke the next morning to a lovely summer day. In the near distance was a farmhouse with smoke pouring from it's chimney, me and another boy agreed to go and ask for some water. By this time we had eaten our sandwiches and drunk the water we had brought with us.

The two of us set off for the farmhouse carrying our empty bottles. We knocked at the door which was opened by a young girl approximately our own age, We explained that we where camping nearby and had run out of water, could she possibly help? she replied, yes of course, and taking our empty bottles from us disappeared into the house. She was very pretty and had a lovely accent. I immediately fell in love. She returned a few moments later with our bottles which were now full of water, accompanied by her father. He wanted to know where we were camping, and when we told him he smiled, and said, it's ok as long as you don't light any fires! I must have gone back to the farmhouse at least three more times that day, with our empty water bottles, just to see the girl. We left later that same day to return home.

Cycling back to Liverpool, we discovered a huge American storage facility in a wood near Bromborough. There must have been hundreds of vehicles lined up in neat rows, all with American stars painted on the sides of them. We climbed over a wire fence into the depot to see what we could scrounge but were seen by a security guard before we could get any souvenirs, we ran away to recover our bikes and decided to continue on our way home. Ten minutes later, we 'found' an orchard and being hungry, again climbed over the fence, we tucked our 'gansies' (pullovers) into our trousers and tightening our belts, first filled our pockets with apples, then filled our gansies to overflowing.

Hurrying from the orchard as quickly as possible, our mouths now full of apples, we must have looked like the Michelin man advert. Not content with that, soon after we found a field full of cabbages, so we stopped and immediately filled the basket on Frank's bike to overflowing. One of my friends had some string from which he suspended a cabbage from the rear of his seat. Returning home through the tunnel to Liverpool, we thought our procession might be stopped by the tunnel police but fortunately for us, it was not.

Arriving home later that evening, we divided our spoils out amongst us, which we then gave to our respective Mother's to make meals with.

Our gang must have been like a plague of locusts, when out in the countryside on our bikes.

I recently walked through the Mersey Tunnel from Liverpool to Birkenhead, to commemorate the 60th anniversary of it's opening. I was accompanied by many thousands of people. Half way through the tunnel, we were fortunate enough to have the unique experience of seeing the Royal Liverpool Philharmonic Orchestra, conducted by the American Carl Davies, the husband of Jean Boht, star of the TV series Bread. The Royal Liverpool Philharmonic is the first symphony orchestra in the world, to play beneath the sea.

It was whilst walking through the tunnel with Charles, I thought of the many times I had cycled through it as a youngster.

Continuing my story, I was now aged fourteen and the government had just raised the school leaving age to fifteen. We were all very disappointed in our class, we had just missed, and would have to spend another year at school! Although now I am pleased to report, that a great many of my school friends became successful business men later in life. Perhaps that extra year at school enabled them to do so.

One evening in our street we were celebrating Bonfire night. For weeks, we had been collecting all kinds of rubbish to burn.

Bonfire night gave people the opportunity to rid themselves of any old furniture they no longer wanted. Sometimes 'Blackie' the local policeman would spoil everyone's fun by asking us to remove the pile of wood we had gathered, He would say. "It's too near the houses". I believe one bonfire night, somebody picked up Blackies waterproof cloak and threw it on the bonfire. after he had taken it off to run after some boys who were misbehaving.

Some times the fire brigade would be called, to put out the fire when it became too dangerous. The day after bonfire night, dozens of smoldering embers would be seen in every street.

On one particular bonfire night, crowds of grown-ups with their families had gathered round our fire, setting off fireworks, whilst an effigy of Guy Fawkes was burning on the top of the fire. Meanwhile other groups of youngsters were swinging fire cans they had made, well away from the crowd.

Suddenly there was a loud bang and Billy Howard who was standing in front of the fire cried out, hands held to his head, blood streaming through his fingers down his face. People ran to help, after a swift examination of the wound, an ambulance was called which arrived minutes later. Billy was then taken to the Royal Infirmary accompanied by his Mother, a wet towel wrapped around his head to stem the flow of blood. Afterwards it was reported, that a round of live ammunition had gone off in the fire, and grazed Billy's forehead just above the eye. Bernie Swan was seen clinging to the rear of the ambulance as it sped away

Apparently Billy was very lucky, another quarter of an inch or so and he would have been killed. Bill still bears a slight scar to this day.

Billy Howard's grandfather, Mr Taylor was deaf and dumb, and from an early age Billy was able to communicate with him and understand the deaf and dumb language.

I was always fascinated seeing him 'talking' to his Grand-Dad with his hands. Much later when we were older, a group of us including Billy would often go to town for a night out, and I have often seen him talking to people afflicted this way. Bill and I still remain good friends to this day.

(I was reminded recently of just how many talented people we have in our city, when being escorted around Liverpool Town Hall by Steve Binns, a blind guide, who unescorted can stand in front of an object and talk so knowledgeably about it . What other city can boast the same?).

I left school soon after the bonfire night incident, now aged 15. My school report was nothing to boast about, it was not unlike all my friend's reports. We used to laugh at a make believe school report which said the following: Who ever gets this person to work for them, will be very lucky indeed!.

By now me and my friends were all anxious to get a job, and earn some money. Fortunately for everybody concerned there was now plenty of work to be had. My first job, was a second man on a horse and cart for British Rail working from Lime Street Station. My wages where fifteen shillings a week. My Mother handed five shillings back to me from my unopened wage packet. I worked Monday to Friday and half day Saturday.

My first task at 8am each day, was to collect 'my horse' from it's stables in Gill Street, near the bullring, and take it to the station.

Once inside Lime Street station, the horse would be hitched to a cart and driven to the loading bay by my driver Mr Jones.

The both of us would then load our cart with parcels.(consisting mainly of Littlewoods catalogue items) Which had been sorted the night before into areas for delivery. Our area being the Wavertree district of Liverpool.

One of our jobs was to deliver goods to the abattoir in Prescot Road. I hated this part of my job. On entering the large ornate gates, we would drive over the cobblestones to the office at the rear of the abattoir, to deliver our parcels. Passing the pens waiting to receive live cargos of animals, for slaughter later that day.

Quite often, huge transporters would be seen backed up to the pens. The drivers inside the rear of the trailers, urging the terrified animals down a ramp to the cages. Occasionally you would see tiny lambs being cruelly thrown from the back of the lorries. Whenever I witnessed this I would feel physically sick. Even our horse pulling the cart, seemed to sense "the smell of death in the air" and would snort and be very nervous until we left

When my driver Mr Jones realised how much this effected me he used to try and drive past the cages as quickly as possible. Once again for long periods afterwards, I would not eat meat.

Another part of our job would be to collect goods, from the old Great Western Railway building in Victoria street, and deliver them to Lime Street Station for onward transmission.

This building was closed for many years, but thankfully has recently undergone a major refurbishment. It is now part of the Museums and Galleries of Liverpool. Here you can see works of art, being cleaned and restored for museums throughout the country.

After loading our cart in the morning. We would exit from the station down a sloping entrance to Lime Street. The policeman on point duty in Lime Street would always stop the traffic to allow a horse and cart the right of way. The horses would be keen to canter, particularly on a Monday morning after being rested, and locked in the stables all weekend.

IN LIVERPOOL

One morning I went to the stables to collect my horse, only to discover it lying dead. It had to be pulled out of it's stable by another team of horses, before being taken away to the knackers yard. It was very upsetting, you soon get very fond of your own particular horse, and the local shopkeepers on our round, missed him aswell, they used to feed him titbits and give us water for him to drink.

There was another boy my age who like me, worked on the horse and cart's, his name was Andy Cunningham. Andy lived in a part of Liverpool known as the Bull Ring, not too far from the station. When we had both finished work for the day, and taken our horse's back to the stable. Andy and I still dressed in our railway uniforms would return to Lime Street station. We would stand as near as possible to platform 9 and wait for the London train to arrive.

When the train arrived, we would separate and walk quickly onto the platform, keeping well away from the older Porters. We would then look for embarking passengers who required assistance. Seeing somebody struggling with lots of luggage, you would presented yourself in front of them and ask. Would you like a porter sir?

In most instances the answer would be yes, and you would carry their suitcases to the nearest taxi rank. Sometimes the passenger would inform you that they were going to the Adelphi Hotel. Then you would reply, "the hotel is only round the corner sir!, I'll carry your bags there if you like, and save you the taxi fare".

If the passenger agreed, you would escort him through the side entrance of the station to the hotel, expecting to receive a much larger tip than usual, having saved the passenger the price of a taxi.

Andy and I received lots of tips. Sometimes far more than our actual pay for working on the carts. That's if we were able to meet enough trains.

The railway porter's employed at the station specifically to handle baggage, resented us delivery boys meeting the trains. They said, it was not our job, and it deprived them of their livelihood. Our reply to this was. "We didn't ask anybody if they wanted a porter, the passenger's asked us to help them, cause we had our railway uniforms on". (Nobody bothered to ask, what we were doing on the station late at night) Andy and I quite often got into arguments with the porter's, and on one occasion I ended up fighting one of them.

One day I had to visit Dale Street magistrates court. I had to appear on behalf of my Mam as a witness, to give evidence against my Dad who had been constantly pestering her. My Mam had been advised to take out an injunction against him. I had been given time off from work by British Rail to attend court and was dressed in my railway uniform.

I sat next to my Mam who had just finished giving evidence against my Dad. My Dad was sitting at the front of the court. My name was called. I stood up and was asked to enter the witness box.

I was very nervous and afraid to look at my Dad. The clerk of the court then asked me to take hold of the bible in my right hand, and to swear on oath that the evidence I will give, will be the whole truth and nothing but the truth. I started to repeat the instructions. It was at that precise moment, that I was rudely interrupted by the magistrate, who looking at me from his seat up on the bench, asked. Have you no other clothing to wear, when you appear in my court? I was initially struck dumb and didn't know what to say. Then I felt my face going red with embarrassment. I thought to myself, I look rather smart, and I intend to return to work immediately after the court hearing. In fact one of the jackets I wore in the evening's when out with my friends, was a British Rail coat, minus it's silver buttons.

I then blushingly explained that I had been given time off by British rail, and intended to return back to work immediately after giving my evidence.

The magistrate then smugly informed me. That if I had to appear in his court in future, then I must be suitably dressed. I was then allowed to continue with my evidence. It just goes to show how some people, are so divorced from reality. Consequently I will never forget that moment in court.

Hughie's Mother, Mrs Smith lived quite near Lime Street Station, at 45 Trowbridge street in the bullring. Mrs Smith sold flowers from a basket in London Road with her good friend Mrs Kelly. Mrs Kelly was the Mother of George Kelly, who was convicted of the Cameo cinema murder, in Wavertree in March 1949 and executed.

His accomplice at the time, Charles Connolly received ten years in prison. George Kelly was a cousin of Hughie my stepfather.

There is a lobby of opinion who say, 'the trial was a travesty of justice', and if all the evidence, would have been produced in court today, George Kelly would not have been convicted of murder. I understand there is a book being written on the subject.

Some days, When my Mam was in town shopping, I would arrange to meet her at Lime Street station, and we would go for lunch in the Railway canteen. On other occasions when we met, we would visit Mrs Smith at her 'patch' in London Road. On them occasions, my Ma would always bid hello to Mrs Kelly and present Mrs Smith with some 'Fine Irish snuff' she had bought for her, which cost seven old pence a twist.

On receiving the snuff. Mrs Smith would say. Ta Mary, and extracting a tin box from somewhere beneath her shawl, would empty the contents of the packet into the tin. My Mam would say. have you had anything to eat yet? Mrs Smith would reply. Not yet! My Mam would then say, come on, we'll go to T J's for something to eat.

Mrs Smith would agree, she would then place her basket of flowers alongside a stack of cardboard boxes on the ground, and carefully place an old hessian sack over them. She would call to Mrs Kelly standing a few feet away. "I wont be long, I'm goin' for a cup of tea with our Hughie's one". The three of us would then walk the few yards to the restaurant in T.J.Hughes' department store.

Once sat in the restaurant, my Mam no doubt feeling obliged to look after her mother in law, would pay for our meal, which invariably consisted of, a round of bread, a bowl of soup and some tea. After finishing our meal, I always became embarrassed watching Hughie's mother putting a pinch of snuff up her nose. The procedure was, for Mrs Smith to take a portion of snuff out of the tin box and place it on the back of her clenched fist. She would then close one nostril with a finger of her free hand, and sniff the contents up her nose. Repeating the exercise with her other nostril until all the snuff had disappeared.

Apparently the 'old people' believed, this cleared the head, and prevented them from getting colds. Unfortunately for them it left a brown stain under their nose.

I mentioned earlier that Hughie was now working on the docks. The men in our neighbourhood who also worked on the docks, with the exception of a few who owned bicycles, would all walk to work. It was much easier to walk, it was all downhill from the heights of Everton. No buses ran directly to the docks from where we lived. Once you arrived at the docks, you could travel on the 'overhead railway' to the ships berthed there.

(The Liverpool overhead railway the first in the world, built in 1893 and demolished in 1957 and known locally as the dockers umbrella) This was another bad example of the unnecessary demolition which took place in Liverpool at that time.

To save money on fares, I also walked to work. Leaving home at approximately 7.15am. Hughie having woken me earlier.

My route to work each day would be as follows. I would leave by the back door leading to the entry, and walk down the jigger to the opening in Beatrice Street. I would then cross the olla's in the streets made by the bombing in the war, emerging at the bottom of Arkwright Street and turn into Great Homer Street. From Greaty I would walk past Paddy's Market to St Anne Street, passing Rose Hill police station and Berry's pawn shop. (Berry's pawn shop stood like a monument all by itself in a sea of debris, as if beckoning to the people of Scotland Road to pawn their wares). I would then cut through Gerrard Gardens, a tenement block designed by the architect Keary and a short cut to Lime Street and my place of work.

For a stranger to Liverpool to see for the first time the magnificent St Georges hall in Lime street, makes me think of Queen Victoria and the impression it made on her. On the opening ceremony in 1854, she declared, it to be worthy of ancient Athens.

(On entering Gerrard Gardens, you would see a statue of a builder, standing with his legs slightly apart holding a spade. The statue was set into the brickwork directly above the entrance to the gardens. On asking some of my friends who the statue was of? they replied. it represented an Irish Navvy who built the flats. Hughie's Mother, Mrs Smith, who once lived in the area, said, it was "her fella, (husband) who helped build the Tunnel", but what was more interesting to me at that age, was that somebody, had thrown a rubber ball and it had lodged exactly where a mans testicles would be. The times I smiled to myself on passing that statue. The thrower's aim was perfect. I wonder what happened to it when the building was demolished in 1987? and what did the statue really represent?).

Hughie had now worked quite a few years on the docks. He also had two close friends who he worked with, named Maxey and Burkey. Apparently they were inseparable and the three of them always chose to work together. They where also his drinking partners and would go for a drink after work, much to my Mothers consternation. Often they could be found in the Rob Roy pub in lodge lane near where Maxey lived. This was when they worked on the fruit berth, at Queens dock, in the South end of the city.

The pay for a dock worker was very poor, about 12/- per day. The docker's where classed as casual labourers. Times were still very difficult for lots of folk, thousands of men had returned home from the war and could not find work.

(It was not until 1968 that dock work became decasualised, after many years spent lobbying Members of Parliament, and going on strike to attain this end. Now thirty years later, since the United Kingdom joined the European

IN LIVERPOOL

Union, Merseyside is in the wrong geographical position, the emphasis now being on the eastern ports of the country.)

A dock worker's day in them days consisted of having to report to 'his pen' at 7.45 am. The 'pen's' were situated along the docks. It must have been rather humiliating, for the docker would have to line up to be selected for work by a representative of the shipping line, and if he was lucky, they might obtain work for a few days on a ship. The docker would have to report each day to the ship, until such time as the cargo had been unloaded and a new cargo loaded. Occasionally this would mean the docker having to work the weekend. Working Sunday was known as the "golden nugget", and would almost double the docker's pay for the week. this was in great demand by everybody who worked on the docks. When the ship was once again re-loaded, it would put to sea, and the whole process would start all over again. If that morning, the dock worker was unable to obtain work from his pen, he would have to report again at lunchtime, and again the following morning, until such time that he was successful.

Sometimes a man would report all week without being able to get work. On pay day he would only receive a signing on fee of five pounds a week.

Leaving the pay queue he would then have to pay from this, his union subs, and any money he may have borrowed from his fellow workers throughout the week, for bus fares and cigarettes etc. You can imagine how much money he'd have left over, for his wife and children.

The docker worked in a gang of eight men. The work being extremely difficult, often in dirty and dangerous conditions.

He also 'handballed' everything. Thousands of sacks each weighing a hundred weight would have to be manhandled, and stacked on boards, then covered in safety nets, ready to be lifted from the ship's hold by cranes. Sometimes accidents would occur and men would get injured.   Unlike today were ships cargo's come in huge containers.

To relieve the monotony and take a break, the docker's worked what was known as the "welt". Two hours on and two hours off. In their 'time off', the docker's would frequent the many dock side canteens for tea and toast. The most popular of these canteens, would be Stan Waters or Big frank's cafe. For lunch you could purchase a bowl of thick and a nudger, for about a shilling. (Pea soup and a french loaf sandwich), and play cards until it was time for you to return to work.

There's many a story been told of Liverpool dock workers, too numerous to mention here, and their various nicknames, who like most Liverpudlians in difficult circumstances, have a wonderful sense of humour.

Hughie would leave home each morning at approximately 7.00am, but more often than not he would return home soon afterwards, not having been able to obtain work for the day.

He soon realised that he would have to do something else, besides being a dock worker, to provide for his growing family. He was a born showman and loved being the centre of attraction and when at work he would entertain his fellow workers by doing tricks.

He sat at home one night and discussed with my Mam ways of earning some extra money, when there was no work for him at the docks. Suddenly he had the bright idea, of entertaining the thousands of people with his tricks, who visited Liverpool city centre on a daily basis, and at the same time make some money for himself .

He gave it some more thought and decided he would expand his repertoire. He then started to collect all manner of things. For example, chains, long handled 22lb sledge hammer's, swords, whips and dozens of old telephone books. When he spread the word about of what he wanted, people would knock at the front door with items for sale.

He also acquired a large tarpaulin from some one, and brought it home with him. He proceeded to cut the canvas into the shape of a sack, large enough to hold a mans body. He wore a pair of thick gloves and stitched the canvas together using large sail making needles. Small holes where inserted in the sack to enable a person to breathe once inside it. I distinctly remember Hughie putting my brother Alec in the bag when it was being made, to try it out. My Mam used to say, I hope nobody calls when your doing all this.

About this time, Hughie also decided to make some dancing dolls. I don't know were he got his ideas from, but all the younger members of our family, and their friends, were given the task of collecting used lolly ice sticks, that they could find lying in the street, and instructed to bring them home. (I was excused because I was now working). Dozen's of sticks were collected, then washed with soap and warm water in the sink.

My Ma's job was to save the feather's from the chicken that had been killed and plucked for our Sunday dinner.

I still disliked the idea of eating a chicken we had reared. Hughie always wrung the chickens neck when I wasn't at home. My Mam would pluck the chicken, and later colour the feathers. She would dip them into a bowl of dye, before hanging them over the fireplace to dry. Later the feathers would be cut into one inch pieces with a pair of scissors. Although I tried hard to have nothing to do with all this, I was asked by Hughie. Jim, on your way home from work, will yer buy a 'John Bull' printing kit, and some glue from a stationer's in town? I'll give yer the money for it!.

He also wanted me to get some "off cuts" of white paper from a printer he knew in Prescot Street. The family was now ready to set up in business.

Every member of the family had a job to do. Hughie had bought a small drill with which he drilled holes in the ends of the lolly ice sticks.

The feathers now dyed different colours, were glued to one end of small blocks of wood, which resembled a dolls head and body, then the lolly ice sticks would be attached to the body by a small piece of wire and secured with pliers. The lolly ice sticks represented the arms and legs of the doll. The finished product looked like two small dolls facing each other holding hands. The legs hanging loose. Black cotton would then be attached to both ends of the doll.

By attaching one end of the cotton to the leg of a chair, and pulling the other end of the cotton towards you, you could make the dolls stand up from a sitting position, by relaxing the cotton you could make them sit down.

After some persuasion, and the promise of a few bob. I was given the job of arranging the letter's from the John Bull kit, into some sort of order, to print the following instructions on the off-cuts of white paper I had bought. 'pass thread through centre hole of arm of doll, tie to chair and pull'.

I was then asked to place the instructions with each completed doll, and carefully wrap them in newspaper, before placing the finished product in a cardboard box ready for sale.

Hughie had already identified a spot for his pitch in the City Centre. It was a bombed site at the corner of Charlotte Street, and Ranelegh Street, facing Lewis's department store, where Samuels the jewellers now stands.

Hughie, besides being a good provider, like I already mentioned was a great showman.

He would prepare his pitch with great care, by drawing a large circle on the ground with a piece of wood, then he would place all of his equipment in the centre of the circle. By this time passers by would stop, to look wandering what was happening. To attract even more attention, he would crack a huge whip in the air. When he thought enough people had gathered round, he would inform them, he had magic dolls he wanted them to see. People would smile and whisper among themselves, before coming nearer. Hughie would shout. Stand back, stand back, let the dog see the rabbit, every one would be laughing by now.

(On a visit to Chester Zoo with my own family many years later, for a joke, I bet my wife that people's curiosity will always get the better of them. I stopped on one of the many footpaths in the zoo, and bent down to stare at the ground as if examining something. After a few minutes, a small crowd had stopped and gathered round me. they also started to stare at the ground. I turned to my wife stood up and said.I've won my bet, then continued walking on our way. Seconds later I Looked over my shoulder and people were still staring at the ground where I had been looking).

One of Hughie's many assistant's was a chap named Johnny Brady, nicknamed (Snowy) because of the colour of his hair. Johnny was married to Hughies sister Maggie.

It was Snowy's job to stand in the crowd with his hands in his pockets, and when Hughie instructed the dolls to stand up or sit down, to unobtrusively pull the cotton attached to the dolls.

(One end of the black cotton would previously have been tied to a brick among the equipment in the middle of circle, making it indistinguishable on the waste ground.)

Hughie would tell jokes and laugh with the crowd, then when everyone was enjoying themselves, he would instruct the dolls to sit, stand or dance. This would result in the dolls performing tricks for him. Hughie, would then extol the virtues of owning one of these magic dolls. Just think how the kids will love them when you take them home, he would say. There only a tanner each. He would finish by saying, How many do you want? I've only got a few left.

Hughie's assistants would hand out the dolls as quickly as possible, to all the eager onlookers anxious to buy them. The money taken, would be handed to Hughie, who would put it in the hat he had been wearing, now held in his outstretched hand. When the crowd had finely finished buying the dolls, Hughie would stop whatever he was doing, and completely ignoring everybody, start to re-arrange his pitch. The members of the public realising the show had ended, would continue on their way

Hughie would now tip the contents of his hat into a large cloth money bag which he kept in his pocket, and when he thought nobody was looking, he would hide the bag under a piece of canvas in the centre of the circle. After a few more minutes had passed, Hughie would start the whole procedure over again with new potential customers.

Hughie soon became well known to the crowds of Liverpool. Amongst his close friends he was also known for his kind generosity. Particularly to the elderly and less fortunate in society. He would always find something for them to do. If he found some one who looked like they needed help, He would ask them to help him with his pitch, even if it meant running errands to the shops for sandwiches. In the warm weather it would be for lemonade and ice cream. He always insisted they "get something for themselves".

I have seen Hughie give money to people he had not even met before, when he came upon them sitting on a bench, or lying in a shop doorway. With the comment, "ere yer are Ma, or Pop" get yerself a drink!.

His generosity would often annoy my Mam, particularly when he was in the pub with her, and she had seen him buying someone a drink.

She would say to Hughie. He's a bloody bum that fella, naming the person, she would continue. He wouldn't give you a push off the side. Later in life, my Mam became hard of hearing and quite often insulted people in Hughie's presence, because she misunderstood what was being said at the time. She thought they where talking about her. It wasn't unknown for people to remark, when they saw my Mam approaching. Watch out here comes Mary, with that a number of them would walk away.

There was one occasion when Hughie had just arrived outside Lewis's, and after marking out his pitch, he started to crack his whip to attract attention. Soon a large crowd gathered round to see him perform his tricks. Hughie was again encouraging the onlookers to purchase one of his dolls. Johnny Brady as usual was following Hughie's instructions, by standing in the crowd to operate the dolls, this time Hughie was asking the dolls to stand up and sit down, and do the Okey Poky. (dance). Consequently Johnny was tugging the cotton rather quickly in his pocket, when all of a sudden he was struck on the head from behind, by an elderly woman wielding an umbrella, who accused him of being a dirty old man.

Poor John was being struck about the head and shoulders. To escape from the woman, Johnny ran through the centre of the ring, the woman in hot pursuit. Hughie soon realised something was wrong when the dolls stopped dancing. The crowd had now turned there attention away from him to see what the commotion was about. Hughie stepped quickly in between the woman and Johnny and tried to separate them, in turn, yelling at the woman, accusing her of ruining his pitch. The crowd now realising what was happening, burst out laughing.

For ease of use, Hughie had made a 'working doll'. This doll had wire hooks protruding from the top of it, which enabled the doll to be suspended quite easily from the cotton. It helped Hughie to be much quicker by not having to tie and untie the doll after each pitch.

On another occasion a Nigerian seaman stood in the crowd and appeared to be fascinated by the dancing dolls. Hughie immediately recognised that he had a possible sale here, and to further entertain the crowd, He focussed his attention on the Nigerian.

Hughie called out to the gentleman, are you a visitor to our town Sir? The visitor replied yes, showing beautiful white teeth emphasised by his black face. Hughie continued. Where yer from Sir? The visitor replied Nigeria! Hughie now playing to the audience answered. I've been to Nigeria I fought with Monty there in the last war! (Hughie never left England in the war) The crowd laughed, Knowing full well General Montgomery served in North Africa.

Whilst the crowd was still laughing and their attention focussed on the visitor, Hughie bent down and quickly switched the working doll, for another one in his pocket, placing it directly on the ground. He straightened up and said to the Nigerian. "Would you like to ask the doll to dance Sir". The Seaman smiled, no doubt conscious everybody was now looking at him. After a moments hesitation he called out for the doll to dance.

Obviously nothing happened! The crowd were enjoying themselves. Hughie then walked over to the doll and picked it up.

Lifting it level with his face, he spoke directly to the doll, instructing it. "To do as it was told for our visiting friend". He then moved the doll to his ear as if listening for a reply. The crowd were even more delighted. Hughie once again bent down replacing the doll on the ground. Again unobtrusively switching dolls, placing the working doll on the suspended cotton. He then informed the Nigerian seaman that the doll had told him, it did not like being shouted at, and it would only dance if it was asked to nicely.

There was a slight pause. The Nigerian smiled again, then in a even voice instructed the doll to dance once more. Of course this time the doll obeyed. courtesy of Johnny Brady. The Nigerian was delighted. The crowd roared its approval. Hughie then persuaded the poor seaman to buy his entire stock of dolls, and had the audacity to take a half a crown deposit on the cardboard box they were in. He then made a quick exit with his friends to the nearest Wine lodge in Lime Street, before the seaman changed his mind.

Occasionally the local Police would move Hughie on but as soon as they had departed, Hughie would start his pitch once again. One day a young policeman asked Hughie to pack all his things together and move away because he was causing an obstruction. Hughie replied, Ok officer and proceeded to gather all his equipment together. The Policeman satisfied his instructions would be followed, then continued on his way.

After a few minutes had gone by, and no sight of the policeman. Hughie once again began cracking his whip to gather a new crowd. Suddenly the young police constable re-appeared and walking straight up to Hughie arrested him on the spot. Hughie tried to reason with him, but to no avail. He was escorted across town to Cheapside police station and charged with the offence. Johnny Brady took care of the money they had taken that day, and all the equipment.

Hughie was ordered to appear before the local magistrate the following day and fined ten shillings. I believe when the new policemen's colleagues discovered that Hughie had been arrested by him that day, they made fun of the constable. They said Hughie should only be arrested if the Sergeant, or inspector ordered it.

Hughie had a good relationship with the Police, although he was breaking the law. They knew he was harmless, and only trying to make a few bob. Apparently the constable was new to the force.

I believe the same young Constable came to see Hughie a few days later, when he was again having a pitch. Taking Hughie to one side, he apologised for the trouble he had caused him. He said. You understand, if I'm ever with my Sergeant, I'll have to move you on. He then insisted on giving Hughie ten shillings to pay for the fine. That's the effect Hughie had on people, he was a likable rogue. Unfortunately, Hughie had now got into the habit of spending more and more of his time drinking with his friends, to the extreme annoyance of my Mam.

My Mam would have prepared a meal for him and he wouldn't return home until late at night, and then he'd be drunk. she would argue with him until the early hours of the morning. I would often have to intervene, it effected every one in the household. The following day I would try to avoid seeing the neighbours because I was so embarrassed.

In the end my Mam would often go to town looking for him.

Quite often Hughie would sell the dolls very quickly and if the weather was good and plenty of people still about, he would continue his show by cracking his whip but this time when the crowd gathered round, he would inform them, "I'm going to perform my strong man act". He would say. "I'll challenge any member of the public to beat me". This is were his collection of telephone directories came in use.

Hughie would pick up a telephone directory from amongst a pile in the centre of the ring. Holding it above his head for everyone to see, He would ask for a member of the public to try and tear it in half.

Unless you are extremely strong this is almost impossible.

After a period of time, when a number of men had tried unsuccessfully to do so. Hughie would retrieve the book and talking non stop to the crowd, place the directory amongst the stack of books on the ground. He would turn to the crowd and say. How did I get from Neddy Road to Lime Street without passing a pub? People would call out different routes, of how to get there. Hughie would reply. Yer all wrong, I went in all of them.(meaning the pubs) The crowd would laugh. Hughie would then pick up a sword laying alongside the books, and in an authoritative voice, inform the crowd. Do not try this, it is very dangerous.

Hughie would then raise the sword and hold it over his mouth, pretending to swallow the sword but stop, just when the tip was about to enter his throat, as if he had suddenly remembered something. Oh yeah, he would say. I've got to tear the directory in half haven't I?. Where's the book! (He was a great showman) He would then replace the sword on the ground, saying I'll do that later. Then walk towards the books lying in the centre of the ring. Selecting a directory from the pile on the floor, he would begin to tear it in half. (Unknown to member's of the public the directory he chose, would have been 'baked' overnight in our oven at home, which enabled it to be torn quite easily, by even the weakest of men.)

Hughie would pretend he was having great difficulty tearing the book, by saying. "this ones a tough one, he would glance at the title and say, it's named Sampson and Delilah". The crowd would laugh. After struggling for a few more minutes, Hughie would eventually tear the book in half, depositing the two half's in a sack held by one of his assistants. He would mop his brow with his handkerchief as if he had really exerted himself. then say to the crowd. Please keep the City tidy don't throw rubbish on the floor. The torn book was put directly in the sack to prevent any one examining it. Having now proved to every one how strong he was. Hughie would then proffer his hat to the crowd, asking them to throw in a little bit of silver. He would continue by saying. It's to buy more books from British Telecom, for my next show. People would again laugh. I often thought to myself, there must have been an acute shortage of telephone books in Liverpool when Hughie was doing this trick.

On other occasions he would produce a six inch nail from his pocket, and ask people to try and bend it. Once again this is extremely difficult.

IN LIVERPOOL

Hughie would get two six inch nails, and by wrapping his handkerchief around both tips of the nails pointing towards each other, he was able to obtain much more leverage on the nails and bend them without too much difficulty. Hughie stood approximately 5"10 in height, and although lithe in appearance he was extremely strong.

Another trick Hughie did, was to wrap nylon cord around the palms of his hands, and apparently without too much difficulty pull his hands apart, and snap the cord quite easily. This is done by the cord being wrapped in a certain way, and the knot being hid in the palm of your hand to take the strain. Unless you wrap the cord correctly, it won't snap and is most painful. Once again he would ask the crowd to 'show their appreciation' by putting a few coins in the hat.

One of his saying's was, I need a few bob today cause the rent man's cumin, and if I get no money here, when he shouts rent, I'll have to say spent. The crowd would love it.

Hughie had now extended his repertoire by a further two acts. One included breaking stones on his chest, and the other, the use of a rope. These two last acts landed him in very serious trouble indeed.

The rope trick entailed him having to place his head inside a noose, with the ends of the rope resting on the ground.

Having put his head in the noose, he would ask for volunteers from the crowd to pull each end of the rope. The noose would tighten around his neck, and the crowd would witness Hughie brace himself and defy death. Under normal circumstances he would have managed to have put a slip knot in the noose to prevented it tightening completely, before it was placed around his neck.

but on this particular occasion, in the crowd that day where two Royal Naval Matelots, slightly the worse for drink, who insisted on placing the noose around Hughie's neck themselves.

When Hughie asked for volunteers, the two sailors had staggered forward to offer their services. They took hold of the rope and started to examine it closely, before placing it about Hughie's neck. Then they quickly took hold of the ends of the rope, and without waiting for the signal to start, began to pull the rope in opposite directions. The rope tightened, and Hughie tried to signal for them to stop by waving his arms about but without success.

He tried undoing the rope around his neck but again without success. The crowd thought it was all part of the act, they were shouting their approval. The next thing anybody knew was that Hughie had turned a funny colour and had collapsed to his knees, his legs giving out beneath him. The sailors seeing him do this, immediately let go of the rope. The crowd then realised something had gone terribly wrong and a number of them rushed forward to help him.

The rope was loosened from Hughie's neck. He was lowered to the ground. Some of Hughie's friends started gently slapping his face, whilst others kept the crowd back to enable him to breathe. After a short period of time he was sufficiently recovered to be able to sit up, and take a sip of water. Later he was escorted to Yates' Wine Lodge in Lime Street, were he made a remarkable recovery, with little more than severe bruising to his neck. He was an extremely tough man.

The other occasion which I distinctly remember, when Hughie got into extreme difficulties, was when he was breaking paving stones on his chest. One of Hughie's favourite expression's at the time, was to ask the crowd for twenty more good sports to put some silver in me hat, then I'll have the slab broken on me chest.

He would start his act by counting the number of people putting money in the hat, then he would deliberately forget where he was up to. Members of the crowd would shout out to remind him, particularly the children. It was like a huge pantomime.

I was always amazed at how easy it seemed for Hughie to encourage people to part with their money. When he decided that he had collected enough money, he would invite a member of the audience to break the stone on his chest with a huge 22lb sledge hammer, lying in the centre of the ring. He would then lift the stone and place it on his chest.

Under normal circumstances, a member of the public would step forward and break the stone.

Immediately afterwards, Hughie or one of his colleagues, would again go round collecting money before the crowd disappeared. Members of the public who had not put any money in the hat, now might do so.

Unfortunately, on this particular occasion, and unknown to Hughie, my Father was in the audience.

My dad quite naturally disliked Hughie, and blamed him for the break up of his marriage to my Mam, although by this time he had also remarried. When Hughie called for a volunteer to break the stone, my Dad stepped forward offering his services. Hughie had already lifted the huge stone on to his chest, and was brave enough to continue standing there ready to have it broken, although by now he had recognised my father.

IN LIVERPOOL

My Dad picked up the sledge hammer, and raising it above his head, deliberately swung it at Hughie, missing the slab completely and striking Hughie's right arm. The force of the blow sent Hughie staggering sideways across the ring, the weight of the slab pushing him to the floor. I believe my Father then calmly replaced the sledge hammer on the ground, looked at Hughie for a second or two, then walked away through the crowd without saying a word. People standing in the crowd watching all this, may have thought it was an accident, and the fella who used the hammer must have lost his nerve and walked away. But Hughie's friend's in the crowd knew otherwise.

An ambulance was called and Hughie was taken to the Royal Infirmary in Pembroke Place, where it was discovered he had a broken arm, and cracked ribs. He spent the night in Hospital before being discharged and returning home the following morning.

Hughie never did complain about the incident. In fact he made fun of it. His arm was in plaster for many weeks and he did not appear to bear a grudge. My Mam seemed more upset than Hughie. calling my Dad all kinds of horrible names. Hughie very rarely did the stone trick after that.

They say, you cant keep a good man down. Although Hughie was in plaster for many weeks after that 'accident', and unable to perform his usual job on the docks. (Dock worker's received no 'sick' pay at that time, being classed as casual labour only).

None the less, quite soon afterwards, Hughie again started to earn some money, only this time he did, what he called the queues.

Hughie bought himself a mouth organ, and through sheer determination, soon taught himself how to play. He had decided he was going to entertain the crowds, who waited in queues outside the picture houses in town. He only learned to play one tune, it was named 'The old rugged cross.' Many years later the family had this hymn played at his funeral in St Georges Church in Heyworth Street.

Being a teenager, me and my friends had now started to go out in the evenings. We would often buy ticket's for the Royal Iris which sailed on a cruise from the Pier Head to the mersey bar, on board ship you could enjoy all the latest music and dance until returning late at night. It was very convenient, the tram took you right to the terminus at the landing stage.

 We had also started to frequent the local dance halls.

Each Friday night a group of us would attend a dance held at Blair Hall in Walton Road. This was something we really looked forward to. Before entering the dance, one of us would to go into 'the pacific' a pub near by, and stretching to our full height, order a bottle of 'bentox' to take out. In the dance you could only buy soft drinks.

Having bought the drink, we would crowd into a nearby shop doorway, and before entering the dance drink the wine, passing the bottle between us. The wine made us feel merry.

Inside the dance hall. Me and my friends would stand together soaking up the atmosphere, listening to the music playing and looking at the girls dancing on the floor. We would compare notes on which girl we fancied. Our group had become quite friendly with a number of girls our own age, who we had learned to dance with. It was nearly time to go home. The last waltz was being played. After a quick exchange of words, Robbie Brougham and I agreed to split up,(excuse) two girls dancing together on the floor and ask, could we escort them home? We stepped on the floor and taking hold of the girls by the arm asked . Can we have the last dance please? The girls replied yes!.

Within a few minutes the girls agreed to walk home with us. both girls lived in Sessions Road, near St John's Church in Walton, which was fine because it was on our way home. Walking along Walton Road we stopped at a chippy, and bought some fish and chips for ourselves and the girls. We continued on our way, now eating our supper from the newspaper it was wrapped in. In between mouthfuls of fish and chips we chatted to the girls, trying to impress them.

Arriving at the girl's destination, we stopped at the end of the road, the girls informed us which house they lived in. Everywhere was pitch black except for the street lights which gave the area an unreal atmosphere. The only sound to be heard was a dog barking in the distance. We stood talking for a few minutes, then gently taking hold of the girl's arms, led them a short distance down the back entry which separated each row of houses. The girls stood with their backs leaning against the wall, a distance of two or three yards separated me from Robbie and his girl. I felt very grown up.

Out of the corner of my eye, I watched Robbie kiss his girl full on the lips, so I did the same and kissed my girl. After a period of time spent kissing and cuddling, Robbie called over to me. Jim, d' yer fancy us all goin'to the pictures together on Sunday? Before I had time to reply, Robbie's girl also called to her friend. Mary, shall we go?. Almost instantly, the girl I was with, replied, yer ok. After a moments hesitation, I also replied, yer, that's smashin. Not thinking of where the money was coming from.

IN LIVERPOOL

We arranged to meet the following night outside the 'Big House', in Lime Street. The Big House is a well known pub in the town centre, which has a large clock hanging over the main entrance, and is situated alongside the Adelphi hotel.

The arrangements being made. We kissed the girls goodnight. They walked up the street and waved goodbye, before disappearing into their respective houses.

Robbie and I then started to walk home, we took a short cut through Kirkdale Park to bring us out at Everton Valley. The park is on the site of the original Liverpool Gaol. We hurried as quickly as possible it was now past midnight. It was rumoured the park was haunted by prisoners who in the past had been hung for murder. On our way home we discussed our 'girls', and the date for the following evening. We were very pleased with ourselves, and full of the joys of spring.

Thinking back to that time. imagine the four of us must have stunk from the smell of fish and chips, and goodness knows what we might have we stood in, standing in that entry. The coats the girls wore that night, must have been ruined from leaning against the dirty wall. But who cares you are only young once.

The next day, I asked my Ma to press me good "kecks" for me, and could she also lend me some money until I got paid next week? She and Hughie asked were I was going, and I replied, just out with Robbie Brougham. They smiled knowingly to each other, but consented to me having some money.

That evening I paid great attention to myself getting ready to go out. There being no privacy in our house, I had to tell everybody not to open the back kitchen door, when I was getting washed from the sink. When I had finished washing. I ran upstairs to the bedroom to get dressed, a towel wrapped around my waist. I stood in the bedroom and popping my head round the door, shouted downstairs. Mam will you bring me "kecks" up to the bedroom? I overheard Hughie say to my Mam, Mary, the Sheriff wants his trousers.

For some unknown reason, Hughie, when I wasn't supposed to be listening sometimes called me The Sheriff, or Big Truck. My brother Alec brought my trousers up to me. I was about to put them on, when I noticed they had been ironed down the seams of the trousers. Instead of a nice crease down the front of the leg, they had been pressed flat, and looked like a pair of bell bottom trousers that sailors wore.

I was annoyed and shouted down the stairs to my Mam, that I was going out soon, and me trousers were all messed up. I did not want to tell them I had a date, and how important it was for me to look my best, although I guessed by now they all knew. I threw my trousers down the stairs in frustration.

The trousers where retrieved from the bottom of the stairs and taken into the kitchen. I heard everybody laughing. Apparently my Mam had given my trousers to Mary my sister to press, and that was the result. My trousers were soon ironed correctly, and returned to me. I dressed hurriedly and left home to call for Robbie. Saying to my Mam on the way out, I'll see yer later. Hughie had left the house a few minutes before me.

Robbie and I caught the tram from Netherfield Road. We got there in plenty of time for the start of the picture showing that night. Soon after we arrived, the girls appeared looking quite attractive in their pretty dresses. They both wore make up and smelled of cheap scent. Feeling nervous in the presence of the girls, I thought to myself. I'm glad I'm with Robbie and not on my own tonight.

Standing alongside our respective girl friends, We crossed the road to the Gaumont cinema and joined the queue that was forming.

The doors of the cinema were not yet open as more and more people joined the queue, the queue began to get quite large. All of a sudden I heard the sound of a mouth organ playing a well known tune. The old rugged cross. The noise was getting nearer and nearer and by now, the familiar sound of a voice saying, thank you Sir, Your a sport.

I said myself, Bloody hell, It's Hughie! What should I do? I was so embarrassed. I didn't want him to see me. How could I hide?. I turned my back to where the sound was coming from.

Suddenly Robbie says, heah Jim, it's your Hughie! I thought to myself. As if I didn't know!. I felt I wanted the ground to open and swallow me up. I also imagined a lot of people were now looking at me.

Hughie had approached us by now playing his mouth organ, one hand still encased in plaster. On recognising Robbie and I he smiled and said, how's the trousers? and continued along the queue collecting money. I could have died, and felt myself going red in the face. I mumbled something or other in reply to one of the girls, who asked, what did he mean about trousers? and how did he break his arm?. A few more minutes passed before Hughie returned, and stopped alongside me. This time he said, "ere yer are Jim, get yerself some ice creams". With that he pressed some money in my hand before disappearing to the next cinema queue. He was a very generous man.

IN LIVERPOOL

I then quietly explained to the girls before going into the cinema, that Hughie was my stepfather, and that he had broken his arm in an accident and could not yet go back to work. Each of them replied, we've seen him in town before! I was not surprised, everybody had seen him. Hughie also gave money to my brother Alec and his wife in similar circumstances many years later.

My two younger sisters Mary and Margaret were now quite grown up, and could help my Mam look after our brother John. I can recall both sisters nursing John, giving him his bottle and changing his nappy. When he was born my Mam bought a huge silver cross pram which enabled the girls to take him for walks in the good weather. John was often left to sleep in the pram which took up most of the room in the lobby.

On one particular occasion I remember. John appeared to be ill. My Mam was so concerned that she wrapped John in his shawl, and carried him to see Doctor McCabe at his surgery in Shaw Street. Mary went with her. The surgery was about a mile from were we lived. Arriving at the surgery, my Mam asked a woman at the front of the queue could she go next?, the woman replied No, I'm sorry, I'm in a hurry aswell. After a few more agonising minutes had passed, my Mam was allowed in to see the Doctor. The Doctor examined John, and informed my Mam. Take him back home and keep him well wrapped up, and give him "a drop of brandy" if you have any. The doctor told my Mam he would call to see John the next day.

That evening John's temperature increased. Mary my sister said John was going a 'funny' colour. My Mam again became very concerned, and not happy with Doctor McCabes diagnoses, decided this time to pay half a crown and take him to see Doctor Strellitz.

Doctor Strellitz ran a private practice and had a reputation as a very good Doctor. His practice was also situated in Shaw Street. Mary and my Mam set off once again to the doctor's surgery and on arrival. John was immediately taken into the consulting room and examined. My Mam was then told that John was extremely ill, and must go at once to hospital. An ambulance was called and John was taken to the Childrens Hospital in Woolton.

The remainder of the family was anxiously waiting for news of John. When my Mam returned home with Mary, she told us that John had gone to Hospital and that she and Hughie would have to leave right away to be near him.

I was told I would have to mind the children until they got back. They both then hurried out of the house to Netherfield Road, where they flagged down a passing taxi to take them to the Hospital.

When they arrived at the hospital, they where informed by a staff nurse that John was seriously ill, and had been diagnosed as having a bowel problem and Pneumonia. He would need to be kept in hospital for some time. She said they where allowed to see him for a brief moment. John lay there unaware of their presence. The nurse said. He will be alright here with us, we'll look after him, you may as well return home, there's nothing more you can do now, come back tomorrow. They were reassured by the nurse and after a short time returned home.

Seeing Hughie and my Mam coming in the house without John, Mary and Margaret burst into tears and began to cry, thinking John was going to die. Later that evening we all retired to bed.

In the early hours of the morning, the family were suddenly awakened by a loud knocking noise on the front door. Hughie went to see who it was, and on opening the door was confronted by a policeman standing at the top of the steps, who informed him that John was very ill. After an operation, John's condition had deteriorated throughout the night, and he was now on an 'urgent note'. The constable said it would be advisable to return to the Hospital right away. My Mam and Hughie dressed hurriedly and returned to the hospital as quickly as possible, only to discover that John was now in the intensive care unit. They spoke to the Doctor on duty who confirmed what the policeman had said. That John was very ill indeed. He also said, the next twenty four hours would be crucial. Unknown to my Mam, the Doctor told Hughie there was a possibility that John may not survive the night.

My Mam and Hughie where naturally heartbroken at Johns condition. The Doctor arranged for some tea to be made for them, and invited both parents to remain by Johns bedside throughout the night. Miraculously John's temperature began to drop, and he started to slowly recover.

When my Mam and Hughie failed to return home by the following morning, I became rather worried. I got ready for work as usual and instructed Alec and the girls to stay off school until my Mam came home. I then went to work. On arrival at work, I informed my driver Mr Jones what had happened to my younger brother, and how worried I was. Mr Jones took me to the general office, and I was made to repeat my story over again to the office Manager. The Manager then kindly telephoned the hospital on my behalf, to be told that everything was going to be alright. I was so relieved.

John spent a number of weeks recovering in hospital. The whole family took turns visiting him, but my Mam went every day. Whilst visiting John, she became very friendly with one of the young nurses who attended to him.

One day my Mam returned home from one of her visits, and informed me that she had 'fixed' me up with a date.

It's with one of the nurses who's been looking after John she said, and you have to meet her on Saturday night outside the 'legs of man' in Lime Street, when she had the night off. My Mam continued, she's a lovely girl and you'll like her. My first reaction was one of complete surprise. Then secondly. To refuse to see her. I had never been on a blind date before. Nor had I been on my own with a girl before. After thinking about it a little longer my curiosity got the better of me, and I began quizzing my Mam on exactly which nurse it was she had made the date with. I was trying to recall wether or not I had seen her on the times I had gone to the hospital. I also thought. What if she is ugly or bow legged?

All the family became involved in trying to persuade me to meet her, particularly my sisters who appeared to know which nurse it was. That evening I stood talking to my mates in the pub doorway, and confided in them about what my Mam had done. I then asked their advise on what I should do?.

A nurse! I wish it was me, they replied.

All my mates agreed I should go and meet her. I did not tell them my mind was already made up, and that I had decided to meet the girl. Instead I told them, I hadn't decided what to do yet, I might, or I might not keep the date. Returning home later that night, and before going to bed. I instructed my Ma, on your next visit to the hospital. Tell the nurse, I'll meet her in town on Saturday night at 8 o'clock. The following day my Mam returned home after visiting John, and informed me that the nurse had agreed to meet me there.

Saturday evening arrived, I had been thinking about the girl all week, wondering what I would say to her when we met, and what will I do if she didn't turn up? I'd feel a right dope. Particularly in front of my mates after telling them all about her.

I got ready that evening paying particular attention to the clothes I wore, and trying hard not to overhear the family whispering about me. I left the house and walked up the street to Netherfield Road to catch the tram to town. Reaching the top road, I stood for a moment before glancing back to our house, in time to see the remainder of the family trying to hide from my gaze at the front door. After a short tram journey, I arrived at my destination, the 'legs of man' pub at the corner of Lime Street and London Road.

I was about fifteen minutes early.

I waited, conscious of every girl who passed by, until eventually this young girl arrived and stood rather nervously on the corner. I tried to see if I could recognise her from the corner of my eye but without success. After a short period of time wondering what I ought to do next, I decided to pluck up enough courage and approach her.

I walked over to where she was standing and said, is your name Joan and do you work at Woolton Hospital?. She looked at me and replied yes! I was so relieved that she had turned up, she also looked quite pretty aswell.

I then explained that I hadn't recognised her in civilian clothes. She smiled and seemed quite pleased to meet me. That evening we visited the Palais de lux cinema in Lime Street. I bought some sweets from the kiosk on the way in. During the performance we ate the sweets, I was conscious of the noise the sweet paper made. I was undecided whether or not to hold her hand, and thought to myself, I better not. Not on our first date.

After the film ended, we went to the 'punch and judy' cafe for a cup of tea, our conversation centered around my Mam and how well John was doing. I was pleased that Hughie had not been playing the cinema queue's that night. It was getting late. We decided to catch the tram home. She told me she lived in Woolton. We crossed the road to the tram stop on the other side of the road, and continued talking until her tram arrived, and she had climbed aboard. I then bid her goodnight but not before we made arrangements to see each other the following week. I then waited until my tram arrived and returned home.

Arriving home, I discovered the whole family was still up, apparently waiting for me. They all appeared to have silly grins on their faces. Hughie said, we've saved you some chips, his breathe smelled as usual of Aussie white wine. I thought to myself, He must have been to town after all. I replied I'm not hungry thanks, I'm going to bed and made the excuse of having to be up early the next morning.

I went upstairs, rather than face a barrage of questions about my night out with the nurse.

The following day after work, I went to see my mates. The first question they asked was, Howd'ya get on last night with the nurse, and what's she look like? I took great pleasure in exaggerating about my night out. Telling them of all the kissing we had done, and how I was going to see her again next week.

IN LIVERPOOL

After my initial date with the nurse, my brother John's health continued to improve, and soon afterwards he returned home completely cured. I continued to see the nurse for quite a long time after on a weekly basis, but eventually we stopped seeing each other. I can't remember why. I started seeing my pals again on Saturday night and made the excuse that I had packed her up. She lived too far away I said.

The following pages show some scenes of the city of my youth.

Once upon a time in Liverpool.

These houses in Cobden Street, pictured above in March 1960, look in good condition, but being in the House Clearance Area they had to go, along with the Bear's Head on the corner (below)

Everton Brow, June 1927

Everton Brow, June 1927

Everton Brow, with its famous Toffee Shop

The junction of Everton Road and West Derby Road, opposite Grant Gardens, June 1937

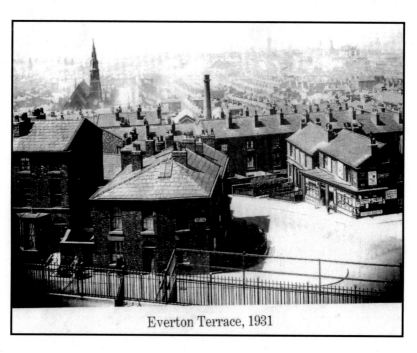

Everton Terrace, 1931

Everton Heights – The Braddocks – in 1959

Everton Valley, November 1904

Everyday life in and around Netherfield Road in 1927

The Juvenile Department at the library

Mere Lane, May 1927

Netherfield Road, 1950

Netherfield Road, July 1913

Prince Edwin Street, July 1920

The hustle and bustle of Prince Edwin Street, September 1920

Prince Edwin Street court houses, March 1924

St Domingo House

St Ambrose Church in Prince Edwin Street
built in 1870 and demolished in 1961

St George's Church

Chapter Six

One evening me and my friends stood talking in the doorway of the Stingo pub, when a group of older lads in their early twenties came towards us. They usually stood in the doorway we were now occupying. One of my friends whispered out of the side of his mouth, look who's coming, we'll have to move. I replied, I'm not moving anywhere, we were here first. The gang approached us, and one or two of my friends moved out of the doorway. The remainder of us stood our ground.

The leader of the gang who no doubt will recognise himself from this description, (It was his two sisters who attacked my mother many years before), came over to where I was standing, and looking me straight in the eye said, "You lot, bugger off or else!"

I stared right back at him and replied,"Or else what?". Both groups of lads anticipating one of us now had to back down or fight, gathered closer. He then answered. Or else we'll knock the living daylights out of all of yer.

I looked round, my friends were all looking at me. I knew if I fought they would fight also, in spite of the other gang being much older than us. I hesitated a moment longer, then said, OK, I'll tell yer what I'll do.

Just fight me. Nobody else, just you and me, in a straight fight! He smiled back at me and said, alright, yer on. I'm gonna kill you Elliott.

That decided, everybody then walked to the waste ground at the back of the pub, a buzz of excitement could be heard from members of each group discussing the forthcoming fight. It was pitch black on the waste ground, except for the light reflecting from the upstairs window of the pub. The floor felt uneven from the mounds of debris strewn about. My eyes were becoming used to the dark, I could now recognise my friends gathered round me, one or two of them volunteering advise. One of my friends held my coat which I had just taken off. I thought to myself, I never did like this fella I was about to fight, nor any of his family. I was reminded of how his sisters had assaulted my mam many years before. This will be my chance to now get even.

We both stepped forward away from our friends to face each other. He had also removed his coat. Both gangs forming a circle around us. I was determined not to give in to this man and confident I could beat him. By now both sets of supporters were shouting encouragement. We stepped closer to each other, hands held in a boxing position trying to anticipate what the other would do. He was taller than me. He stepped closer intending to hit me with his fist, Suddenly I dropped my guard and charged forward in a rugby tackle, striking him with my shoulder, all my weight behind me. It was a matter of self preservation.

The force of the blow made him fall backwards, both of us now locked together. He had lost the height advantage and I knew I had winded him. We rolled on the floor striking each other about the body oblivious to the rubble lying on the ground. I thought about my mother which seemed to give me added strength. We continued to grapple with each other for what seemed ages, rolling over and over, I received a number of blows to my face and body, eventually I managed to pull myself free. He was in a kneeling position about to stand upright, I quickly grabbed him from behind in a headlock. I could hear my friends shouting instructions. I squeezed his neck as tight as I could with my left hand, at the same time pressing my left knee into the small of his back. I rained blows to his face with my right fist. He continued to struggle but he was in a hopeless situation, I continued to squeeze his neck harder and punch him about the face.

He cried out for me to stop but I continued striking him, not wanting to lose the advantage. Suddenly he went limp and collapsed in my arms.

I shouted to him, d' yer give up? my fist raised threatening to strike him again. He replied yeh! I released him and he leaned forward, one hand on the floor steadying himself, the other hand holding his throat.

The fight must have lasted less than ten minutes.

I was still very angry. I could feel the adrenaline surging through my body. I turned round to face his friends, and standing upright adopted the boxers stance once again. I shouted out, does anyone else wanna go? There was a moments silence, then one of his friends said. It was a fair fight. The tension was broken, with that his friends stepped forward to assist him, My friends gathered round to congratulate me and help me on with my jacket.

My legs were still shaking, I was breathing heavily and trying hard to compose myself. I walked over to my opponent who was now standing upright, his right eye swollen. He was holding a handkerchief to his face to prevent it from bleeding. My whole feelings had now suddenly changed towards him, in fact I now felt sorry for him.

I offered him my hand in a handshake and asked, are you ok? He replied yeh I'm alright, extending his own hand to shake mine. To make him and his supporters feel less embarrassed, I said, I was very lucky yer no, I jumped yer because you would have beaten me in a proper boxin match! He did not reply.   Both groups of supporters where now talking to each other, something they rarely did in the past. We continued speaking for a few more minutes, deliberately not mentioning the fight, before bidding each other good night.

Both gangs separated, each going our own way.

Now walking home and out of earshot of the other gang, my friends started to congratulate me on how well I had fought. By saying, did yeh see the big eye he's got? yeh nearly killed him, and he wont be so quick at offering you out in the future. We stood in the doorway of Ben's shop and spent what seemed hour's talking about the fight. Being the topic of conversation I bathed in their admiration before we all decided to go home.

I climbed the steps to our front door and entering the house, crept along the lobby, it was late, everybody had gone to bed. Good, I thought to myself. I can examine my face in the mirror without being disturbed. I noticed bruising on my face and decided. Tomorrow, I'll disguise that with some of my ma's make up before I go out.

From that moment on. I often met my opponent and his friends and we used to stop and talk to each other. Both gangs now tolerated each other's presence but because of the age difference between us, we never really became good friends.

LIFE'S BUT A WALKING SHADOW, A POOR PLAYER THAT JUST STRUTS AND FRETS HIS HOUR UPON THE STAGE, AND THEN IS HEARD NO MORE : SHAKESPEARE, MACBETH V. V.

One of the highlights of the year for most people in Liverpool is the Grand National. It is a unique occasion in the horse racing calender, and not unlike today, in the past, thousands of people would come to see the World Famous race. Every available space on the main roads leading to Aintree, would be filled with huge signs advertising the different daily newspapers. Outside the racecourse, dozens of temporary stalls would be erected selling all manner of things. The pubs in the area would be packed to overflowing with lots of customers stood outside drinking on the pavement.

Hundreds of people would be mingling outside the entrance to the racecourse. Many looking at newspapers trying to identify the winner of the race. Some people would be eating hot dogs or drinking tea. Whilst others would be watching the various entertainer's, all of them soaking up the unique atmosphere of this special day.

Young boys would be seen running amongst the crowd selling the Liverpool Echo and programmes. Whilst every few minutes Aintree station, the local bus service and taxi cabs would continue to disgorge their passengers by the hundreds.

A regular visitor each year to the race was a huge black gentleman known as 'Prince Monolulu', who had a zebra skin cloak draped over his shoulders. He wore a large silk top hat with a feather stuck in the side. In his hand he carried an African fly swat. He would shout. "I've got a horse, I've got a horse". People would rush to buy a ticket from him in the hope his tip would be the one to win. It was a carnival atmosphere and Hughie took full advantage of the occasion.

On the day of the race, Hughie and his helpers would leave for Aintree early in the morning to secure his pitch. My mam would follow later with a shopping bag packed with sandwiches and the kids. I would go separately with some of my mates. On arrival Hughie would head for the car park of The Sefton Arms, which is immediately outside the famous race. He would go behind the pub and borrow some empty beer crates to place on the ground were his pitch would be, as if waiting for a delivery. The Police wouldn't realise what was happening until it was too late. When Hughie thought enough people had gathered for him to have a pitch. He would suddenly appear and start cracking his whip, informing everybody that he was Liverpool's official street entertainer. I'm here every year he would say, and I've permission from the Lord Mayor to perform here today. He would wave a piece of paper in the air.

I would travel to the National the same time as my mam on a tram. On the way to the races I would sit upstairs with my mates away from the rest of the family. Alighting at the races I would always stand a few feet away from the family as they watched Hughie do his tricks, pretending I didn't know them. I always felt rather embarrassed in the presence of Hughie and my mam but at the same time very protective. This may seem strange but now I was older, I felt the responsibility for the family had shifted to me. No longer were my parents protecting me as they had always done, our roles had now changed and now it was me who was protecting them.

After attracting a crowd in his usual manner, Hughie would perform the bag trick. He would crack his whip and welcome the visitors to Aintree as if he personally had been nominated to do so. Telling the crowd he performed this trick all over the world, and that he had just returned from Las Vegas. He would continue by saying. He hoped the crowd would be generous today because the man in the bag has a large family to support. The people in the crowd who knew Hughie from his performances in town, would all be laughing and smiling.

Hughie would try and have as many pitches as possible before the race began, and would be constantly looking at his watch. When he thought he had collected enough money, he would start the count and Johnny Brady would escape from the sack. He would then quickly start another pitch and Johnny would escape once again.

In between pitches, my mam would have sent one of my sisters over with sandwiches for me and my mates to eat.

At about 2.30pm, the National started at 3.15pm, Hughie would announce that this would be his last performance today, and would everybody kindly throw as much money as possible in the hat, because the money collected this time was for the blind, under his breathe he would say, stinkin drunk. Everyone would laugh. He would thank the crowd and say he hoped they had enjoyed his act and would they tell their friends all about him. "You can send me postcards when you get home" he would say. "Just address it to Hughie, the man in the bag, Liverpool".

Having collected as much money as possible, this being his last performance. Hughie would thank the crowd once again for their kind generosity. Then he and his helpers would start to collect all the equipment together, wrapping it inside the canvas bag.

When he had finished, he would carry the bag to one of the nearby car park attendants, and ask. "Will yer mind it for me"? He would tell the attendant. "I'll be back after the race and fix yer up"! (reward him).

After arranging to have his gear looked after, Hughie would return to his friends, and a small crowd of us would walk to Melling Road and climb up the slope to the railway embankment, from there you had a good view of the race without having to pay. Hughie would have helped my mam up the slope by pulling on her arm. By this time she would be weighed down with all the loose change he had put in her shopping bag from the day's performances. Before the day was ended, my Mam would have helped herself to some of the money, before she returned it to him.

After the race had ended, we would return to the car park. Hughie would collect his bag from the attendant fixing him up as agreed. The pavements would once again be packed with thousands of people, this time hurrying home or crowding into the local pubs. The stalls which hours before where bustling with activity were now being dismantled and loaded onto lorries. Discarded newspapers and debris would be spread everywhere waiting to be cleared away. My mam and the rest of our company would stand waiting for

Hughie to return and when he joined us, we would cross the road to the railway station.

From the station we would take a train to the centre of Liverpool. On arrival at Central Station, I would say to my mam before leaving. "Ma, I'm goin'now"! which would be a signal for her to say, "Hughie, Jimmy's goin'now". Hughie would then put his hand in his pocket and retrieve a handful of silver coins, and thrusting them towards me insist, "Here yeh are, here's a couple of bob for you and yer mates before yeh go".

All my friends thought the world of Hughie and would tell me so. I used to reply. "Yeh but you don't have to live with him do yer"! By this time Hughie's helpers had separated from us and were making there own way to the pub. Hughie would escort the family to Lime Street from where they would catch a tram home. He would say to my Ma before he left. "I'll see yer later Mary, I'll just sort the lads out". My mam would reply, "don't you go leavin me on me own in the pub again".

Hughie would head for the American bar in Lime Street were his friends would now be waiting for him. The manageress of the pub allowed him to store his bag there until he needed it once again. Hughie would order a round of drinks and take his own drink to one of the alcove seats, which afforded him a little privacy in which to count the days takings.

The manageress would take all Hughie's loose change in exchange for pound and ten bob notes. After a short period of time, Hughie would 'share out' the days takings amongst his assistants. He would then order another round of drinks, making sure the manageress was fixed up before going next door to the wine lodge, were he intended to have a few Aussies whites before going home.

More often than not, he would stay in the wine lodge with his friends until just before closing time, then hurry out to catch a taxi to take him to the Stingo in Netherfield Road, in time to meet my Mam for the last order.

On some of these occasions when she was sitting alone waiting for him, friends of theirs who knew how angry she became when she was waiting, would often tease her by saying, hasn't he arrived yet Mary? and continue by saying. I think he's got another woman! My mam would reply, I'll other woman him when he gets here. They were very jealous of each other.

When Hughie did eventually arrive. My mam would shout at him asking, "Where'd yeh been till now?" people in the pub would start laughing. Hughie seeing people laugh, and to make matters worse would just grin back at her, making her even more angry. Hughie would then start acting the fool by balancing a pint of beer on his head. He loved to be the centre of attention. He always carried with him a bunch of pennies tied together with string, which he would throw on the floor when some one passed on the way to the toilet. The person would think they had dropped some money and turn round. Everybody in the immediate vicinity would laugh. If my mam was still angry she would continue to nag him. Telling him to sit down and behave himself. Friends would say, leave him alone Mary, He's doin no harm.

If I was ever there when this happened, I would tell my mam to keep quiet, and say to her, everyone is laughing at yer!. I would sometimes become so embarrassed at their antics that I would leave the pub to go somewhere else. (I realised many years later that people were not laughing at them but with them). My mams nagging would sometimes continue back to the house and quite often end up in a full blown argument upsetting the rest of the family. In fact the rows in our house had became a way of life, and I always had to intervene.

Sometimes when Hughie was working the bag trick, he would make arrangements with my mam to meet her later in town, this would be instead of him returning home first to wash and change. After finishing work for the day, he would go to Lime Street station where he always kept a change of clothing in the gentleman's wash room. The attendant obviously knew Hughie well and would always pay lots of attention to him when handing him the soap and towel. Hughie would remove his clothes from the waist to wash and shave. When he had finished washing he would enter a cubicle and change into his clean clothes, on emerging from the cubicle the attendant would produce a clothes brush and then brush him down. Hughie naming the attendant would say, Ta, Ere yer are, get yerself a drink, and give him a generous tip. Hughie would then leave the wash room to meet my mam, leaving his dirty clothes with the attendant until sometime later.

Working the bag trick each day in town, and with ships from all over the world docking at Liverpool. Hughie naturally received lots of foreign coins in his collections. At the end of day when counting his takings in the American bar, he would separate the foreign coins, and put them in a pocket of his coat. On returning home later that evening, he would put the coins in a large empty glass bottle he kept in the parlour. After a period of time the bottle became quite full.

I remember Alec my brother stacking the coins in piles in different currencies and totalling them up on a piece of paper. He would then say to my ma. "A Ma how much is this worth in English money?" My mam would have no idea how much it was worth but reply, about a hundred pounds.

Alec would be delighted. And when his friends visited the house he could be heard telling them how much the coins were worth.

I remember occasionally looking through the coins myself, to find any that resembled our own money, which I could pass to some unsuspecting person in the cinema, or on dark nights to Jagga the paper man. Poor Jagga he must have received dozens of foreign coins in the dark nights, and I think I was mostly responsible.

Sometimes Hughie would go out of town to have a pitch, and spend the day at Haydock races or Manchester, often taking Alec my brother with him, but more often than not he preferred to stay in Liverpool where everybody knew him, especially the police. He had now discovered a number of good sites in town where he could do his tricks. One of these was a bombed 'olla' situated between two cinema's, The King's in London road and the Majestic in Daulby street.

The Majestic cinema was demolished many years ago, and the site is now being developed for the Roy Castle cancer research centre.

London road and the adjacent area at that time was very busy, with hundreds and hundreds of small shops.

One day Hughie was sitting in a pub named The Prince Of Wales having a drink with some friends. The pub is situated at the corner of London road and Moss street. He always had a quick glass of beer there before preparing to do his show across the road. Suddenly the door of the pub opened, and one of his many acquaintances entered, pulling after him, what appeared to be a dog on a lead.

The dog it was soon discovered was in fact a fox.

A conversation took place between Hughie and the owner of the animal, and it was suggested, it would be a good idea for Hughie to buy the fox. One of Hughie's friends said. "You can use it to attract the crowd to yer pitch". "Think of all the people yer'll get watchin yer, if they know yer've got a fox". Hughie's mind was immediately made up. He bought the fox there and then.

Soon afterwards Hughie took the fox to the waste ground near the Majestic cinema were his pitch was being held that day. He handed control of the fox, which by this time must have been terrified, over to the care of Johnny Brady. Hughie then started to crack the whip in the usual way, to attract the attention of the people who were doing their shopping. Having now got their attention as they gathered round, he paused and shouted at the top of his voice. 'At great expense to myself, I have bought a fox'. Pointing to the cowering animal in the centre of the ring, 'and the fox is going to be put in the bag with my assistant, who will be bound and chained before making his escape.'

'Forget about ferrets down yer trouser leg,' he went on to say, 'this is a real fox. Come and look.' The crowd pushed forward to try and see the fox.

You can imagine the interest this aroused with everybody. People gathered closer and closer round the circle. I can assure readers that Hughie had no intention of putting the fox in the sack with Johnny. In fact. Hughie was a great animal lover, and would often bring stray animals home with him. However, unknown to Hughie, Somebody, quite rightly telephoned the RSPCA to complain about him, and soon after, an inspector arrived accompanied by a policeman, and a reporter from the Liverpool Echo.

The fox was duly removed from the ring, and taken into safe keeping by the RSPCA. Hughie was interviewed with a view to being prosecuted for cruelty, but was able to convince the inspector, that he had only just purchased the poor animal that afternoon, and he had no intention of being cruel to the fox. It was only to drum up the crowd he said.

Apparently no offence had been committed. The following day there was an article in the Liverpool Echo all about it, and a photograph of Hughie with the fox. Hughie was quite thrilled at seeing his photograph in the paper, and when asked the question. 'Won't people think your cruel when they read about you in the paper?' Hughie, in his own inimitable way replied, 'There's no such thing as bad publicity!'

I often wondered what Hughie would have done with the fox at the end of the day, if the RSPCA Inspector had not taken it away from him.? He could not have brought it home! Our house was already home to chickens, pigeons, two dogs and a cat.

I will now take reader's on a tour of Hughie's favourite pitch the Pier Head, which stands directly in front of the magnificent 'Liver Buildings.' Synonymous with Liverpool's waterfront, and known throughout the world. Alongside the Liver buildings, with it's clock face which is larger than Big Ben, stands the beautifully designed Cunard Buildings, the Custom House and St Nicholas church, known as the seamans church. If you travel south, from the Liver Buildings three hundred yards further along the dock road, you would see the fruit ships being unloaded at Queens dock, and the smell of oranges, bananas and tomatoes would drift pass your nostrils.

Standing next to Queens dock, is Albert Dock, named after Prince Albert who was present at it's opening in 1845, and now restored to its former glory. The Albert Dock is a beautiful example of dock architecture and was the first dock to be totally enclosed by five storey warehouses, to handle goods from Britain's growing empire. It was designed by Jesse Hartley, Liverpool's dock engineer, who began his working life building bridges. The dock is built of granite with the ground floors open, supported by doric colonnades. Today the dock, like similar dock buildings in Liverpool, has been converted into beautiful apartments with their own garages at the rear. The Albert Dock's ground floor is a mixture of hotels, the northern "Tate Gallery" and dozens of shops selling all kinds of merchandise. It is a wonderful place to be especially when the tall ships race is on, with thousands of people crowding the dock, it is a real tourist attraction.

To return to Hughie's favourite pitch the Pier head, on a sunny day this would also be packed with people, some sitting down and picnicking amongst the statues and the memorabilia for the seamen who lost their lives in world war two, and the Titanic shipwreck, whilst others would be feeding the pigeons or just out for the day strolling about.

Others would be waiting for the ferry to dock to take them over the water.

It was a really wonderful place to be.

Just imagine for one moment, a bright sunny day and hundreds of people crowding the Pier head, with various "tradesmen" and crowds about them listening to what they had to say.

All kinds of people would take it upon themselves to speak out about the worlds problems, and large crowds would gather round them to listen.

Men could be seen walking up and down, holding placards above their heads, declaring the end is nigh, and that the world could be saved by Jesus.

Looking out to sea from the Pier Head, you have a wonderful view of the river, with Liverpool bay in the distance.

At that time, huge passenger liners, the Irish boats, and the Isle Of Man ferry could be seen almost any day tied up alongside the floating Landing stage. Passengers for the ships could be seen emerging from the carriages at the Riverside Railway Station. The passengers arrived directly at the dockside from all parts of the country.

All types of ships could be seen on the river, travelling to the south docks, and Ellesmere Port, or further upstream to the Manchester Ship Canal.

Facing you from the Pier Head but this time looking towards the Wirral, is the world famous ship building company, 'Cammell Laird', which launched some of the finest ships afloat. Alas no more, although recently a number of small companies have amalgamated, to form a new company, to bring ship building once again to the Mersey. To the left of Laird, is Tranmere Oil Terminal, capable of handling some of the largest tankers ever built.

In these idyllic surroundings, with hundreds of people bustling about their different business, each day at one o'clock precisely, you would hear the sound of a gun being fired 'over the water', indicating the time of day.

If you where fortunate enough to be at the Pier head on a lovely summer's day, sitting witnessing all these activities about you. It must have been quite a simple task to close your eyes, and imagine all the wonderful places the ships could take you to. On a hot summers day, the Pier head is one of the nicest places to be at. It was in this carnival atmosphere that Hughie decided to have his regular pitch.

He would arrive early at the Pier Head travelling by tram, and recover his kit from under the stairs of the tramcar, were it had been placed.

His friends would appear as if by magic to welcome him. Where presumably they had been patiently waiting to greet him. They would carry his gear and ask, could they help with his pitch that day? Hughie would reply "yeah", he always found something for them to do.

Sometimes, my mam would follow Hughie 'down to the Pier Head' on a later tram, for a day out with the kids.

The tram stopped at the terminus directly outside the landing stage. Quite often my mam would take the family on the ferry to New Brighton without embarking, just crossing backwards and forwards, taking in the sea breezes. Often some of the passengers would have a piano accordion with them or a banjo which they would play, and the rest of the passengers would join them for a sing song. I often travelled with the family but as I previously mentioned. I tended to sit away from them with friends of my own.

Large queues of people would form at the landing stage waiting to board the ferry. A chain would prevent you from boarding the boat until all the alighting passengers had embarked. When the boat was empty, a seaman would release the chain, and there would be a mad scramble to get aboard to find a good seat.

I cannot ever recall, paying the fare on the ferry. I think me and my mates used to 'dodge' the attendant collecting the fares.

I remember an occasion, when the family was crossing the water on the ferry to New Brighton. This time Hughie was with us. He lifted John on his shoulders and said to the ticket collector that John was only three years old, when in fact he was about seven. I also recall a special labeling machine at the entrance to the ferry terminal, a cast iron monster, and for the price of a penny, you could punch out in raised letters your name printed on a strip of aluminium. There was always queues of children waiting to use it.

I believe this particular machine was a relic of the first world war, and was used for identifying casualties from the trenches.

Quite often when Hughie arrived at the Pier Head to have a pitch. He would invariably upset the religious speaker's. Who would already have a crowd gathered about them. The crowd would be listening attentively to the speaker talking. Hughie would say to his friends, nodding in the direction of the speaker. "Lets use that crowd over there, the Jesus freak has got". With that he would pick up his gear and walk over to where the crowd was standing.

He and his assistants would start laying out all his gear right next to them. The canvas bag, the chains, ropes etc. He would then pick up his whip, and whirling it in the air start making loud cracking noises with it.

Other times he would simply set fire to a newspaper to draw attention to himself. He would then say to the crowd, who had now turned away from the speaker to face him. "If you want to be saved, come over here and give us a few bob". The crowd would begin to laugh, and wander over to see Hughie begin his act. Leaving the religious speaker standing alone, and shaking his fist in frustration at Hughie.

On one such occasion Tony Jacques arrived accompanied by his father. Tony sometimes assisted Hughie in his act. He walked up to where Hughie was performing and said. Hughie, can yer let us have a pitch with yer today, for our ale money? Hughie quite naturally agreed.

It was decided on this occasion, that Hughie would be the one to escape from the bag. Consequently the crowd gathered round to watch Hughie being bound with rope. He then stepped in to the open bag laying on the ground, which was then pulled over his head and tied tight at the top.

A chain was wrapped around the bag and secured with a lock. Finally a sword was inserted through the chain, and Hughie was gently lowered to the floor.

It was Tony's job this time to entertain the crowd, and collect the money. A count of ten would soon begin. Under normal circumstances Hughie would escape from the bag before the count had ended. Unfortunately, on this occasion the police arrived and immediately arrested Tony Jacques and his Father. Two policemen then took hold of Hughie who was still lying on the floor tied in the bag, and without further hesitation, threw him into the back of the police land rover. They climbed in after him and the vehicle drove off to Cheapside.

The crowd watched all this in amazement, as if it was part of the act. then began laughing and talking amongst themselves for some time after, before finally drifting away.

Mr Jacques was often mistaken for Hughie's Father, and Mr Jacques's son Tony, for Hughie's Brother. The three of them looked alike, each having black wavy hair and pencil thin moustaches.

Much later when speaking about this incident, Hughie laughed and said. "I think, the reason we where locked up that day, was because the church people had moaned about us. They must have gone to the cop shop on the landing stage to complain". He concluded by saying. "Anyway, I escaped from the bag before we got to Cheapside!".

There were many other occasions when Hughie was arrested.

Occasionally Hughie would receive 'fan mail', addressed to the man in the bag, Pier Head, Liverpool. Sometimes there would be photographs enclosed from people who had watched his performance. They would write to thank him, for the wonderful time spent in Liverpool, and how much they had enjoyed his act.

Hughie was always very pleased to receive letters. He would proudly mention this at the start of his act by saying.

"I receive fan mail from all over the world, even from Russia, but I don't know what it says, can anyone here read Russian?" Youngsters in the crowd who had seen Hughie perform his act many times before, would repeat the message, word for word.

One photograph sent to Hughie by an admirer, shows Hughie about to swallow a sword, and in the back-ground is my young Brother John. He is sitting in front of the crowd, still in his school uniform, peering intently at his Dad.

There was a period of time in Liverpool when Davy Crocket was very popular. I think they were showing a series of his films at the local cinemas. Children playing Cowboys and Indians in the street, either wore a Davy Crocket hat, or a feathered head dress like a Red Indian.

I remember our mam making John a Davy Crocket hat out of the sleeve of an old fur coat. John loved it. We would stand at the front door and watch him play in the street with other children, the hat stuck firmly on his head.

About that time. Hughie had once again to appear at the Magistrates court in Dale Street, for 'doing his bag trick'. He had been arrested a few days earlier for obstruction. (Incidentally Liverpool City Council, now encourage buskers and the likes to perform in the street to entertain the crowds). On this occasion, Hughie was sitting outside the court room waiting for his case to be heard, telling jokes as usual and showing the recent tricks he had purchased from the wizards den, to the people sitting near by. Everybody was laughing at the stories he was telling. Hughie treated life as one huge joke and did not seem to worry about anything.

He always used to say, "enjoy yourself, yer dead a long time". On this particular occasion he entered the court room with people also waiting to have their cases heard. He sat at the rear of the room listening for his name to be called. When the Magistrate was about to enter the court room, the court usher asked everybody in the room to stand. Everybody stood.

It was at that precise moment that Hughie called out. "Here comes Davy Crocket"! Everybody including the policemen, and solicitors representing various clients, burst out laughing. Suddenly every one went silent. The Magistrate must also have heard it. The Magistrate addressing the clerk of the court, then wanted to know what had caused everybody to laugh. Hughie was finely identified as the culprit by one of the policemen in the room. The Magistrate instructed Hughie to come and stand before him in the dock. Hughie was escorted to the dock by a Policeman, and was then asked by the Magistrate to explain what had caused the laughter. Hughie informed the magistrate, that he was talking to his friend about the recent craze, in which all the kids wore Davy Crocket hats, and you just happened to enter the room, when I said Davy Crocket he explained. But I didn't mean no offence to yer, yer honour. He went on to say.

None the less, his explanation was not accepted, and he was cautioned about his future conduct, and the possibility of being fined for contempt of court if it ever happened again. Hughie pretended to people in authority that he was quite stupid, and they very often believed him.

He would pretend that he could not read or write, and when asked to sign his name, He would put a cross where his signature should be. You had to see him to believe it. He was very convincing. I believe the Magistrate had difficulty keeping a straight face when fining him for the real reason he was there that day, the obstruction offence.

Another favourite saying Hughie had when doing his tricks. Was to ask the crowd. "To put a little bit more silver in the hat this time please, cause it's to pay me fine". Human nature being what it is, the crowds were always attracted by Hughie's performances, which were quite theatrical and ranged from the comical and absurd to the sometimes very sad.

Which brings me to my next part of the story, which took place at the Pier Head.

Chapter Seven

George Smith, Hughie's brother, had served in the Merchant Marine during the war, and whilst at sea, his ship had been torpedoed and sunk within minutes.He and a number of other survivors took to the life boats, and spent eight days in the Atlantic Ocean before being rescued. Soon after, George like many others in similar circumstances, returned to sea, and continued to serve as a stoker right up until the end of hostilities in 1945.

After the war, George continued in the Merchant Navy for a number of years, but had to retire prematurely due to ill health. He suffered from bronchial problems, due mainly to the time he had spent in the open boat at sea. On his doctors advice, he moved with his family from an old damp dwelling in Liverpool, to a new overspill housing estate in Winsford Cheshire.

One day George appeared at the Pier Head, when Hughie was doing his usual bag trick. Hughie was very pleased to see him and asked. how are you fixed? meaning did he have any money for himself! George replied that he was skint, and had come to Liverpool to see the old lady. George continued, "I've seen me Ma and she's okay. She told me that you wus down at the Pier Head, doin the bag trick. So I thought I'd come and see yer".

Hughie then suggested to George, that he could earn himself a few bob, by 'getting in the bag', George looked puzzled and replied 'I know nothing about it.'

Hughie said, 'don't worry, I'll show yer how to escape. It's dead easy.'

After some brief instructions on how to escape. George was persuaded to get in the bag. Hughie now started his usual spiel to the people waiting for the act to begin as George nervously entered the ring, were he was ceremoniously tied-up and placed in the bag. Once again the bag was laced firmly at the top, and a chain wound around it and locked. Finally the sword was placed through the chain, and George was lowered to the ground. The act was now ready to begin.

Hughie then gave his regular sales pitch to the gathering crowd. At the same time walking round amongst them collecting money, and saying. "Ladies and Gentlemen, the man who's going to escape from the bag today is a war hero, who's won lots of medals, but has now fallen on hard times". "His kids are starvin, with only jam bread to eat". Be a sport, Sir, just a few more coppers in the hat before he escapes, make it worth his while, give a little silver just a tanner or two more.

IN LIVERPOOL

Hughie would be conscious of how much money he had collected, and would not start the count, until he thought he had taken enough money.

Meanwhile George was struggling to untie himself inside the sack. He was having some difficulty breathing. Being asthmatic he suffered from a very bad chest.

Hughie was prolonging the agony by asking for more money. Sometimes when the person escaping from the bag was inexperienced, they would be much slower than usual. When this happened, Hughie realising this would start counting, one, one and a half, two, two and a half, three, three and a half etc, the crowd would laughingly shout their protests but it was all part of the act and in good fun.

Poor George was becoming desperate. He could stand it no longer. Suddenly there was a tearing sound followed by gasps for air, and the cry of "get me out of this f...... sack". George had slit the bag open with a pen-knife, and was struggling to get free. His head peered from the torn sack gasping for breath. On seeing this, Hughie addressed the crowd by saying. "Due to technical difficulties today's show is cancelled, but the good news is that next week's first performance will be free".

Hughie had collected enough money and had no intention of giving it back. He went on to say."I've not got any tickets to give you for this cancelled performance, but your all invited back next week" . Hughie would make fun out of any situation. He then invited the crowd to give George, who was now sitting amongst the remains of the sack still gasping for air. "A big hand for a fine effort". The crowd responded by cheering and clapping George. Hughie then went amongst them collecting more money.

George did end up with his 'few bob' after all. Once again the crowd was entertained and thoroughly enjoyed themselves.

I think it was on another occasion when George visited Hughie. This time he had with him a new pair of shoes still in the box, that he wished to sell. Hughie said he would buy them from him to help him out. He thought they would fit our Alec. Returning home that night with the shoes, Hughie said to my mam, Mary these shoes might do Alec, and handed her the box.

Alec was asked to sit down and try the shoes on, they were the correct size and seemed to fit perfectly. Unfortunately it was discovered too late that when he stood up, Alec was about two inches taller than he should have been. The shoes had built up insoles hidden inside them.

He refused to wear them, although my mam tried to encourage him to do so, by saying, they'e alright, honest, you can't notice anything! but Hughie spoilt it by saying. Alec pass me that book off the top shelf will yer? Then everyone burst out laughing.

The shoes were never worn in our house again, and if I remember correctly. Hughie pawned them in the local pawnshop, and sold the ticket to somebody else in Yates' Wine Lodge in town.

One day Hughie surprised us all by returning home with a moped.

He said, He had bought it to take him to work at the docks, and wanted it to be a surprise. We all went outside to look at it. It was silver in colour with L plates on the front and rear.

After discussing where he had bought it and how much it had cost, Hughie invited my mam to go with him for a ride later on, "for a run out to Southport". She replied, will you be alright to drive? and when he answered yes of course I will! she smilingly agreed to go with him.

That night after the family had finished eating our tea. Hughie and my mam got washed and changed into the clothes they wore to go out. When they were finely ready, they went outside to the moped which was leaning against the wall by the front door. We all followed them out to look. Hughie climbed on the bike, and switching on the engine, kicked it into life with his foot. The bike started first time. He now started to rev the engine.

Some of the neighbours had now appeared at their front door attracted by the noise. As usual I felt embarrassed, but it didn't appear to worry Hughie. In fact, Hughie tended to show off when people where taking notice.

Hughie then invited my mam to sit behind him. After some hesitation, she laughingly adjusted her skirt and mounted the bike. I felt even more embarrassed. They prepared to depart. My mam looked at me and said, I'll see you later, we wont be long. They then drove off, my ma clinging to Hughie's waist so it seemed, for dear life.

It was now late at at night. they had been gone for hours, and I was very worried about them.

In those days the law did not require you to wear a crash helmet, and to my knowledge Hughie had never been on a bike in his life. Both Hughie and my mam drank rather heavily. We youngsters where terrified in case they had been involved in an accident. I imagined all kinds of things had happened to them. They should have been back by now I said. We each took turns going to the front door looking to see if it was them returning home, every time we heard a noise that sounded like a motor bike.

I could stand it no longer. I instructed the rest of the family to stay indoors and not to go out. I decided to go to the top road, to see if I could see them.

IN LIVERPOOL

I walked up Robsart Street to the Stingo in Netherfield Road, to see if they had gone straight to the pub. Turning the corner to the side entrance of the pub I opened the door. I looked inside the lobby, and seeing someone I recognised, asked whether or not my mam and Hughie were inside? they replied no. I walked back to the street corner and stood in the pub doorway. Standing here enabled me to see down to our house in Robsart Street, in case they came up the street from Greaty. From this vantage point I could also see along Netherfield road. I was now sick with worry. It was just after 10pm and the pubs were beginning to let out, the pavement was becoming quite crowded. Just about then, I heard the sound of a motor bike, and Hughie rode into view from the direction of Everton Valley, my mam sitting on the seat behind him.

I was so relieved that they had arrived home safe and sound. My relief quickly turned to one of anger, because just then Hughie started to show off to the people standing outside the pub now watching. He mounted the kerb with the bike, and started to drive slowly along the pavement.

People were moving out of the way, and laughing at his antics.

My mam was shouting for him to stop. He eventually stopped the bike and both he and my mam dismounted to talk to their friends. They both smelled strongly of drink. My mam continued complaining to Hughie, calling him stupid, for riding on the pavement, but at the same time smiling.

A group of people now gathered round the bike, some asking questions, like, Where d'ya get the bike from Hughie? and where've yer been?.

Some youths in their early twenties who had been standing outside the pub, watching all what was happening. Now walked over to where Hughie was standing. they appeared to be drunk. One of them asked Hughie. Can I have a little ride on yer bike?. Without hesitation, Hughie agreed. The man who asked permission mounted the bike, and one of his companions climbed on behind him. The engine was switched on and they drove quickly away.

By the time I realised what was happening, the two youths where riding up and down the road, their friends shouting encouragement after them.

I was very angry and thought, there taking the mickey out of us, they must think where bloody stupid!. I walked up to my mam and said. Why did Hughie let them have the bike? Come on, lets go home, them fella's are goin'to wreck the bloody thing! I then angrily ran up to the men on the bike as it pulled in to the kerb, and standing in front of them, held the handlebars. I then said. Where goin' home now. I had no intention of letting hold of the bike. I was so angry at the situation, I was willing to fight them if necessary.

Hughie walked over to where we were standing. He must have realised how angry I was. He laughingly said to the youths. The boss said we have to go home now. They laughed, the tension was broken, the men dismounted from the bike remarking how good it was, and walked over to join the remainder of their friends standing outside the pub. I still had hold of the bike.

By this time my mam had now joined us, they both called out. Goodnight every one. Their friends replied goodnight Mary, goodnight Hughie. Hughie took the bike from me, and mounting it, began to free wheel down Robsy to our house. I walked down the street, my mam walking besides me, steadying herself on the steep street in her high heels, by holding onto my arm. I angrily told her how worried we had been waiting for them, and how stupid Hughie was for loaning the bike to people he hardly knew.

Reaching Ben's shop, Hughie turned left steering the bike into Sanderson Street, so he could enter our house from the entry, and park the bike in the back yard. Me and my mam climbed the front steps and entered the house through the front door. My mam went and unlocked the back door for Hughie to come in.

On entering the house, Hughie produced the inevitable bags of nuts and crisps from his pocket, which where gratefully received by the rest of the family, all thoughts of them being involved in an accident now forgotten.

My mam then started to tell us where they had been that evening, and what they had done since leaving the house. Completely forgetting how worried we had been. I went to bed in disgust, still angry with both of them.

Hughie still continued to work at the docks and in winter because of the dark nights, was only able to do the bag trick in town at weekends. One day he had reported for work as usual but there was no work available, so he decided to have a pitch at lunchtime in front of his fellow dock workers on the dock road.

He had persuaded one of his colleagues to have a collection for him whilst he escaped from the bag. Once again volunteers where invited from the crowd to secure the rope and chains which were wrapped around the bag. Unknown to Hughie his friends had arranged to place him on the back of a lorry which was going to Manchester. Hughie having stepped inside the bag and the bag tied securely was then placed him on the vehicle which immediately drove away. Hughie realising a trick was being played on him made his escape from the bag and managed to stop the vehicle at the Crown public house on the East Lancashire Road before returning home.

Hughie quite liked playing tricks on people and often joked about this incident to his friends. He never objected when tricks where played on him. He had now started spending more time with his friends and going for a drink with them after work, very often he came home drunk, it was more worrying now because he drove the moped to work. He was tipsy most nights. Particularly in the winter time, when it was too dark to do the bag trick in the evenings. If he had signed on that day, he would sometimes spend the remainder of the day with his friends on the booze, visiting shebeens (drinking clubs) in the south end of town.

Quite often when he did obtain work, he would be given the job of 'bogey' driver. The bogey was used for transferring goods from the ship to the warehouse for storage. I was told that on one occasion when he was working nights, Hughie accidentally drove the bogey into the dock. He might have been killed. I imagined he must been drunk again. When I asked him what had happened that night, he assured me that he hadn't had a drink all day. The brakes had just give out, he said.

At about the same time, Hughie seemed to be suffering from a spate of injuries. He never complained. At home you would often find him bandaging nasty cuts to his arms and legs. When he was questioned about how he had hurt himself, he would reply. I did it at work, It's nuthin.

It was very worrying. We all guessed how he had received the injuries. He must have fallen off his bike when drunk. Everyone in the family was always telling him to sell the moped.

Each night we would wait to hear the sound of the moped approaching the house. Sometimes he would arrive home sober. It was quite a relief when that happened. After his meal, he and my mam would go to the Stingo for a drink.

There they would sit in the parlour with some friends and Hughie would invariably take charge of 'backing the fire' with coal from the bucket and entertain everyone with his various tricks.

But more often than not he would arrive home smelling strongly of drink, and still insist on going out to the pub with my ma for more drink.

We all thought it was just a matter of time before he had a serious accident driving the bike. His friends in the pub would say. Hughie yer gonna kill yerself on that bike!.

On one such occasion Hughie drove to work and parked the moped somewhere down at the docks. That day he and his two close friends were given the job of working on a Yankee boat, whose cargo consisted of scotch whisky. You can imagine what happened next. A case of whisky went missing and some of the dock workers including Hughie got drunk, in fact Hughie got so drunk his friends hid his bike to prevent him from driving it home. That evening he came home in a taxi and my mam argued with him for the rest of the night. The next day he returned to work and recovered his bike.

I was always amazed at him, no matter how much he had drunk the night before, Hughie always managed to get to work on time.

The arguments at home where becoming more and more frequent, not so much because of Hughie's drinking, but because he didn't come home to take my mam out. He preferred to drink with his friends in town instead. The rows when he came home late at night would disturb the neighbours, who would knock on the wall to show their disapproval at the noise. The arguments were now becoming a way of life, and I would be often forced to intervene.

I was conscious of the effect the rows were having on me and the rest of the family, and truly wished for a normal family life.

It was soon after one of these rows that Hughie returned home one evening, he was sober. He was carrying a parcel wrapped in newspaper, which he deposited on the table. Steam was rising from it, it was full of freshly cooked fish and chips.

He then informed us, that he had sold his moped that day to a workmate. At first, we didn't believe him, thinking he had been in an accident and the bike had been wrecked beyond repair. He smiled, and pulled out a wad of bank notes from his inside pocket. Here's the money to proof it! E' are Mary, here's a few bob fer yer, he said, peeling some money from the bundle and handing it to my mam. It was true, he had sold the bike!. I breathed a sigh of relief. We where more than pleased to see the back of that bike.

The family then sat round the table, and concentrated on eating the meal he had brought in. That night, I'm sure we all had the nicest sleep in weeks.

One day the fair returned to our area. My sister Mary and her friend June Allen had offered to take our brother John to see it. He was quite grown up now.

My mam and Hughie were going out together that night, and Mary as usual, was left in charge of Margaret and John. Hughie gave Mary some money to spend on the fair. He advised both girls to be careful, and warned them about gangs of boys who roamed the likes of fairgrounds.

I had made arrangements that evening to see my own friends. We would all meet up in the doorway of the Stingo pub in Netherfield Road, before catching the tram to town for the night out. My friends and I had now started going to pubs in town where nobody new our true age. Our favourite pubs at the time, were the Duck House and Lulu's. We also used to visit the Magic Clock, where artists from the local theatre's seemed to frequent. Lots of men appeared to be very effeminate. One chap in particular who used this pub quite often was named Johnny Lyonas, a seafarer, and was known in town as the Queen Bee. We used to smile amongst ourselves at the mannerisms's of some of the men, and jokingly tried to act more masculine ourselves by talking in a deep voice.

Returning home later that night, I was met at the door by my mam, who seemed reluctant to tell me something. I said, What's the matter? She replied, "John's been in an accident and had to go to hospital"! I was shocked for a moment, then said. What happened? My mam continued by saying, "He got knocked down by a bumper car at the fair and he's hurt his leg".

I had walked in the kitchen by this time, and could see Mary sitting on a chair sobbing. John was laying on the settee, his leg heavily bandaged.

I was told much later that Mary had apparently gone to the fair with her friend June, taking the two younger children with them. Mary had taken John for a ride on the bumper cars and after sitting down, John then became frightened and wanted to get off. Mary asked the operator to allow them to leave the car before it started. The man agreed. They were making there way back to the safety of the boardwalk, from where she intended to watch June and Margaret drive in one of the other cars.

Unfortunately, the attendant had completely forgotten that Mary and John were making their way back to safety, and switched on the electricity which started the ride. A car parked quite near them started suddenly, and leaped forward, trapping Johns leg between the car and the stage. The force was such that the bumper bar on the car had sunk into John's flesh. The attendant supervising the ride, on discovering what had happened, immediately switched off the power.

Some grownups standing near by seeing the accident, ran to John's assistance. John was crying out in pain. Mary was crying herself now. Mary was assured by a number of people that John was going to be alright, and not to worry. They said it was not her fault and blamed the attendant. John's leg was eventually freed and he was taken to Hospital, Mary and June went with him. Margaret was taken home by one of our neighbours. They spent some time at the hospital, were John had to have stitches put in a deep wound in his leg. Fortunately the leg wasn't broken.)

Arriving home later that night, my mam and Hughie discovered a neighbour sitting at home with Margaret, who told them about John's accident.

They were about to rush to the Hospital when Mary arrived home with John. She explained all that had happened. After hearing what Mary had to say, and making sure John was comfortable, they sat down to have some tea. Hughie said he would visit the fair the next day, to see "that fella on the bumper cars". The fair had long since closed for the night.

When I arrived home I naturally knew nothing at all about this, and seeing John injured immediately thought Mary was to blame. Not waiting for an explanation. I ran up to Mary and started to strike her about the head, accusing her of not looking after John properly. I accused her of being more interested in bloody fellas! Mary became more and more frightened and started to cry louder.

I continued to strike her about the head, she crouched low in the corner, both hands over her head trying to protect herself, crying out for our mam to help her, until eventually, Hughie managed to put himself between us.

I was very angry and felt Mary hadn't done her job properly looking after John. I would have continued striking her if I had been able to reach her. I wanted to teach her a lesson. Mary still crying, was ushered upstairs away from me by Hughie.

My mam tried to explain, that it wasn't Mary's fault. It was the fella on the fairground, she said and Hughie's going to see about it tomorrow!

A few minutes passed. I was still very angry.

I walked to the back kitchen for a drink, still threatening what I would do to Mary when I got hold of her. Unable to release my pent up feelings on my sister, and possibly more angry now with myself for hitting her. I raised my left hand and punched at a pane of glass in the back door with my fist.

The glass broke on impact, then fell shattering into a hundred pieces on the stone steps leading up to the door.

When I think about it, I must have known exactly what I was doing, because I am normally right handed. I realised that I would hurt myself quite badly, and therefore didn't want to use my right arm.

My hand initially felt numb, then the pain swept up my arm. Warm blood was pouring from a deep cut on my wrist. The blood spattering all over my shirt and down the front of my trousers, it was gathering in a pool on the floor. I didn't seem to care, I was angry with myself.

On hearing the sound of breaking glass, my mam ran to where I was standing in the back kitchen. Seeing blood, she shouted for Hughie to come quickly. Discovering what I had done, she took hold of my hand and placed it over the sink. The blood began running in a stream down the plughole. She then snatched the face flannel hanging from a nail over the sink, and turning on the tap, soaked the flannel in cold water before placing it around my wrist to try and stem the bleeding.

I was led into the kitchen and persuaded to sit at the table, whilst the cut was examined by Hughie and my mam. All thoughts of revenge now completely gone from my mind. My mam suggested that I ought to go to Hospital. The cut would require stitches!. I refused. I had calmed down now and wasn't angry any more. I somehow felt some justification in injuring myself, As if I had been 'paid back' for what I had done to Mary. By this time Hughie had brought cotton wool and some hot water in a bowl, which he placed alongside me on the table. My mam began to bathe the wound. I was now able to see it more clearly, it was a nasty cut.

After drying the wound. My mam, using the tip of her finger, gently smeared some germolene, (an antiseptic ointment) on the cut to stop the bleeding. More ointment was then spread on a strip of clean linen, before it was placed over the wound. She then completed the task by wrapping a bandage round my wrist. Amid all this commotion poor John had been completely forgotten. Meanwhile Hughie had made some tea and toast and Mary was invited to join us. We all sat down to eat. Everything was now back to normal.

I was told afterwards, that before I arrived home. Mary had been complaining, to the rest of the family. "Our Jimmy will kill me when he comes home".

That night I had a terrible sleep. The pain kept me awake most of the night, and I prevented Alec who shared the bed with me from sleeping aswell. The next day at work. I told my workmates who could see my hand heavily bandaged. That when I was going to the toilet in the dark the night before , I had fallen down our back steps, and cut my wrist on some broken glass. They replied. You must have been drunk! Well it was half correct wasn't it.

Returning home from work later that day, I walked up the entry as usual to go into the house through the back door, and on entering our back yard I immediately noticed that Hughie had repaired the window, broken the night before. A reminder of the occasion, is the scar I still bear to this day, it's almost three inches long.

Meanwhile Hughie had visited the fairground, and asked to see the owner of the fair. Apparently he was already expected and was taken into the office right away.

Later that same evening. Hughie smilingly told us what had happened when he visited the fair.

Once inside the office Hughie informed the owner. "I've got a dozen witnesses who saw what happened to my son last night, he could have been killed! and what are you going to do about it? He continued, I can get you closed down for what your man did to my lad."

After listening to Hughie's tirade for a few more minutes, the owner of the fair accepted that it was possibly one of his staff's fault, and apologised profusely for the accident. He said he had been operating the fair for year's and had never had an accident in all that time. He offered Hughie free use of the rides for the family, but Hughie insisted it wasn't good enough. My poor lad's now got a broken leg, and will be in Hospital for weeks.

He went on to say. "My kids have been to your fair each night and spent a small fortune on the rides". The owner then understood what Hughie was saying, and after a short consultation with a colleague, gave Hughie some money. Hughie finished his conversation to us by saying. I had the poor fella crying. Anyway yer ma can buy yer all something now. Hughie knew perfectly well how to turn a mishap into an advantage.

I had decided to change jobs. You could in those days, there was now plenty of work to be had. I wanted to become a driver. So I got a job working for Dover's furniture shop in Moss Street, I was the drivers assistant on the delivery lorry. The pay was much better than on the railway. I was almost seventeen and the driver at Dover's had recently been demobbed from the Royal Air Force. I was fascinated listening to him tell me about service life, conscious that I would be called up one day myself, for National Service. After finishing deliveries for the day, we would park in a side street and he would instruct me on how to change gear. He was always very smartly dressed and wore a collar and tie. After I had been working there a short time, he suggested that now I was earning more money, I ought to buy myself a good suit from Abram Brothers, the tailors round the corner from the shop in London Road. "You can get one on the weekly you know. That's were I buy my clothes" he said!

I told him that I would think about it. (I was still wearing my railway uniform, minus the silver buttons).

Strangely enough, soon after my conversation with my driver, I met one of my former classmates, named Joey Piggott who had joined the Merchant

IN LIVERPOOL

Navy on leaving school. He worked as a steward, and sailed on the Cunard boats from Liverpool to America. At our meeting we had spoken for some time about our school days, but what impressed me most about him, was the clothes he wore. I liked the way he was dressed.

When I asked him were he had bought his suit he replied, "In New York, and everybody who goes to sea all wear the latest fashions". It was true, you could always identify a seaman. Even the work clothes they wore looked different, and what was known as 'Jeans'. They were so unlike our bib and brace overalls. They were made by companies named Wrangler or Levi, and could not be purchased at that time in England.

The story I was told is that the name 'Jean's' came about, because seamen purchased their work clothes from a particular shop in New York, and the lady who owned the shop was named Jean. Seamen would say to one another, "I'm going to Jean's to buy my work clothes. This was eventually shortened to: I'm going to buy some Jeans", (hence the name Jeans, to describe what we in England called Overalls).

After my chance meeting with my friend, my mind was now made up. I would go and see about buying a new suit.

After finishing work one Saturday afternoon, I decided to visit Abrams the tailors.

I stood outside the shop admiring all the different bolts of cloth on view in the window, wondering whether or not I could afford it. After some hesitation I plucked up enough courage to nervously open the door and enter the shop.

A short stocky man approached me who I later discovered was Mr Abram (one of the owners) who asked, "Can I be of any assistance to you?" I informed him blushingly, that I worked for Dover's the furniture shop in Moss Street, and my driver, mentioning his name, "told me to come here to buy a suit, on the weekly,! I added quickly Mr Abram smiled knowingly and seemed to know my driver, and replied, "that is correct".

He suggested that I look at some suit lengths and choose the one I liked best. (I was more interested in the price.) Eventually I chose a cloth and Mr Abram then worked out exactly how much it would cost me to repay it each week. I was pleased with the amount. I decided I could afford it and signed the necessary agreement and paid a small deposit. I was then measured for my suit, and asked to call back the following week for a fitting. It was then I realised for the first time what it meant, when asked the question, "which way do you dress Sir"?.

I returned home and told my mam what I had done, she seemed to be very pleased. Hughie said he knew the shop very well, "it was near were he held one of his pitches, and he would visit them and get something knocked off the price for me". On hearing this I nearly burst a blood vessel, and replied. "Don't you dare go near the place".

The following week I returned to the shop for my fitting. There was chalk marks all over the cloth. It felt good putting it on. I was pleasantly surprised to discover the price included a waistcoat. I had never worn a waistcoat before. In fact I had never worn a new suit before. After some slight adjustments, and more chalk marks added to the cloth, I was told that I could collect the suit the following afternoon.

The following day could not come quick enough for me. That day after work I went to collect the suit. I was thrilled to bits, a new suit. I must now make sure I saved enough money from my wages each week, to pay for it.

Arriving home with my precious parcel, I placed it on the table. Everyone gathered round to see what the suit looked like.

I cut the string around the parcel with a pair of scissors, and opened the package. I then picked up the jacket and held it against my chest. My mam said, "It's nice, go and try the suit on". I gathered up the parcel and went quickly upstairs to the bedroom to change. Two minutes later I was back down stairs again standing in my new suit. They all agreed it looked nice. Alec said I looked like Burt Lancaster the film star. I felt so pleased with myself.

On Friday evening I wore my new suit for the first time. All my mates where impressed. We had met outside the Stingo pub before going on to Blair Hall as usual. Inside the hall I was conscious of people looking at me. It felt good. I hoped I looked as smart as my friend Joey the seaman.

Chapter Eight

It was now my birthday. Hughie and my mam had bought me a watch. I was thrilled to bits. I felt like I now had everything, a new suit, a watch and a job which allowed me to travel to parts of Liverpool I had not seen before. What more could I want?

Soon after, my friends and I decided to go to the Grafton Ballroom in West Derby Road. Like most people I worked half day Saturday, and we had arranged to go to the dance that afternoon. I hurried home from work at lunchtime and quickly getting washed, put on my new suit.

It was the first time I had ever been to the Grafton. I was amazed at how much it resembled the dance halls of the Hollywood films I had been watching for years. Your feet seemed to float on thick carpets as you walked in through the door, and beautiful chandeliers hung cascading from the ceiling. After you entered the dance hall from the reception area, the orchestra could be seen sat facing you, under a large canopy at the rear of the dance hall. Members of the orchestra were impeccably dressed as where all the staff, wearing dinner jackets and bow ties. I thought it strange at first to see a woman conducting the orchestra, until I was told it was the wife of the late Wilf Hamer the dance band leader.

Two dispense bars ran parallel to the dance floor supporting the upper floor, and there were tables and chairs placed along the wall for people to sit at. A staircase at either end of the hall allowed access to the floor above, from which you could view the dancers below. there was also another small bar. Upstairs afforded you more privacy, and couples would be seen sat engaged in conversation, usually oblivious to every one around them.

The Grafton Ballroom became another world when you entered it's door's. It was quite unique, and had a sprung dance floor unlike the Locarno rooms next door, which was another wonderful place we used to visit. I used to love standing on the edge of the floor, feeling the floor bouncing up and down to the different dance tunes being played.

Me and my mates would stand looking for pretty girls dancing together, so we could 'split them up'. Sometimes you would see American servicemen from Burtonwood, the nearby air force base doing the jive.

Hughie and my mother visited the Grafton at least once a week. People used to tell me they were lovely dancer's. I suspect that is where they first met.

Me and my friends had now started to visit the Grafton regularly each Saturday night. It became customary for us to try and take a girl home after the dance. We would try to make it a foursome if we could, but this was not always possible. On one occasion I asked the girl who I had been dancing with, could I take her home? And she replied yes! She was alone. Her friend who had accompanied her to the dance had met an old boy friend and they had gone off together. The girl said she lived in West Derby. I waited for her in the foyer whilst she collected her coat from the cloakroom, then we walked outside the dance and caught a tram heading out of the city.

We were joined on the tram by groups of people returning home, all dressed in their finest clothes.

The tram set off, stopping every few minutes along the way at each stop. Fifteen minutes into the journey the girl I was with looked out of the window and said, this is my stop!. We stood up and made our way between passengers to the exit, and descended from the tram outside a pub named the Royal Oak. We then walked in the direction of the girls home exchanging small talk, before reaching a block of shops. I thought to myself this will do nicely, thank you. I then took hold of the girls hand and led her into one of the shop doorways out of view of any passers by. At least I'm entitled to a kiss after seeing her home, I said to myself.

We began kissing and cuddling in the privacy of our little den, until she reminded me, that if I did not leave soon I would miss the last tram back to town. I looked at my watch and asked her. "What time does the last tram leave?" She mentioned a time. Another glance at my watch meant I had a few more minutes yet! I continued kissing her some more before deciding to stop and bid her goodnight. I then asked, can I see you again? she hesitated a moment, obviously thinking about it.

I could hear the rumble of the tram in the distance. She replied, you wont turn up! I answered, I will! She said. Would you come all the way from Netherfield Road to see me? I insisted I would. She paused a minute longer then said, Prove to me you'll show up by giving me your watch, and if you do I'll see you here next week and return it! After a moments hesitation on my part, I agreed and handed her my wrist watch. We began kissing again. Subconsciously I heard the tram arrive but I was enjoying myself too much now. The girl pulled away from me and said hurry or you'll miss the tram. Trying to impress her I said, don't worry I'll catch a taxi home. Little did she know I had no money for taxis. We continued kissing some more before stopping and agreeing to meet outside the Royal Oak pub next Saturday at 8pm.

I had one final kiss before parting and going our separate ways. The girl disappeared down one of the side streets with my precious watch, and I to a long walk home having missed the last tram.

That week I tried desperately to hide the fact from the family, that I no longer had my watch. I kept trying to convince myself that it would only be a few days before I had it back again.

Saturday evening eventually arrived. I had planned my journey well. I left early and walked from Netherfield Road to Brougham Terrace, from there I could catch a tram to the Royal Oak.

That evening I had paid particular attention to myself before setting off from home. I had my best suit on and had even used some of Hughie's old spice after shave lotion. I knew that if I took a tram from the bottom of West Derby Road to Muirhead Avenue, I would arrive with plenty of time to spare. The tram practically stopped outside the pub.

I arrived at the pub at approximately a quarter to eight and stood outside the same shop doorway the girl and I had kissed in the week before. the pavement was quite busy now with people going about their normal business. Unlike last week when the place was almost deserted.

I waited and eight o'clock came and went. People who had passed me earlier. No doubt on errands, now walked past me again. I imagined they where smiling at me. It was fairly obvious why I was standing there. I continued waiting. Then I began thinking to myself. Had I got the time wrong? or had I got the day wrong? I waited some more and thought. And why didn't she agree to meet me in town? I was left with a lot of unanswered questions.

I began to feel quite stupid and asked a man who happened to be passing, do yer know the time please? He replied. twenty past nine! I had been there for over an hour and a half. I had been stood up. But worse still, I had given my watch away. What a bloody fool I'd been. I didn't even know where the girl lived. I felt so stupid. What would my mates think? they knew I was coming here tonight. I caught the next tram back to town, then wandered into different pubs having a drink in each of them. I hoped none of my friends would see me. I returned home later that night when I thought all the family had gone to bed.

A few days after my mother asked. Where's ye watch? I haven't seen it lately. I then admitted that I had mislaid it somewhere and didn't know were it was!

I was a long time after before I told my mates the truth about my watch. When they had asked me about my date that night, I had lied to them and replied, it was okay but I don't think I'll see her again. When I eventually told them the truth, they all laughed their heads off, and for a long time afterwards they made fun of me, by saying , what time is it Jim? knowing full well I no longer had a watch, and on other occasions they would ask, have yer got yer watch back yet? I went to the Grafton every Saturday evening for months after that, but I never did meet the girl, nor did I see my watch. In fact I probably wouldn't have recognised her again, it happened so quickly.

I often wondered what really did happen that night? Did she give my watch to another boy? or did something happen which prevented her from meeting me? I can laugh about it now but at that time I was as sick as a parrot.

I had now found myself a regular girlfriend. She lived off Smithdown Road. After we had been out for the evening, we would go back to her house after her parents had gone to bed and spend hours kissing and cuddling on the settee in the parlour. Until her mother came downstairs in the early hours of the morning and chased me, when I would leave to walk back home to Neddy Road. Sometimes I would borrow her fathers bike, if he didn't need it the next day for work.

It was about this time that I was called up for my National Service.

Unlike many of my friends I had already decided to become a regular soldier.

I received notice to report for my medical examination to Pownall Square and along with dozens of other young men, experienced the embarrassment of being examined from head to foot by a panel of doctors.

At my interview I had informed them that I wanted to be a driver. Having successfully passed the medical, I signed a document committing me to serve in the Army for the next six years. I initially joined the Royal Army Ordinance Corps, later I transferred to the Parachute Regiment. The extra money I would earn would allow me to send a £1.00 a week to my Mother. A few days later I received my rail warrant to report to the barracks at Aldershot to undergo eight weeks basic training. I had not been in the Army very long. And like most new recruits I made the common mistake of saluting anybody in a peaked cap, including members of the regimental band. The saying goes. If it moves salute it. If it stands still paint it. One day our platoon was put on fatigues, (given various jobs to do) and I and another recruit was told to report to the guardroom.

The Sergeant in charge of the guardroom gave us the task of painting the gates to the entrance of the barracks. He handed me a ball of string and instructed us to tie the string across the gate diagonally, to enable straight lines to be painted. The end result would be a white cross, similar to the x in oxo on a black background.

The tying of the string was done quite quickly. We then stood about waiting for some one in charge to return with the brushes and paint so we could continue with the job. We waited a while longer, and still there was no sign of the corporal. Neither of us liked the idea of returning to the guardroom to enquire about the paint, this would be asking for trouble. Soldiers were often seen being marched in there at double quick time, accompanied by lots of bawling and shouting, and they didn't seem to come out again.

Being raw recruits, and not wanting to get into any trouble, we discussed with each other what we should do next. Had we misunderstood the sergeant? Perhaps we had to fetch the paint ourselves? After a few more minutes of conversation and still no sign of the corporal, I offered to try and find some paint myself.

I left my companion and walked smartly over to the administration block. I thought, some one here should be able to tell me were I can get some paint. I entered the building through the main door which led into a large hall. A number of rooms lead off from the hall.

I looked at the names over the doors before deciding which one to knock at. A large sign above one door said O.C. This one should do I said to myself. I knocked at the door and a voice inside invited me to come in. I entered and saw an officer sitting behind a desk. I immediately froze not expecting to see an officer but saluted immediately. I was asked what I wanted, and blurted out my reason for being there. The officer smiled, stood up and invited me to stand easy.

He then crossed the floor to another door leading off from his office, and opening it slightly, called out. Sergeant Major. A voice replied Sir, and moments later the Sergeant Major appeared. I was then invited to repeat my reason for being there. I could see them both smiling at my explanation. The Sergeant Major then said. Your a scouser aren't you? I had never heard this expression before, and obviously looked puzzled. The Sergeant Major seeing my puzzled look continued. Are your from Liverpool? I replied. Yes Sir. He appeared to smile knowingly. then asked, how long have you been in the Army soldier? I replied 'two weeks Sir.'

I was then informed by the Sergeant Major. That I should not approach the Officer Commanding directly. If I required anything in future, I should seek out my immediate superiors, the lance corporal, or the corporal in charge he said. I nodded my agreement.

I eventually got the paint I wanted and I believe my colleague and I made a good job of the gates.

Some time later I was on guard duty at the main gate. It was just before Christmas, and most of the occupants of the camp had gone home for the holidays. Just then a car approached the guard house. It was the O.C. himself, Major Redwood. I darted forward and quickly lifted the barrier to the entrance. I then stood smartly to attention and saluted.

The car stopped alongside me and the window wound down. I wondered to myself, what have I done wrong now? The Major, now peering from the window said, "well done Elliott"! (He remembered my name).

He continued. How much longer have you got on duty? I replied this is my final day sir. He then said. Are you going home for the holidays? I replied no sir. He then said, come to my office within the next hour, when you get stood down. I answered yes sir.

On being relieved, I inspected myself carefully in the guardroom mirror, making sure no buttons were undone. I then hurried to Major Redwoods office not knowing what to expect next. I entered the building and knocked at his door. The knock was answered by the words "come in". I entered the office and saluted. Major Redwood looked up from his desk and said stand easy. I relaxed.

Looking directly at me, He asked, "have you ever been to Devon"? I replied no sir! He then said.

"How would you like to spend Christmas with my family in Devon? I have a daughter about your age and I'm sure she would like to meet you"! For a moment I was lost for words and didn't know what to say. I had expected to be given some sort of job to do.

I hesitated a moment longer before answering. "I'd like that sir". Major Redwood replied, "good. See the duty clerk about a rail warrant and I'll sign it for you".

I left camp the following morning armed with an address of a village named Ottery St Mary, in Devon. I was alone. Major Redwood had travelled home the night previously. I arrived after a train journey lasting about two hours and was met at the station by Major Redwood and a young lady who he introduced as his daughter. He was in civilian clothes which made me feel more comfortable. We drove a short distance to his home were I was introduced to his wife, and shown to the room I would be occupying.

Later that same day his son also arrived, dressed in a naval officers uniform.

IN LIVERPOOL

He was also on leave. That evening we all sat down for dinner at the table. I was initially very nervous but they soon made me feel most welcome. That night I was asked lots of questions about my family and home life in Liverpool. (I never mentioned my stepfather who earned his living by escaping from a sack) His daughter then took charge of me. The following day we went exploring the village, and the surrounding countryside.

Before I returned to camp, Major Redwood and his family took me to visit Honiton a nearby town were the local cider is made. I was told that once a year, I can't recall for what reason, a 'tar barrel' is set on fire and ceremoniously rolled down a hill.

I don't know why I was invited to Major Redwoods home. It was most unusual. Perhaps he felt sorry for me being away from my family at Christmas. It was not unlike the occasion when I was invited to stay at the 'School boards house,' many years before.

When visiting Devon on holiday years later with my own family. I once again visited the beautiful village of Ottery St Mary. I stopped at the local post office and enquired the whereabouts of the Redwood family. I would have loved to have seen them again, but unfortunately they could not help me. Apparently they had left the village many years before.

After my basic training I was posted to Germany, where I continued to write and receive letters from 'my girl friend' in Liverpool. Being a non smoker I would sell my cigarette allowance to members of the German public for a profit. Soon I had enough money to buy two ladies watches, one for my mother and one for my girl friend. I carefully wrapped them up and sent them via the Army postal service separately to Liverpool.

I was therefore most surprised to have one returned soon afterwards, by my girlfriend, who had refused to pay the duty on it. I did not even receive an explanation from her. I was so disappointed. On my next home leave I was told by one of my friends, that she had been seeing some one else in my absence. So that was the end of that romance.

I was glad she hadn't accepted the watch, which I had now given to one of my sisters. I met her coincidentally many years later when shopping in town. She informed me that she now had five children. Except for putting on a lot of extra weight, she had not changed at all. It appeared to me, that she had been stuck in a time warp all those years. Phew what a narrow escape.

Whilst home on leave, I was told that some of my old school friends who where also doing there National Service, were stationed in different parts of the world. Jimmy McConn, nicknamed 'Macca' was stationed in Cyprus,

Robbie Brougham was stationed in Trieste, and Kenny Gibbons was stationed not too far from me in Germany. On returning to Germany I telephoned Kenny's barracks, and we arranged to meet and spend a weekend in Hanover. We would both wear civilian clothes.

In my opinion, one of the silliest things the Army ever did. Was to issue all new arrivals from the UK, a detailed street map of all the premises 'out of bounds' to British Army personnel. The map gave you the addresses of all the best bars in the red light district of town, which in ordinary circumstances would have taken you months to find, suddenly it was presented to you like mana from heaven. Retrieving the map from were I kept it, I looked at it and said to myself. That's where Kenny and I will be spending our weekend.

We would just have to make sure we not caught by the 'redcaps' who quite often patrolled the area.

When the military police entered the bars looking for military personnel, to prevent being discovered, you could sometimes bluff your way by speaking a few words of German. But more often than not your Army haircut, English clothes and Army issue grey socks would give you away.

Fortunately for Kenny and I we were not discovered and we had a fantastic weekend. Like most soldiers away from home, we met two frauleins who invited us back to their place. The inevitable happened. We got stinking drunk and fell asleep. Needless to say, the following morning when we woke up, the frauleins had disappeared and so had our wallets with the remainder of our money. I distinctly remember Kenny and I staggering out of the room still under the influence of alchohol, in the middle of nowhere, trying to find our way back to town, and asking a scarecrow standing at the edge of a field, directions back to town, and being quite annoyed when it wouldn't answer us.

We eventually managed to hitch a ride back to the centre of town, there we met some sqaddies who gave us a lift back to our respective barracks.

Each October in Germany they hold a carnival called a 'wine fest', to celebrate the 'tasting' of the new wines. It's a lovely festival, and an excuse for the local girls to don a mask and enjoy themselves. We 'Tommies' always looked forward to this occasion, which we named 'shagfest', it gave us the excuse to get drunk and hopefully, get ourselves a girl. Unfortunately on this particular occasion I was on 'jankers', (confined to barracks) for something or other I had done.

None the less I was determined not to miss the Festival, and after roll call at

IN LIVERPOOL

10pm, when you reported in full MSO kit to the guardroom, for inspection by the duty officer, I hurried back to my room and changed into my civilian clothes and left the barracks. Having thoroughly enjoyed myself, I returned to camp at about 2.30 am, and was informed by one of my friends on guard duty, that the duty officer was looking for me.

What could I do, I asked myself. I'd be in serious trouble if it was discovered I'd left the barracks. I hurried back to my bunk and quickly changed out of my civvies, putting on my pyjamas. I then hurried to the ablutions and removed every toilet roll from all the cubicles and put them in the stove to burn. (Each barrack room had a stove to heat the room). I then went to bed. Not long afterwards the duty officer entered the room and approached my bed. Using the cane he was carrying, he pushed it under the bed clothes and threw back the blankets, no doubt expecting to find me still dressed. I sat up in bed rubbing my eyes as if roused from a deep sleep. What do you want sir? I said innocently.

"Where have you been Elliott?, I've been looking for you". With a puzzled look on my face I replied, I must have been on the toilet sir, I had an upset tummy. "don't give me that nonsense, I went to the toilets and you were not there", the officer insisted.

I answered, "Sir, I went to the toilet in the other block, because there's no toilet paper in our toilets".

I could sense a sound of gloating in his reply when he said. "Right Elliott get dressed and come with me, and I must warn you, if I find one toilet roll in any of the toilets, you will be before the C.O. in the morning on a charge of absence without leave."

I donned my greatcoat and walked behind him to the toilets.

Flinging open the door of the first cubicle he came to, he was unable to find any toilet paper, he then tried the remainder of the cubicles without any success. I could see the look of bewilderment on his face, that I had tricked him somehow. He turned to face me and said. "Go back to bed". I answered. "Yes Sir", (and no doubt rubbing salt in his wound) "goodnight Sir".

On another occasion me and my platoon had been sent to Bad Hartzburg a small town in the mountains of southern Germany, to learn to ski. Our tutor was an ex German olympic gold medallist. We had been there about two days and had progressed to the nursery slopes, when a number of us decided to take the chair lift to the top of the mountain, to see what the view was like from up there.

After about twenty minutes we arrived at the top and embarked. We stood in a group gazing about us at the view, and at the tiny ant like people in the valley below. The scenery was magnificent. Standing there in our white combat gear, precariously balanced on our skis, unable to ski, we thought we were the bees knees. From time to time expert skiers would pass by us and pause for a moment, before skiing down a long jump protruding out from the mountain top.

Having leapt from the jump the skier's would disappear from view for a few moments before re-appearing once again further down the mountain side.

Suddenly we were approached by a women who on hearing us speak English, introduced herself as some Colonel or other's wife. We engaged in polite conversation until she suddenly asked, how long had we been skiing? Two day's Marm! we replied. We could see the surprise on her face at our answer. Two days! She replied a look of astonishment now on her face, and your up here on top of the mountain? "Yes Marm I replied, and Taffy's just about to jump". With that I reached out and pushed Taffy Giggs who stood facing the jump, gently in the back.

Taffy let out a yell and began to slide towards the slope. Unable to stop himself, he sat down on his backside and slowly slid towards the edge of the jump, letting out one final yell, he disappeared from sight.

Realising what I had done, I said to my companions, "I'm going next are you coming"? I then stepped forward, sat on my backside, and slid forward over the edge in a similar fashion to Taffy.

Flying through the air for what seemed like ages, (in fact it was only a second or so), I hit the ground with a great bump, the thick snow breaking my fall. I continued to slide downhill my legs and arms going in every direction until I eventually managed to stop.

I regained my footing with some difficulty and felt for any broken bones, everything seemed to be okay. I looked for Taffy, he was standing ahead of me, I waved to him, and was relieved to see him wave back.

Suddenly two more huge snowballs came sliding down the mountain towards us, it was our other two mates. Fortunately for everyone concerned, we were all able to stop at a slight bend in the run, before it turned and headed straight down a much steeper slope.

Nobody suffered anything more than a few bruises and we were all elated at what we had just done. Later we had a good laugh about it drinking in one of the local bars, but having pushed Taffy over the edge I thought to myself, I better go as well. There's no way I could have gone down in the chair lift. My mates thought the same and followed me. Goodness knows what the officers wife thought about us, she must have thought we were mad.

Unfortunately Taffy Giggs who came from Cardiff was later killed in a road accident, when the Army truck he was travelling back to camp in, skidded on ice in the road and crashed.

Much later I was promoted to corporal and put in charge of the stores. This was a 'cushy number' especially on Army excercises (manoeuvrers). Part of my job was to issue jerry cans of petrol to the hundreds of vehicles on the scheme. Unfortunately for the Army, many of the contents of the cans found there way in to farmers tractors and the like, in exchange for schnapps, chickens and eggs, the German farmers being strictly rationed at that time. I also sold my cigarette allowance to them, and made a handsome profit.

Soon after on a visit to Belgium, I met some one very special and fell head over heels in love, her name was Maria.

When I returned to my unit we kept in contact with each other by letter, and when I had some weekends free I would go to visit her.

It was about this time also, that I received a letter from my mother informing me that a school friend, Joey Piggott, had been accidentally killed. He was the merchant seaman who I mentioned earlier, who impressed me by the way he dressed.

Apparently Joey had hitched a ride on a vehicle travelling from the docks to Great Homer Street, and on jumping from the vehicle, he had stumbled and fell beneath the wheels and died instantly.

Poor Joey, when I think about our school days, and the dozens of times we 'skipped' the lorries travelling from the docks.

I had some leave due to me so I returned briefly to Liverpool. My intention was to visit my family for a short visit, then return soon afterwards via the Hook Of Holland to Belgium, where I would spend the remainder of my leave with Maria. I had told my mam and Hughie all about Maria, and they both seemed pleased. My final day at home. I had spent most of the day with friends drinking in a shebeen in the south end of town, before saying goodbye to them and returning home. I had promised Hughie and my mam I would have a drink with them before I caught my train.

That evening I finished packing my case and after eating my meal and saying goodbye to the younger members of the family, me Hughie and my mam caught a tram to town. I was dressed in my Army uniform.

It was early, the London train wouldn't leave until just before midnight.

We visited the American Bar in Lime Street and had a few drinks, Then later, we went next door to the Wine lodge. As usual Hughie took great pleasure in introducing me to his friends. "This is my lad from the Army he would say". they in turn insisted on buying me more drink, until finally I became completely sloshed. It had been almost non-stop drinking for most of the day. Finally it was time to leave. I was practically carried to the train by Hughie and my mam, they found a seat for me in a compartment with other military personnel returning from leave. Before saying goodbye, Hughie handed me a bottle of Aussie white and said. "Here share this out with everyone".

I vaguely remember unscrewing the top and taking a sip before passing it to the next person. I'd had enough. I don't remember much else after that, I must have fallen asleep, except that one of the WRACS in the carriage asked, could she try my beret on.

Arriving at Euston station in the early hours of the morning. I was awakened by a porter. The carriage was empty and my beret was missing. That WRAC must have pinched it I thought. I felt terrible, my head was aching and my mouth felt like hair was growing on my tongue. I collected my suitcase and headed for the exit. The platform was empty, the passengers having left before I awoke.

I needed to wash and freshen up and rinse my mouth. I walked through the barrier and handed my ticket to the ticket collector.

I crossed the station causeway heading for were I knew the toilet was.

Suddenly from out of a doorway stepped two military policemen, heading straight towards me. Just my luck I thought, this is all I need.

They had obviously seen me, I stuck out like a sore thumb, wearing no beret. I tried to ignored them, and continued walking towards the toilet. I was almost abreast of them when one of them said.

"Where d'ya think your going to soldier, and where's your beret"? I stopped, put down my suitcase and looked towards them. They were both lance corporals.

I was superior to them in rank being a corporal myself. I replied. "First of all, when you speak to me, address me by my rank. And in answer to your questions, I'm travelling to Belgium and I've lost my beret"!

The taller of the two then stepped forward and said, rather sarcastically. "Corporal, you wont be travelling anywhere, your improperly dressed and you appear to be under the influence of drink".

I looked at them both and replied. "Just leave me alone. Let me travel back to my unit, I'm doing no harm". With that I lifted my case and took a step forward as if to continue on my way. With that the taller of the two grabbed hold of my arm to prevent me from leaving.

My reaction to this was to instinctively drop my suitcase, pull my arm free, and turning slightly sideways to face the redcap, punch him on the jaw. He fell to the floor as if poleaxed and lay still. It was all over in a split second. I realised immediately what I had done and bent over him to see if he was hurt badly. I was now completely sober. With that the other redcap jumped on my back and proceeded to arrest me. I offered no resistance but shouted out. "Help your mate on the bloody floor, I'm not gonna run away"!.

Soon after I was taken under arrest to the guards barracks at Chelsea, and placed in a cell. About ten minutes later the cell door was flung open and there stood before me, was one of the biggest men I'd ever seen in my life. A Regimental Sergeant Major from the guards brigade and directly behind him, six guardsmen holding pick axe handles.

I stood up from the bunk I'd been sitting on. The RSM bellowed. "Who's the hard case we've got here then"? I said. "Corporal Elliott Sir"! I then kept completely quiet. I was no fool. I knew I was in big trouble, and there was no way I was going to argue with seven men. The RSM replied, "any trouble from you corporal whilst your in my custody, and I'll soon sort you out". I again kept quite.

That same day I was escorted back to my regimental headquarters at Aldershot, to appear before the Commanding Officer.

I was pleased Major Redwood was no longer there. (I found out later that he had been seconded to the Rhodesian Army).

After the charges were read out to me, (Drunk and disorderly, conduct prejudicial to military discipline, improperly dressed and fighting) I pleaded guilty. I was then confined to barracks on 'open arrest' to await a court martial. I was so annoyed with myself, and what I had done, here I am awaiting a court martial when I should have been enjoying myself on leave in Belgium. Some weeks later I was sentenced to be 'reduced to the ranks' and 90 days detention at Colchester Military correction unit.

When I arrived at the 'Glasshouse' under escort, I could not help but notice a lot of the King's Liverpool regiment already there. They had just come back from a tour of Korea and some of them had gone absent without leave. I recognised two of my mates from school, Georgie Pugh and Chuck Brougham.

Military detention is something I would certainly recommend to the authorities, to straighten out some of today's youth who break the law.

On completing my sentence I was escorted to the main gate and released. At that time the railways were on strike and I had to make my own way back to the barracks. This was not difficult when dressed in uniform.

When I eventually arrived at headquarters, I was informed that I would not be returning to my unit in Germany but instead, become one of the many permanent staff at the camp. I soon settled down once again to the routine of Army life and was promoted to lance corporal. I wrote to Maria and asked her to come and join me, she arrived soon afterwards. We rented a house and soon after bought ourselves a Boxer dog. It was something I always wanted a boxer. In fact. I have even got one to this day. We named him Bruce. He was a lovely animal.

Things were progressing well. Maria had obtained a part time job and I had been given the task of teaching new recruits 'how to drill'. Then one day I found my name on the notice board for a posting to Korea. Apparently I was due for service abroad once again. I did not want to go to Korea. It meant parting from Maria again. I was perfectly happy where I was and had recently been awarded my second stripe.

I had embarkation leave due to me, so I arranged to take my dog to Liverpool to be looked after by my mam. Maria reluctantly returned home to Belgium. I took the train from Aldershot changing trains en-route to arrive at Euston station, from were I could catch a train to Liverpool. Because of some slight delay in crossing London, I arrived at Euston station rather later than expected.

Hurrying as quick as I could, I arrived at the platform. I could see the doors being closed on the Liverpool train, and the Guard looking at his watch in preparation to signal it's departure. If I hurried I could still catch the train. I ran up the platform pulling the dog on his lead after me. The guard blew his whistle and the train started to pull slowly away.

A passenger leaning out of the train window waving goodbye, and realising I wanted to catch the train. Kindly opened the train door for me.

I picked up my dog and running alongside the train, threw him through the open door. He landed on his feet and turned round to face me. I was just about to jump on the train myself, when suddenly the dog no doubt thinking he was being abandoned, sprang out of the door back on to the platform. I hesitated momentarily, letting go of the door, and turned round to see where he had gone.

It was then I was struck by the open carriage door, knocking me to the ground.

I remember a blow to the back, then finding myself stumbling to the ground, and thinking to myself, I'm going to fall between the train on to the track. I came to a stop face down near the edge of the platform.

I remained completely still where I had fallen afraid to move, I could see the wheels turning, carrying the weight of the train on the lines below. I lay a moment longer my heart pounding, then looked up to see the rear of the train just disappearing out of sight. It had all happened so quickly.

Breathing a sigh of relief I got to my feet and quickly examined myself. luckily I seemed to be okay. Regaining my composure, I started to brush my clothes with both hands to rid them of dust.

My dog was now circling me, wagging the stump of his tail. One or two people had also gathered round, asking, are you alright? I replied "yes thank you". The guard approached and said, "you were very lucky, you could have been killed"! I said to myself. Don't I know it! I made an excuse and retired to the toilet to clean myself up. The next train to Liverpool was not for another three hours.

Arriving home later that evening with my dog, the whole family immediately fell in love with him, having had dogs all their life.

It was nice to see the family again. I never mentioned my narrow escape a few hours earlier. After enjoying my home leave and seeing some of my old mates again. I left my dog with my parents and returned to Aldershot before my leave was up. I wanted to see the company clerk, he was a friend of mine and had helped me in the past. I wanted to concentrate on 'getting out of going to Korea'. Eventually after a great deal of wheeling and dealing, I was able to 'wangle' it with the company clerk, so that my name was exchanged with another corporal on a draft going to Belgium instead.

It was at headquarters that I met Rocky Seddon a professional boxer who later became a bodyguard to the stars. We became very good friends but unfortunately he died rather mysteriously many years later in Liverpool.

I had now got myself a nice cushy posting to Belgium.

Chapter Nine

Things had worked out much better than I first imagined, but more importantly, I would be stationed near Maria.

For the next six months things couldn't have been better. Maria had rented a flat in Antwerp and I was able to see her almost every night.

One day I received a letter from my mam, informing me that my dog had gone missing. 'Everybody's been looking all over for him, she said, and I've placed an advert in the Liverpool Echo, offering a reward for a boxer dog named bruce, with an Aldershot address on his collar'. She then went on to say, 'I know who's taken him', naming one of the neighbours.

'He always stops to admire him, and he always says, that's a smashing dog you've got, he looks like a show dog'. She continued, 'I bet He's taken him to breed off'.

The dog was never seen again.

Maria and I had decided to get married, it was a simple affair with Maria's parents and her cousin in attendance.

Once again I found myself being posted. The Army required a sergeant at an ex Luftwaffe airport on the border with eastern Germany. Unfortunately I was unable to do anything about it this time. It was now near the end of my six year engagement, so it meant I would have to serve the remainder of my time there. Meanwhile I promised Maria I would return to Belgium whenever I could.

Returning to Belgium one weekend, I found myself late at night at a train station in Holland. I always found the Dutch to be extremely friendly, and on this particular occasion the train driver invited me to sit in the cab with him, perhaps it was because I was wearing my uniform. It was a wonderful experience travelling at high speed in the dark, with only the occasional signals being visible.

Towards the end of my service, I declined an offer from my commanding officer to extend my Army service, even though I had a good rank and the possibility of being promoted further. Maria and I now had a baby boy. He was born in Belgium, and was named Jim after me, and quite naturally I wanted to be near them. I decided to take my discharge and seek employment in Belgium. Maria's Father had made some enquiries for me and had arranged a job interview with a shipping company in Antwerp. On being discharged I went to see them and soon after my interview, I was offered a job, which I readily accepted.

IN LIVERPOOL

Our flat at the time was near Central Station in Korte Kevit Straat, just behind the zoo and the diamond centre of Antwerp. It had been very convenient for when I returned home on leave. Now I had left the Army, we decided to move nearer to Maria's parents and we found a flat in Rupel Straat near the Velodrome , (Indoor cycle track). Maria's parents lived in the next street, Twee Neten Straat.

(The first time I ever went to meet Maria's parents, I noticed a blue plaque attached to the wall of the tenement block where they lived, it was in memory of the many civilians killed there in the war from a direct hit by a flying bomb in 1944. At that time the German Army was retreating from Antwerp. Towards the end of the war, the Germans fired hundreds of flying bombs which killed lots of civilians. One flying bomb in fact killed many British soldiers when it landed on the Rex cinema in the centre of Antwerp, whilst they were relaxing there watching a film.)

(To commemorate the liberation of Antwerp by the British Army, a Churchill tank now stands to this day in the centre of the main road leading from Brussels to Antwerp.)

I believe it is one of the original tanks that entered the city.

Maria and I had now moved into our new flat. It was here that Maria's father taught me how to paint and decorate, and do odd jobs about the house. I had never done anything like that before. Wim was like a father to me and I'll always be grateful to him, for all the help he gave me.

Throughout the war, Maria's mother also named Maria belonged to the Belgium underground movement, the resistance, and when Wim, Maria's Father, went on duty as a fireman. Maria's mother used to meet up with other members of the resistance, to sabotage German military equipment. I loved to sit and listen to her tell stories of her experiences during the war.

Alec my brother came to stay with us on holiday. This was his first trip abroad. He had brought with him the name and address of a friend's sister who lived in Antwerp. Our friends name was Sammy Nielson. Sammy's sister had married a Belgium seaman many years before. We visited them on a number of occasions and they were delighted to see us, making us very welcome indeed.

Alec was learning to speak the language, and Maria was able to send him to the local (winkel) shop on errands. Even today Alec can still recall the following sentence. Madame, Twee kilo potates aster bleeft en nee fergater de zegelt's. Something quite unique to Belgium at that time was being able to purchase hot soup from a man in the street who rode a bicycle cart, and rang a hand bell to inform people he was there.

Maria and I had a really good time showing Alec the delights of Antwerp, which is not unlike Liverpool in many ways.

We took him to visit the jungle bar, owned by a friend of ours named Albert De Vader, He was a homosexual and had the nickname Mitzi. He was a wonderful dancer. Alec could not believe his eyes, seeing men parading around dressed as women. (unheard of in Liverpool at that time).

We also took him to another bar we often visited in the town centre, in this bar they had a five piece robot band, who looked unbelievably lifelike. The robots seemed to stare straight at you, whilst sitting motionless behind their various instruments.

When you placed five francs in the machine, there would be a sound like a hiss of steam, followed by the robots standing up from their seats to play a tune. At the end of the tune they would sit back down in their seats again, unbelievable!.

They where so real looking. And not like anything I had ever seen before.

Alec came to stay with us one more time after that.

I had settled into my civilian job quite nicely, and had made a lot of friends. I had also met another scouser, who came from the south end of Liverpool and had married a Belgian girl. Maria and I were very happy. Unfortunately the Belgium congo crisis had just developed, and being a foreigner, I was soon informed by the police that my work permit would not be renewed. This I understood, was to make jobs available for Belgian nationals returning from Africa.

I was desperate. What could I do? I would have to leave Belgium very soon. My work on the dock entailed me meeting lots of British seamen and it was suggested by one of them that I visit the 'Flying Angel', to enquire about becoming a seaman on one of the British ships which docked regularly at Antwerp.

I soon visited the Flying Angel, and was informed by the union representative there, that it was possible, but before I could become a seaman, I would first have to join the seamans union in England. Maria and I discussed what I ought to do next, and we decided that the best thing for me to do because I had to leave Belgium anyway, was return to England and join the union. Perhaps then I could get a job working on one of the 'beaver' boats sailing from Antwerp to Montreal and back.

I packed a bag and returned to my parents home in Liverpool, and immediately applied to become a seaman. I was told to visit the union office in Park Road Toxteth, which is practically next door to the Norwegian church. Being an ex serviceman, I was able to join the union quite easily. Having joined the union, I was asked to report to the Merchant Marine office at Mann Island to seek employment. It was on my first visit to the shipping office that I was offered a position on deck, as a DHU, 'deckhand uncertificated', on a 32,000 ton shell tanker named Venessa, which was leaving Tranmere oil terminal at Birkenhead in two days time. This trip would give me the experience I needed, I was informed.

At that time, provision was made for ex servicemen to become trainee able seamen, and obtain their steering ticket and life boat ticket whilst at sea.

The big day finally arrived. Hughie, and my mam accompanied me to the dock. En route we stopped and like in the past, we had a few drinks in Yate's wine lodge in town. Once again Hughie introduced me to some of his friends with. "This is my lad from the Army, he's now going away to sea".

Everyone would smile, because one of Hughie's favourite saying's when performing the bag trick, was to say to the crowd, "I have three sons, one in the Harmy, he would pronounce Army with an H, one in the navy, and one in the bag". Hughie's friends always seemed pleased to see me. This time I didn't drink too much.

I could see my mam and Hughie where disappointed that I was leaving so soon. They both looked older, and I wished I could have stayed a little longer. We had not seen a great deal of each other the last two years, and I knew they worried a great deal about me. We took a taxi through the Mersey tunnel, and within minutes arrived at Tranmere oil jetty.

After saying goodbye. I was just about to mount the gangway leading to the ship, when Hughie took me to one side, and insisted on giving me some money. "You'll need a few bob for yourself" he said. Same old Hughie he hadn't changed at all, he was also correct, I was flat broke.

Sailing out of the Mersey later that evening, I stood on deck with a slight lump in my throat. I was choked, and wished things could somehow be a bit different. I hoped they would both look after themselves. I also imagined them standing at the Pier Head waving me goodbye.

What I understood to be a training run to the Middle East, then returning to the United Kingdom, turned out to be a trip lasting much longer

I soon adapted to navy life and concentrated on learning my job. Part of my duties entailed me being on lookout at the fo'c'sle head throughout the night. This part of my job I enjoyed very much, standing there all alone with nothing but my thoughts and the stars for company, watching the bow of the ship cut through the water like a knife through butter, flinging aside the luminous sea creatures in their hundreds. I had also arranged with Maria that each night before we went to bed we would both look at the moon. It was so peaceful and it gave me a great sense of well being.

We sailed non stop travelling east past Gibraltar through the Mediterranean sea, then on through the Suez Canal, until finally arriving at Kuwait in the Persian Gulf. I had never seen so many oil tankers anchored together from all parts of the world waiting to take on oil. They stretched as far as the eye could see. I was glad. This was our first port of call and it enabled me to visit the town,(Mena Al Amadi) whilst we were waiting.

It was extremely hot in the gulf. Dressed only in flip flops and shorts, we deckhands carried out our various tasks, taking on board fresh provisions and painting the outside of the ship. After our cargo of oil had been loaded, we headed back out to sea.

Passing through the Straits of Hormuz to the Arabian Sea, we received instructions to proceed across the Indian Ocean to Australia. Lying low in the water now that we had a full cargo, dozens of flying fish could be seen hurtling through the air, some to land on deck, no doubt trying to escape from predators.

Trips like this continued for weeks on end, collecting our cargo of oil from one producing country for delivery to another.

At each port of call, our mail would be waiting for us and the letters we had written to our wives and families would be taken from us to be posted home. The voyage reminded me very much of what it must have been like on a tramp steamer years before. Not knowing which country you would be visiting next.

On one such visit to Yokkaichi in Japan, we berthed about a mile from shore and were met by dozens of boatmen, each of them offering to row us ashore. Me and my friend named Joe Connolly hired a boat and asked the boatman would he be willing to come ashore with us and show us the sights if we paid him. He agreed.

That day we had an escorted tour of the town and in each bar we visited we drank saki, a potent rice wine, and so did our boatman. He was only a small chap and we had become quite fond of him. After about seven or eight hours non stop drinking, it became time for us to return to the ship but our boatman was in no fit state to row us back. Joe and I quite literally had to carry him back to the quayside were his boat was tied up. Unable to rouse him from his stupor, we sat him down with his back against a wall, making sure he was as comfortable as possible, we then emptied our pockets of all the yen we had left, putting it in one of his coat pockets. We then borrowed his boat to take us back to the ship.

On reaching the ship we placed the oars carefully inside the tiny boat, and proceeded to climb up the Jacob's ladder to the deck above, once on deck we looked back in time to see the small boat bobbing aimlessly in the water below.

Soon afterwards the ship put to sea. I wonder, did the boatman ever recover his boat?

On another occasion we were sailing up the west coast of America having recently discharged our cargo at San francisco, when all of a sudden there was a huge explosion in the engine room. A boiler had burst showering boiling hot water over one of the crew, a Scots engineer. We all ran to help him, he lay screaming on the floor, his clothing torn from him by the blast. He was scalded from head to foot, his skin a bright orange colour, some hanging from him in long strips. A radio request for help was made and he was airlifted by helicopter to a San Diego hospital. I don't know what became of him after that.

Eventually we were ordered to sail through the Panama Canal to the Atlantic Ocean, collecting our cargo's of oil this time from Venezuela, for delivery to the Caribbean islands and the east coast of America.

It was whilst sailing in the Caribbean that we came quite close to HMS Ark Royal, and watched her aircraft landing and taking off, it was a lovely sight, and made you feel proud to be British, we exchanged signals with each other before going our different ways.

Although I visited many different parts of the world, and made many new friends. I had made my mind up. A seamans life was not for me. I wanted to be near my family. I was worse off now than when I was in the Army. Finally we received instructions to proceed to the United Kingdom and home.

On docking at Thames haven, (The ship by now having completely circled the globe). I collected what money was due to me and headed for my parents home in Liverpool. (I had made provision to send money to my wife each month) The whole trip had lasted twelve months.

My close friend aboard ship who I had mentioned earlier was a chap named Joe Connolly. He worked below deck in the engine room. He was also a married man with a family and lived in Kirkby, a district of Liverpool. We used to go ashore together when ever we docked. On one of our last ports of call in South America, Joe had bought a small monkey which he kept in his cabin, it was for one of his children. Just before we got paid off at Thames Haven the poor creature died. On the train to Liverpool, Joe unpacked one of his bags and produced the dead monkey. I asked him why he still had the monkey? and he replied. "I've written home telling my kid I've bought him a monkey, and unless he sees it, I don't think he'll believe me".

That was Joe's last trip to sea. he had also decided to work ashore. Afterwards, Joe and I would meet occasionally in Town for a few drinks. Unfortunately we lost touch with each other when I later moved house.

Many years later, I remember seeing Joe briefly, he was driving a Liverpool Corporation bus. We managed to wave to each other before driving in opposite directions.

When the train arrived at Lime Street station bringing us home, I dismounted from the train and looking round, beckoned for a porter to help me with my luggage. I needed a taxi to carry all my baggage. It felt strange asking for assistance. I did not recognise the porter who approached me, and smiled to myself, thinking of the times when Andy Cunningham and I, many years before would have been carrying other peoples luggage.

Arriving home half an hour later I was shown to my room, the parlour, which had been converted into a bedroom for me. It had been decorated since I was last here. It was nice to see everyone again. I immediately started to unpack my cases looking for the presents I had brought home for each of the family. On one of my visits to Japan, I had purchased three beautiful dinner sets, which were hand painted, and when you lifted up one of the cups to the light, you could see the face of a geisha girl in the bottom of it.

I had already decided who they were for. One set was for my Mother and Hughie. One set for Alec and his wife, (Alec was now married), and the other set was for my own family in Belgium. I had also bought a Japanese kimono for my mother in law, and a musical cigarette box shaped like mount Fujiyama, for my dad and my step mother Eileen who both smoked, they now lived in Catherine Street in the south end of the city.

Little had changed since I'd been away, except that my brothers and sisters had now grown up.

Alec my brother had married his childhood sweetheart Margaret, and they were now living in a flat in Great Mersey Street. His wife had recently given birth to a little boy.

Soon after my arrival. Maria and the baby came to stay with us, with a view to staying permanently, but it did not work out very well.

IN LIVERPOOL

The family still lived in Robsart street an overcrowded house in the slums, and the living conditions there were most unsatisfactory. We still had to use a cold water tap and an outside toilet. Maria was like a fish out of water, especially with a young baby to look after.

We went to visit Liverpool city council housing office and applied for a house, but to no avail, although they put our name on the housing list, they informed us that there was a huge waiting list and it would be many years before we would be housed. The slums were being demolished at that time, and you needed a certain amount of points to qualify for accommodation.

friends of the family offered us a room at their house, which we gratefully accepted. It was less crowded, but after a short period of time, we decided it was not what we wanted, and that we ought to return to Belgium to see if circumstances had changed and if I could get a job there again.

We packed what few things we could carry, and returned to Antwerp to stay with Maria's parents.

It wasn't long before we found ourselves another flat. Once again, it was quite near were Maria's parents lived. My savings where almost gone now, and we found I still required a work permit, without this you could not get a job or obtain any benefit. We were up against officialdom and wondered what would become of us. Maria was obliged to take a part time job whilst I looked after the baby. I felt so useless. The money Maria earned was just about enough to support her and the baby.

One Sunday afternoon, Maria and I took the baby to see the caged birds for sale at the Vogel market, and from there we visited the Steen and took a trip by ferry on the river Scheldt. We used to do this quite often in the past. The Steen reminded me very much of Liverpool's Pier Head. On this particular occasion I took lots of photographs of Maria and the baby, somehow realising that it may be quite some time before I saw them again. I would soon have to return to Liverpool. At least I could obtain work there.

The day arrived for me to leave Antwerp. I had already said goodbye to Maria's parents the night before. I looked round our flat and wished I could just pick it up and deposit it in Liverpool. I took hold of our son and hugged him close to me. I kissed Maria goodbye and insisted on her staying at home, she wanted to come with me to the train station. I walked down the stairs and out through the front door into the street, I looked up at the window, Maria was leaning out to wave goodbye.

I could see the tears streaming down her face. I waved back to her and turned away to walk to the bus stop, trying hard not to look back and forcing myself not to cry also.

After an uneventful journey I once again arrived back in Liverpool.

My intentions were quite clear, to get a job, work hard, and save enough money to buy a house. Only then could I send for my family. I couldn't help thinking, life can be so cruel sometimes.

I could see by the looks on their faces, that Hughie and my mam felt sorry for me. At that time, I don't think I was very good company, and although they tried to cheer me up by inviting me to go out with them for a drink, I always refused. Instead I would sometimes go to bed quite early. In spite of that, Hughie always remembered to bring me back some bottles of beer.

Hughie told me, that they had just been promised by the corporation, one of the new houses being built in the vicinity."Perhaps you can bring "Maria" back then" he said. I appreciated his kindness but knew that would be impossible. Soon afterwards I applied for a job with S.P.D Ltd. and was asked to start right away.

The company name of SPD stood for 'speedy prompt delivery'. We drivers called it St Patrick's day, or short paid drivers. The depot was in Sefton Street on the dock road. My job was to deliver margarines and soap powders for Lever Bros Ltd to shops on Merseyside. The main factory being over the water in Port Sunlight.

One of the staff working at SPD at that time was a person named John Lennon, later to become famous as a member of the Beatles. He helped load the vehicles although I didn't know him very well.

Each year the company held a 'do' at 'Lever hall' in Port Sunlight, when members, their wives and friends got together. I had invited my mates to meet some of the girls who worked in the office. (Many years later one of my pals Dave Ormesher married June Ashworth one of the girls from the office) We had a fantastic time. The group who entertained us that year was named the Beatles.

I had also joined my local football team. The Albion, named after the pub in Netherfield Road in which my friends and I now used to meet.

The Manager of the team was named Tommy Cooper, a huge man, an ex regimental sergeant major who had served many years in the Army. Tommy looked remarkably like Victor McGlauglin the Hollywood film star.

Our team played in the Liverpool Sunday league at Kirkby. One of the biggest leagues at the time in the country. After each match we would return to the pub for a drink, or sometimes a 'stay behind'. One day Tommy Cooper gave me a wallet which I still have to this day. He said to me.

IN LIVERPOOL

"You'll never be skint if you always keep something in your wallet, no matter how little." occasionally I only have a penny in it, but it's never left completely empty. Quite often in the pub we would play darts or a game of dominos or just listen to Tom speaking about the time he was stationed in India. He was a fine big man and we all gathered at his funeral many years later when he died.

I had now started 'going to the match' on Saturday's with a group of lads from the pub to support Liverpool Football club. One day a friend named Billy Campbell said he knew a man who had a car for sale for £50.00 and if we bought it between us, it would work out much cheaper to travel to the away games to watch them play. At that time not many of my friends had cars. After a short discussion we decided to buy the car and Billy would collect it for us.

Liverpool was playing away that weekend at Nottingham.

The day of the match arrived and Billy came with the car. It was an old model reminiscent of the Al Capone's era, it had dark tinted windows. (Heads turned when we drove by, we must have look like gangsters). There was eight of us all together and it was decided I would drive. Billy would drive his own car. We split into two groups four of us in each car, and set forth to the match.

The car ran well, although there was lots of smoke coming from the exhaust, it got us there in plenty of time to see the game.

After the match we visited the city centre. As was usual in our case we looked for a Yates' Wine lodge to have a drink. Driving along the road I spotted two Pakistani gentlemen and suggested we stop and ask the way. My brother Alec and Macca got out of the car to ask for directions. (I intended to play a joke on them), I beeped my horn and indicated to Billy in the other car to follow me and we drove away, leaving them stranded.

Ten minutes later we returned to collect them, only to find them drinking in a nearby pub with the two Pakistanis, enjoying themselves with not a care in the world.

Eventually we found a wine lodge, and on entering it we were most surprised to discover a small orchestra playing music on the balcony overlooking the bar. It was a little bit more up market than we were used to in Liverpool. In our five Yate's wine lodge's in town, they only had sawdust on the floor to entertain the customers.

Returning home along the M6 motorway in the early hours of the morning, we had just reached the turn off for Haydock when there was a loud bang.

The big end had gone!. (no oil) There was smoke everywhere. Pulling onto the hard shoulder we stopped. Billy following in the other car seeing our predicament also stopped. We all got out of the cars. Unable to do anything about it and knowing it would be expensive to be 'towed' from here, we decided to push the car off the motorway onto the East Lancs road, were we found a spot to park it.

The eight of us now had to crowd into Bill's car for the journey home. The next day we returned and towed the car back to Liverpool for scrap.

When Liverpool played at home. Immediately after the match it was customary for us to go to the pub for a drink, there we would discuss the game before returning home. Occasionally we would just sit there drinking and talking until closing time at 10.00pm.

By now I was in the habit of visiting the local most nights for a drink with my mates, except at weekends when we would go to the town centre.

I've already mentioned that we would play darts, cards or dominoes, and sometimes we would have a sing song, particularly if some one had brought an accordion with them, or a set of spoons.

One of the nicest persons in the pub at that time, was a chap named Sammy Neilson, who you could always rely on, to give a song. Sammy knew the words of all the old Liverpool songs. I had mentioned him earlier when me and my brother Alec had visited his sister in Antwerp.

Sammy was blind in one eye caused by an accident on the docks many years before. One day he was returning home from town on the bus with his wife. Alighting from the bus in Netherfield Road on his blind side, He walked into the road with the intention of crossing to the other side, and was struck by a car killing him instantly.

It was very sad, and all his friends from the pub attended the funeral.

One day I returned home from work to discover my brother John had been taken to hospital. This time he had broken his arm. I found out later he had been collecting wood for the fire, from the old houses that were being knocked down. This was a chore he inherited from Alec and I. He had tripped over when running from the cockey watchman guarding the site. At that time, John was in the school boxing team and was becoming quite good at boxing. For the time being he would have to wait until his arm was mended.

Our neighbourhood was slowly being knocked down brick by brick, to make way for new houses. Whole communities were being broken up. Some families would be never seen again. They were being moved to Speke,

IN LIVERPOOL

Huyton and Kirkby, the new housing estates being built on the outskirts of Liverpool.

I had now been working at SPD for about nine months, when a vacancy occurred for a salesman. It was to sell Birds Eye frozen food products to shops in West Lancashire. The pay was the same but you could earn commission on the sales you made. I applied for the position and got the job, so I transferred over to that section of the company.

I soon became comparatively successful, and started to earn more money, which enabled me to save a little extra each week.

Although we wrote to each other at least once a week. My trips to Belgium were becoming less and less frequent. It was impossible for me to take time off work. Maria had now got herself a full time job, and appeared to be managing alright. We seemed to be in a hopeless situation.

All my colleagues at work had their own cars. So I decided to buy one aswell. It was much more convenient for getting to work. I thought to myself, If I had a car I could give a lift to Hughie who worked down at the docks. That decided, one weekend I visited a local garage and bought a second hand ford on hire purchase.

It was now our turn to be offered a new house by Liverpool Corporation. We were more fortunate than most families. We would remain in the locality and had been offered a three bedroom flat in a block of maisonettes in Petton Street, next to the free library in St Domingo Road.

History records. That a Mr George Campbell, a wealthy West Indies merchant bought this particular piece of land in 1757, and built a fine house there, naming it St Domingo House. It was purchased as a result of one of his many privateers capturing a rich French merchantman off the island of St Domingo. Hence the name St Domingo Road.

Almost opposite Petton Street, is St Georges Church. The Church is actually in Heyworth Street, and is known locally as the cast iron church. the first church in the world to be built entirely of cast iron. St Georges Church stands on the highest part of Liverpool, and from this vantage point you have a magnificent view of North Wales, the Wirral and the ships entering and leaving Liverpool bay.

I understand, the church built in 1812, is on the site of a former beacon. The beacon was a signal fire which could be lit in times of emergency, and formed part of a network of beacons covering the whole country.

Many is the time I have wandered through the church grounds, looking at the grave stones of prominent families buried there. Many having died in the

West Indies, or America and brought back to Liverpool for burial. Some prominent families even had their black servants buried along side them. (presumably ex-slaves), who must have lived in the area more than a hundred years before.

I also read somewhere that in the Royalist siege of Liverpool, Prince Rupert had his headquarters quite near to the church. I used to imagine him at that very same spot,

looking towards the town and remarking to his fellow officer's. "The town is but a crow's nest that a parcel boy could take". In fact I understand he lost over 1500 men capturing Liverpool.

At the time my family moved to Petton Street, it was customary each year on New Year's eve, for hundreds of people to gather outside the church to welcome in the New Year.

The church bells would ring out and ships sirens on the river could be heard indicating the approach of the new year. Just before midnight there would be a final, ten second countdown by the crowd. Then at the exact stroke of midnight. Everyone present would turn to the nearest person to them, perfect strangers included, and wish them a "Happy New Year". The girls would be kissed and mens hands would be shaken.

It was after one of these such occasions, that Hughie and my mam invited some of our friends back to our 'new house' to continue letting in the New Year. Once the guests had arrived, crates of ale that had been bought days previously appeared as if by magic, the bottles were opened and distributed to everyone present. The volume on the radio was turned up and people made themselves comfortable on various pieces of furniture.

Hughie and my mam disappeared into the kitchen to make sandwiches. Everyone seemed happy and slightly the worse for drink.

Hughie soon appeared carrying a huge plate of sandwiches which were quickly eaten up by everyone present. When the sandwiches had all gone, a friend of Alec's named Ronnie Williams said, "hey Hughie them sarnies were great, is there any more left"? Hughie looked at Ronnie and smiling at him, replied, "I'll get some more, specially for you Ron". He once again disappeared into the kitchen and returned soon afterwards with a small plate of sandwiches. "Ere yer are Ron he said". With that, Ronnie jumps up from his chair, says "Ta Hughie", takes the plate from Hughie, sits down once again and within a few minutes has eaten the lot.

After a few minutes had passed, Hughie said to Ronnie. "Ron, yer don't wanna go outside yet do yer"? Ronnie looks quizzically at Hughie and says, "what for"? Hughie replied. "For a piss"! Ronnie then says. "What do I want to go outside for a piss for? There's a piss house upstairs isn't there"? Hughie then says. "Because you've just ate the dogs food on yer sarnies and I thought you might want to go outside and cock yer leg up". Everybody bursts out laughing. Poor Ronnie had been given a tin of the dogs food on his sandwiches and had eaten them not realising it. Hughie was always playing tricks like that on people.

We always had lots of visitors to our house. I remember another time we had a party. On this occasion a friend of ours named Hughie Dainty had drunk too much and had gone to sleep on the settee.

When my stepfather realised he was asleep, he went to the broom cupboard and returned with a tin of black boot polish. Then without disturbing the sleeping man he carefully blackened his face all over with the polish.

When Alec's friend finally awoke later that evening, he yawned and immediately decided that he was going home to sleep. My mother trying hard not to laugh, asked, did he want a drink of tea before he left? Every one present had now gathered round all smiling and waiting to see his reaction. Hughie still blinking from sleep looked around, he must have thought he had been snoring to attract so much attention to himself, and in answer to my mother's question, he replied. No thanks Mrs Elliott I'm goin'straight home. (All our friends still called our mother Mrs Elliott although she had been married to Hughie Smith for many years now). To further increase his victims embarrassment and make everyone laugh, Hughie Smith dropped down on one knee in front of young Hughie Dainty, and in a poor imitation of the late Al Jolson, started singing. "I'll walk a million miles for one of your smiles". Everyone present was now laughing out aloud. The poor victim smiled back at Hughie not quite understanding what was happening. He then stood up, staggered to the door and called out. "I'll see yer all termorra" and closed the door behind him.

The house was in uproar when he left, every one now laughing uproariously. My mam was saying to Hughie, "are yer shouldn't let him go home like that, what will his ma think"? Everyone in the room then crowded over to the large window overlooking the street below. Seconds later, Hughie Dainty came into view walking drunkenly home.

The window was opened wide and shouts of, see yer termorra Hughie, called out. Hughie Dainty waved his arm in reply, no doubt wondering why he had suddenly become so popular.

Apparently he didn't realise his face had been blackened until he got home and looked in the mirror. I would have loved to have seen the surprise on his face when he found out! It was all in good fun and nobody ever took offence. My stepfather was a person who loved life to the full and you could never really get annoyed with him. Although, when I was in his company, I often became embarrassed by his antics. When I complained about it, people would say to me. "Leave him alone, he's doin' no harm".

I mentioned earlier that in spite of Hughie's happy go lucky attitude, very often it would end up with him and my mam arguing with each other. More often than not it would be my Mother who would start it. She would get particularly angry if Hughie came home drunk and she had been waiting for him to take her out, or if she had gone to meet him in town and he hadn't turned up. At home she would throw the first thing that came to her hand at him. Hughie would often get cut, and in turn would grab hold of her to protect himself and a fight would ensue.

Like my brother's and sister's, I was a bag of nerves when they rowed. It would be impossible to sleep and I would have to get out of bed to try and stop them. Very often the neighbours would complain and occasionally the police would be called. I was always very embarrassed seeing the neighbours when this happened. This was also one of the reasons why Maria couldn't come to live with us.

Chapter Ten

John my younger brother had now joined the Army cadets, he always looked very smart dressed in his uniform. He was also doing very well in the boxing team at Roscommon Street school.

Rossy school regularly produced good boxers, whereas St Anthony's produced good footballers. Many years later some ex pupils would receive silver medals for boxing at the olympic games in Moscow. One evening John was appearing at Arnott Street School in a title fight, and me, my friends and family all went to cheer him on. We were so proud of him when he won his fight and was presented with a championship medal.

One evening John hurriedly donned his uniform, intending to go to drill practice with his friends, who were now waiting for him at the nearby bus stop.

Opening the front door He shouted out, "I'll see you later" and ran from the house closing the door behind him. Hughie once again playing one of his tricks, opened the window and waited until John came into view, he then called out. "John you've forgotten something". John stopped in his tracks, and looking up to the window replied, "What is it dad"? Hughie said, "stand underneath the window and I'll drop it to yer". John walked beneath the window and looked up in anticipation. Hughie then produced a toy plastic rifle from behind a chair were it had been hidden, and said. "here's your gun". With that he dropped the toy from the window to John standing below. John now realising a joke was being played on him and on hearing the word gun, stepped aside to allow the toy to hit the floor, it broke on impact into a dozen pieces. Without saying another word, John then ran off to meet his friends at the bus stop.

Once again my mam complained to Hughie about making John look foolish in front of his friends but we were just as bad, because we all laughed aswell. Mary my sister had now started to accompany my mam and Hughie when they went out to the pub. One night the three of them visited the Blue Ball in Prescot Street. In the lounge of the pub, a pianist would play a piano on a small stage, and invite people to 'get on the mike' and give a song. My friend from my railway days, Andy Cunningham and his brother Tony often sang there, it was a very popular pub and at weekends it became very crowded.

On this particular night a group of American Airmen had come to visit the pub, from the nearby Burtonwood air force base.

One of the airmen sat at the table were my family were sitting and quite naturally started to speak to them. Hughie immediately stood up and asked Mary to exchange places with him, so that she sat next to my Mother and he sat next to the airman.

Hughie then said to the airman, "hey yank, this is my daughter! I don't want any funny business from yer! I know what you yanks are like" The poor man was so surprised, he couldn't quite understand what Hughie meant. My mam had to intervene and say. "Take no notice of him, he's always like that".

When ever Mary was in their company, particularly in a crowded pub, Hughie became very protective towards her, and acted like a mother hen with chicks.

One day Alec's wife Margaret who was now expecting a baby, became ill with stomach pains and was rushed to the Royal Infirmary for treatment. Alec was assured by a doctor not to worry but to return home, "she was going to be alright" he said. The next day he again went to visit her, and was told by a nurse that the sister wanted to see him before he returned home.

After spending some time with his wife who appeared to be making good progress, and not knowing what to expect next. He asked to see the ward sister and was directed to her office. The sister was waiting for him when he arrived and invited him to sit down. She then explained to Alec that the baby they were expecting had unfortunately died. She then went on to say that his wife Margaret was suffering no ill effects and would soon be able to return home, "your both young enough, and there's plenty of time for you to have children in the future" she said. Having said that, she picked up the telephone and spoke briefly to some one on the other end, then gently replaced the receiver back on its hook.

Moments later there was a knock on the door and a hospital porter entered carrying a small cardboard box. The sister by way of introduction then said. "This is Mr Elliott" and gestured towards Alec. The porter nodded a greeting to Alec and without saying a word, handed him the box.

Alec was then informed by the nursing sister, that the box contained the body of his dead child, and that he would have to take it to Smithdown Road cemetery. She then went on to explain. That at the cemetery he would have to see the attendant there, who would make arrangements with him for the child's burial.

Alec being only seventeen at the time was dumbfounded and didn't know what to say. He took hold of the box and left the office in a slight daze. Outside the hospital he was able to catch a bus going past Smithdown Road cemetery. Holding the box securely on his knee he was conscious of it's contents, and was very pleased when he eventually arrived at his destination, imagining all kinds of things that could go wrong.

Entering the lodge at the entrance to the cemetery, he reported to the attendant in charge and explained his reason for being there. The attendant didn't seem at all surprised by his errand and replied. "That's Ok son, leave it with us", and apparently as an after thought he said. "What's your religion"? Alec replied "Church of England"! "Fine" said the attendant, scribbling C of E on the box, we'll make sure it gets buried with the same religion!.

When Alec returned home later that day and told us what had happened, we were very surprised, and at first we didn't believe him. Eventually after more questioning, we realised it must be true and that this must happen quite regularly. I wonder if it still happens to day?.

A few months after this incident Alec decided to join the Army. And on completing his basic training he was posted to Chester. Each weekend he would return home,and to earn some extra money he would help Hughie with his pitch.

On one such weekend, Hughie was performing the bag trick at the Pier Head and Alec had been asked to get in the bag. It was a beautiful warm summer day and very hot inside the bag. Hughie was doing his usual sales spiel to the crowd. Asking for "just a few more shillings for the poor man in the bag, who's souls of his shoe's are so thin, that if he stepped on a 'tanner' he would tell you if it's heads or tails". The crowd as usual was enjoying every minute. Soon it would be time for Alec to escape, but before he did so, he would take another deep breathe of fresh air from the tiny holes in the bag. Bending his head slightly forward, he was just about to breathe in through the tiny holes, when he noticed his commanding officer standing in the crowd.

What could he do? He was on weekend leave and didn't want any of his Army colleagues to see him. Certainly not the Commanding Officer. Hughie had now started the count down!

Every one's eyes were now fixed on Alec.

Alec started to struggle inside the bag, untying his hands. He was still thinking to himself, what can I do? the officer is bound to recognise me. Suddenly he thought to himself. He's only seen me when I'm in uniform, I know what I'll do, I'll dirty my face, then he'll not recognise me.   He completed freeing his hands and then undid the rope around his body.

Still enclosed inside the bag, Alec now started to squat on his legs to enable him to reach under his feet. Forcing his fingers under his shoes he extracted some dirt from under them. Still bent almost double he pulled his arms up to his mouth and spat into the palm of his hand, then he rubbed the mixture on his face.

The count had reached ten and Alec should now be stepping from the bag, instead he was still inside bent almost double.

Hughie realising something was wrong leaned over the bag. "What the hell are yer doin? yer should be out by now he whispered".

Alec whispered back. "There's an Army officer from our camp in the crowd who knows me and I don't want him to see me". Hughie looked into the crowd and spied the officer. "Leave it to me" he said. With that Hughie walked over to were the officer was standing and called out to him, at the same time extending his arm which held the collecting hat. "Would you like to put a few bob in the hat general"? The crowd began to laugh knowing full well Hughie had exaggerated his rank. Hughie continued "if you put £5.00 in the hat, I'll come and live with yer". The officer initially appeared slightly embarrassed, everyones attention now focussed on him.

But after a moments hesitation he smiled and dropped some coins in the hat.

Whilst all this was going on Alec had quickly struggled free, and stepping from the bag his face now streaked with dirt, walked quickly away in the opposite direction to where the commotion was taking place.

The crowd as was usual clapped their hands in approval on his escape, and wrongly assumed Alec required the toilet in his hurry to get quickly away. The show now being over, the crowd started to disperse.

A few more minutes elapsed before Alec returned. On seeing him, Hughie said. "Come on Alec, lets have another quick pitch, while there's still a lorra people about"?. Alec replied "I'm not chancing it, that officer may still be hanging around and he might see me"! Hughie looked hard at Alec and said. "He'd never recognise yer, even your own mother wouldn't recognise yer now, you look like a bloody gipsy with all that dirt on your face".

None the less Alec had had enough excitement for one day and decided to return home. Sitting on the bus he watched Hughie gather a new crowd by placing a cigarette between the lips of one of his helpers, and pretend to extract it with the aid of his whip.

Soon after Alec was posted to Germany accompanied by his wife and new born son.

The remainder of the family including myself had now settled in to our new home. I remember passing our old neighbourhood, it wasn't far from where we now lived, and seeing the contractors knocking our old house down. I felt rather sad and thought about the good times we had spent there, and the time Maria had come to stay with us. Maria and I still wrote to each other regularly and although I had my name down on the housing list for re-housing with Liverpool Corporation, it would be many years in the future before we would be offered a house of our own.

One day we had just sat down to our evening meal when there was a knock on the front door, on opening the door I was confronted by two of Hughie's sisters who seemed rather upset. They asked if Hughie had arrived home from work yet? and I replied yes and invited them in. They walked into the living room and on seeing Hughie and my mam sitting there, they cried out, "Me Ma's dead"! They then both burst into uncontrollable tears. Hughie and my mam jumped to their feet and putting their arms around both sisters, tried to console them, at the same time asking, "what happened"?

In between sobs the sisters explained, earlier that day, whilst crossing Renshaw Street, Mrs Smith had been knocked down by a bus and as a result of that had died of her injuries. She was 96 years old.

Both my parents were terribly shocked by the news but immediately donned their coats and left the house quickly to visit the hospital.

It was very sad, I was very fond of Granny Smith.

Soon afterwards the funeral took place. Alec had managed to get compassionate leave from the Army.

The service was held in the Metropolitan Cathedral of Christ the King.

Being a devout catholic Mrs Smith regularly attended 'Paddy's Wigwam' as it is known to most liverpudlians. The Cathedral is quite near to were she lived in Trowbridge Street. Up until that time I had never been inside the Cathedral, and on the day of the funeral, I was most impressed by the works of the many contemporary artists, whom I was to discover later on a visit, were named, John Piper, Patrick Reyntiens, Elizabeth Frink and Ceri Richards.

It was a beautiful day that day, the sun shone directly through the glass roof, reflecting it's many ray's on to the huge Yugoslavian marble altar in the centre of the church. Apparently the Cathedral besides having a unique ten ton bell, contains the largest piece of marble of any church in the world.

The church was absolutely crowded, with hundreds of people coming to pay their last respects. Granny Smith was a well known figure in the town and loved by almost everyone.

I recognised a lot of the 'hand cart' women there that day.

After the service, everybody including the priest was invited back to the 'Bronte club' which is near the bullring, for a buffet and a chat with each other. At the club I was introduced to Hughie's relatives, some who I had never met before. I didn't realise he had so many. Everyone agreed it was a sad occasion, and that Mrs Smith would have lived until she was a hundred, if she hadn't had the accident.

The day after the funeral Alec returned to his barracks in Germany.

Back home my mam and Hughie speaking of 'how nice the service had been' consoled themselves with the thought, that Granny Smith had had a good innings, and that right up until her death she had been very happy and had not suffered much.

Both Hughie and my mam had now started to visit the 'Albion', the pub I drank in in Netherfield Road. To get to the pub from our house, you have to walk down Havelock Street which runs alongside the John Bagot fever hospital.

Havelock Street must be the steepest street in Liverpool, and to assist you in walking, the powers that be had fitted a handrail at the edge of the pavement running the entire length of the street. I don't know of another street like it.

I mentioned earlier, alongside our new house in Petton Street stands Everton library. Carved above it's doors in the ornate brickwork are the words 'Free Library'. It was very convenient for me and I used to use it quite a lot. It had a warm welcoming atmosphere and in the winter it would be crowded with elderly people reading the daily papers but if the truth be known I suspect they went there more to keep warm. Each night when the library closed, one of the elderly men would settle down on the front steps to spend the night huddled in the doorway.

He was of an indeterminate age and wore an old Army overcoat. He also boasted a thick greying beard. He was known locally as 'badgie' because of the dozen or so campaign medals pinned to his chest.

When ever Hughie and my mam went out for a drink, before returning home they would invariably stop at Maggie's chippy in Netherfield Road to buy fish and chips for the family.

Quite often they would buy some for badgie, who would be found sleeping on the steps of the library. He always seemed very grateful. Hughie would sometimes give him money aswell.

IN LIVERPOOL

By now both my sister's Mary and Margaret had left home. Margaret had got herself a flat in the South end of Liverpool, and Mary had married her boyfriend Robbie and moved to a house in Howe Street, which was quite near the Albion pub.

Like myself, Mary's husband Robbie played football for the Albion, and one of his close friends was named Joey Meacock. Joey worked as a carter for 'Harpers' on the 'horse and carts,' delivering goods to the market in Great Homer Street. Quite often at lunchtime when passing Howe Street he would call to my sisters house for something to eat. He would tie the horse's reins to the railings outside the house and being rather a steep street, he would place a brick under the wheels to prevent the cart from rolling downhill until it was time to go. The horse would not be entirely forgotten, having had it's nose bag placed over it's mouth to feed. When Joey was ready to leave, he would remove the nose bag and give the horse a drink of water from a bucket which hung from beneath the cart.

Another character who frequented the Albion was a chap named Johnny Walker. Who had lots of brothers and sisters. Johnny sometimes helped to collect the glasses when they were empty, but besides collecting them, Johnny's "forte" would be to eat broken glass. Occasionally a glass would get accidentally broken, and Johnny would put a piece in his mouth and chew it. He would then pick up a pint and swill the contents down his throat, as if finishing a meal. Everyone would advise him not to do it, but he never took any notice. He was a fanatical Liverpool supporter and was well known by the police at Liverpool Football club, for running on the pitch dressed completely in red, whenever Liverpool scored a goal.

To my knowledge John still goes to the match and the glass eating period doesn't seemed to have effected him.

John my younger brother had now left school and had got a job with Scott's bakery in Great Homer Street, helping to deliver bread to shops on Merseyside. I was very proud of him, he had to be in work for seven am and getting out of bed early didn't seem to bother him at all.

Each morning Hughie would be first out of bed to prepare the breakfast, no matter how much he would have drunk the night before. (In winter time he would also have to light the fire).

In the morning Hughie would wake John early and they would breakfast together before John left for work, not wanting to be late

I would leave later with Hughie in the car, hoping his breath wouldn't smell too much of alcohol.

Suddenly John had grown up. He had even got himself a girlfriend. He was a very loving and generous young man, and would always remember everyone's birthday in the family and buy them a small gift. I remember the time he came home from work one day carrying a potted plant for his Mother, it was Mother's day. He was also very fond of animals, and Hughie had bought him two rabbits for his birthday which he kept in a hutch in the garden which was separate from the house.

When he was not in the garden attending to his pets, he and his friends would go to the Victoria Settlement, the local youth club in Netherfield Road, were they would play records, and dance to the music until 10pm..

I had some holidays due to me so I decided to visit my family in Belgium. To save money Maria had now moved back into her parents home. It was lovely seeing every one again but our relationship wasn't the same anymore. We were like strangers with each other. I assured Maria that it wouldn't be too long before I had enough money for a deposit on a house, but in my heart I knew it would be a long time yet. I realised it must have been very difficult for her with a child to look after. In Liverpool, I had my work and my friends who I could go out with for a drink in the evenings. She really had no one.

I suggested that perhaps she and the baby might join me in Liverpool but because of the situation at home, she decided it wasn't a very good idea. We discussed our situation until the early hours of the morning and both of us cried a lot, before finely deciding it might be a good idea if we stopped seeing each in future. It was a hopeless situation, I couldn't obtain work in Belgium and Maria didn't want to live in England.

I was heartbroken but she seemed to have made her mind up.

I returned to Liverpool and for a some time afterwards I felt really depressed. Eventually I managed to push everything to the back of my mind and get involved once again in my every day work. I also started to go out again in the evenings with my friends to try and forget everything.

One summer night Bill Howard, Dave Ormesher and I arranged to drive to Ainsdale. We had been told that there were some good clubs near the beach. On this occasion we were in Dave's car. Leaving Formby by pass we drove along the coast road which is very pretty in the summer with its sand dunes leading down to the beach. I had been to Formby beach many times before as a youngster with the family, and had been fascinated by the sight of the old recluse who lived on the beach in a old tin hut he had erected.

Arriving at our destination we parked on the beach alongside other cars whose occupants were enjoying the view, it was a lovely evening with the sun on the horizon about to set.

We got out of the car and walked the remaining few yards to where the two night clubs were situated, they were named the Sands and Toad hall. On this occasion we decided to try Toad hall first.

Entering the club we enjoyed ourselves so much we decided to stay until near closing time. Leaving the club about midnight we walked towards the car only to discover that the tide had come in and completely submerged it. It was unbelievable! If you have ever been to this part of the world you will understand, when I say that you need a pair of binoculars to see the sea, its such a long way off and now here it was completely covering the car. Unfortunately we could not do anything about it that night, the only thing we could do was return to the club and telephone for a taxi to take us home. We returned the following day to try and recover the car but it was hopeless,it was damaged beyond repair and if I remember correctly we had to pay to have the car towed away for scrap. That was an expensive weekend for us.

With my friends from the Albion I had now started to frequent the different pubs and clubs in town. It was the time of the swinging sixties and Liverpool seemed to be at the forefront of most things. It was nice seeing the town so full of people. One evening in the Chequers club I met two people who became great friends of mine, one was named Chris Woods and the other Albert Dunlop. Chris Woods was to remain a personal friend of mine until his sad death quite recently. Chris was well known on the club circuit throughout Merseyside for being a singer cum club compare, and of his impression on stage of Frankie Vaughan. I always felt good in Chris's company, he had some very funny sayings and a huge repertoire of jokes.

The other friend, Albert Dunlop, had been a professional footballer and played in goal for Everton Football Club. We had some good times together too. He was then working for a double glazing company. When poor Albert passed away it was as he would have liked to, with a blonde on one arm and a baby in the other, no doubt still in debt to the world. That was one of Albert's failings, his weakness for betting. Now, I think I'm the only one left. Whereas in the past when Liverpool was a magnet for people from all over the world, it appeared to be like that once again with hundreds of people visiting and wanting to become part of the city life.

Unfortunately it was also the start of the troubles in Northern Ireland and a good friend of ours named 'Babs,' a lovely woman and the manageress of the Bears Paw pub, received news that her son serving with the Army in Northern Ireland had been shot and killed by a sniper, one of the first British soldiers to be killed in this long and bloody campaign.

Things were progressing well at home until one Saturday afternoon in late January, when John asked our mam would it be alright if he stayed at his friends house that night . Naturally my mam answered yes, she knew the boy well, He was always in our house. That evening John got ready to go out, when he had finished getting ready he came downstairs. He looked very smart, he was wearing his new suit which he had recently purchased from Jacksons the tailors. His shoes were highly polished, and he had on a white shirt and one of my ties, which I had loaned him. His hair was brushed back and still slightly wet from having just been combed.

I was also going out later that night, and before I went upstairs to use the bathroom. I said to John, "Enjoy yourself and don't get into any trouble whilst your out"! John looked at me with a look of utter disgust on his face and replied. "I wont, don't worry! I'll see you tomorrow". I remember thinking to myself he's growing into a fine young man.

That evening my friends and I went to town and did what we usually did each Saturday evening, visiting our favourite pubs, before finally meeting my father and his wife Eileen in Yate's wine lodge in Lime Street for a drink. After spending some time with my father and his wife, we left to spend the remainder of the evening in a club named the Indiana, in Berry Street, which was owned by someone we knew. It must have been about 3am when I finally arrived home after taking my friends home. I parked the car in my usual place and noticed a police car parked outside the house.

I suspected something was wrong, the lights in our living room were still on which was unusual at this late hour.

I said to myself. I bet they've been arguing again! (Meaning my parents)

I ran up the stairs and along the passageway to our house, feeling angry. The front door was open. The first thing I noticed on entering the house were two policemen in the living room, and my Mother on the settee sobbing her heart out. She was being comforted by one of them. Hughie sat in a chair holding his head in his hands.

My mind was racing ahead of me trying to determine what had happened. I looked round the room for breakages, perhaps the neighbours had complained about the noise I thought before blurting out. "What's going on"? The two policemen had now turned to face me and one of them said. "Mr Elliott"? I replied. "Yes".

IN LIVERPOOL

He then stepped towards me and said in barely a whisper. "I've got some bad news for you. your brother John has met with an accident and I'm afraid he's dead"!

For a moment I was struck dumb and unable to comprehend what had been said, I thought, I must be hearing things or maybe it's a bad dream.

I looked once again at my mam and Hughie sitting there and realised it must be true. They were both in a state of shock.

I could feel the pain and anger now surging through my entire body. Not our poor John. Why him? I asked myself. I gazed at the policeman and said. "What happened"? He replied. "Your brother and his two friends were found dead in a caravan by the father of one of the boys".

He continued. "We need a member of your family to come and identify the body". Body, body, I thought, perhaps he's not really dead. I looked once again at my parents and replied. "I'll go". There was no way I was going to put them through more pain than was necessary. The policeman said, "we've sent for the doctor for your Mum and Dad, he should be here any minute, my colleague will stay with them until he arrives". I nodded in agreement then said. "Lets go".

We walked out the front door and down the flight of steps to the waiting car, before being driven away. I was in a sort of trance.

The journey didn't take long, less than five minutes, we drove in silence.

I looked out the window as the car slowed down and recognised where we were, it was just before the Kirkdale Homes in Westminster Road. The car turned into a Cul de sac I discovered later was named Mayfields and stopped. I expected to wake up at any moment and find it had all been a bad dream.

A policeman stood outside the entrance to a contractors yard, as if on duty. I was ushered through the door to a caravan parked inside the yard. I don't remember if any one else were there at that moment. I was in a complete daze and told by the accompanying policeman, "to brace yourself for quite a shock, the three bodies are inside the caravan, and would you go and identify your brother"?

We climbed the steps together, and the policeman opened the door for me and I stepped inside. The scene that met my eyes was one of absolute horror, a black soot like substance lay everywhere. Two bodies lay on bunk beds as if asleep. I recognised them immediately as being Charles Stocks and Paul Blanchard the inseparable friends of my brother John. One of the bottom bunks lay empty.

The body of a young man lay slumped over a calor gas heater, suggesting he must have had breathing difficulties, been alarmed and stood up from his bunk to try and open the door, before becoming overcome by the fumes and falling over the stove. Part of his 'pac a mac' coat had melted from the heat of the stove, no doubt accellerating his death .

I bent over the body not wanting it to be John. I had now started to cry. I turned him to face me. It was John. I hardly recognised him, his face was black from the soot. I kissed his cheek, He didn't seem dead. I put my hands beneath him and tried to lift him up.

In my shocked state I wanted to take him home, but was prevented from doing so by the policeman standing behind me. I kept repeating out loud, why God, why did this have to happen.?

Finally, I was persuaded to return home in the police car. I was told, I would be much better there, looking after my parents. They really needed my help now.

I don't recall the journey back home, but I do remember seeing Hughie still sitting in the chair starring into space. I walked over to him and placed my hand on his shoulder, this seemed to bring him back momentarily to reality, he seemed most concerned about my Mother and informed me that she had gone to bed, and that she had been given a sedative by the doctor. We spoke for a short time before I finally persuaded him to go to bed aswell. The remainder of the night passed very quickly, I don't think any of us slept at all.

That day the shock really hit us. I insisted that my mother stay in bed. Hughie appeared to be crying inwardly but without tears, I had never seen him like this before. The news had spread like wildfire.

A reporter from the Liverpool Echo knocked at the door and kindly asked could he ask me a few questions, and did I a have a photograph of John I could let him have?. Friends and neighbours flocked to the house to offer their help. Later that day a police inspector arrived and informed me what he thought must have happened.

Apparently, the boys had spent the previous night in town at a beat club which finished late, and rather than disturb their parents, the boys had gone to sleep in the caravan which was used for family holidays.

The caravan had been stored in the yard for the winter and unknown to the boy's, the father of one of the boys had completely sealed it to prevent any damp entering. Naturally because of the cold that night, the boy's had lit the stove to keep warm, without making sure that there was sufficient ventilation available.

I thanked the Inspector for this information and he left. I now took control of everything. Hughie and my Mother were still in shock and would be for some time yet. It would be better if I left them to mourn. My sisters where now here if they needed anything. I walked to the post office at Everton Valley to send telegrams to Alec and Maria informing them of Johns death. Nothing seemed to have changed. I half expected people who I passed to recognise my terrible loss by the look on my face, instead the traffic still ran and people were going about their normal business. I stood at the post office counter, a radio was playing in the background. I informed the clerk of my requirements. He took my instructions and whilst writing them down looked up and informed a colleague that it was his turn to make the tea.

I was so disappointed by his remark, I expected every one to feel the same pain as me. I'm sure he didn't mean any disrespect but at that moment I felt like shouting at the top of my voice, "that my brother your writing about and he and his friends have just died, and would you be a little more respectful". but life goes on just the same. I also felt very sad for the other boys parents who must be suffering exactly the same as our family. That day the *"Liverpool Echo"* featured a story. *'Three boys found dead in caravan'*.

The next day Alec arrived home on compassionate leave. Seeing him was a great comfort to me, up until then I had deliberately avoided meeting anyone I knew. Together over the next few days we managed to complete all the tasks necessary for the funeral of some one you love. Finding ourselves in town we sought out a pub were nobody knew us, and without being disturbed, have a beer and talk things over between us.

Our Mother seemed to have aged quite considerably and against all our advice, insisted on John being brought home before he was finally laid to rest. Consequently the undertaker was instructed to bring his body home. The coffin was placed in the living room on two iron stands under the large window overlooking St George's church, were the service would be held later that week.

I dreaded having to look in the coffin, remembering how I had last seen John. But with Alec alongside me I gathered enough courage together to do so. John had been cleaned and looked very peaceful, as if asleep but then I noticed a tiny piece of cotton wool protruding from one of his eyelids. I turned away and asked Alec to follow me into the kitchen. Alec had noticed it also. We discussed it briefly and decided the sooner John was buried the better.

From then on I was a bag of nerves. Dozens of people came to pay their last respects. My sisters, and family friends helped tremendously by making plates of sandwiches and gallons of tea for all the visitors.

Then the unbelievable happened. John's girlfriend arrived with some friends. She was heartbroken, sobbing her heart out. She entered the room and seeing the coffin immediately ran across to it, practically throwing herself across it. I rushed alongside her holding her back, terrified that she may knock the coffin off the stand in her grief.

The funeral service was held at St Georges church, the church was full to capacity, with many hundreds of people standing outside. The internment being at Anfield cemetery. My parents received many letters of sympathy, some from people we didn't even know. I'm sure it helped them a great deal knowing that people cared. I was pleased to receive a telegram from Maria telling me how sorry she was. Later my Mother answered each letter personally, thanking everyone for their kindness at our loss.

That occasion must have been the longest seven days of my life and Alec and I breathed a sigh of relief when it was all over.

I made a promise to my brother Alec. I said I would never look into an open coffin ever again, no matter who it was, and I would rather one's loved one's be taken to a chapel of rest, instead of being brought home. It's too emotional. To this day I have kept my promise on both counts and much prefer to remember my friend's the way they were.

What was quite obvious to us all in this difficult period, was just how much John had been liked by everybody. His friends at the youth club all signed a commemorative plaque which was handed personally to my Mother, and the club committee authorised the purchase of a wooden bench to be used in the club, on which the three boy's name's were inscribed on a brass plate.

Later at the autopsy, the home office pathologist doctor Charles A St Hill confirmed. "The boys had suffocated due to carbon monoxide poisoning". Ironically, I had also discovered that the name of the beat club the boys visited that evening was 'The Iron Door' in Tempest Hey, and the name of the group playing that night were the 'Undertakers'.

Just before Alec returned to his unit in Germany, I received a letter from the police asking us to collect Johns belonging's from Westminster Road police station. At the police station Alec and I were handed a parcel which contained the clothing John wore that night, there was also an envelope containing some loose change he must have had in his pocket when he died. Before leaving the police station Alec and I opened the parcel. It was very stressful examining the contents, I must admit I had tears in my eyes.

The suit had hardly been worn, it would be too distressing for our parents to see it and be reminded again of John. Walking home we decided to visit the local Corporation tip in St Domingo Road, and throw the parcel in the incinerator for it to burn.

I kept the few pennies that were in John's pocket, and I still have them till this day.

Later when Alec had returned to Germany and I was alone in the house. I went into Johns bedroom and emptied it of all his clothing which I took to the incinerator for burning.

Some time afterwards a letter arrived addressed to John, it was from Jacksons The Tailors. I opened it and read the contents. It was advising him that he had fallen into areas with the payments on his suit. It was a very sad reminder of his death, I was glad I was the one who opened the letter. Soon afterwards I visited the shop and explained what had happened to John, before paying the outstanding balance.

They say that time heals all wounds and eventually you are able to carry on as before. This was the case with my family, the person you loved and lost is never quite forgotten. I know my mother never seemed to be the same again, and whenever John's name was mentioned, she would have a tendency to cry.

Alec and his family returned home briefly to Liverpool for some embarkation leave, prior to leaving for a new posting to Malta. He had now been promoted to Corporal and his new job was clerk to the G. O. C. the Middle East, later he would travel quite extensively with the General, to Cyprus, Aden and throughout the Middle East.

I was doing quite well at work and had built up a good relationship with my customers. One day I received a telephone call from a customer in Leigh. Who informed me that on my last visit to see him, he had not ordered enough fish fingers, and would it be possible for him to increase the order and receive them on his next delivery? I replied. Yes of course it would. I'll see to it right away. I then went to the Manager of the Cold Store and explained about the telephone call I had received, and what was required.

Unfortunately the Cold Store Manager's reply was. "That it would be impossible. The vehicle was already loaded, and the customer should have ordered sufficient quantities in the first place". Perhaps it was because of the recent death of John, or the breakdown of my marriage, or maybe my frustration at not being able to keep my promise to the customer, or even the culmination of all three, I don't know, all I do know is that I was psychologically mentally drained, and we argued about it, and in the end I did a very foolish thing. I took my vehicle keys, and threw them at the Manager. I told him "he could keep the bloody job". I then went home.

I was only home about an hour when there was a knock on the front door. It was a colleague from the depot who had been sent by the General Manager to ask me to come back to work.

I had already decided I wasn't going back. Although I had made provision with my bank to send money to my family each month, I had been thinking about them a lot recently, finishing work now gave me the opportunity of seeing them again. I informed my friend that "I had made up my mind and wouldn't be returning to work".

I asked him to convey my apologies to the General Manager Mr Monroe, who I got on rather well with, and to tell him I would be going to Belgium as soon as I got a few thing's sorted out. At that time I felt really depressed and just wanted to get away from everything.

Later that evening choosing the right moment I told Hughie and my mam what I had done. I asked Hughie would he be able to make his own way to work the next day?. He replied. "Yes it wouldn't be a problem".

I felt rather guilty leaving them. I hated the sweet smell of white wine on Hughies breath in the morning's but already I knew I was going to miss it. I also told them I was thinking of visiting Maria and young Jimmy in Belgium and trying to soften the blow, I said, "I wouldn't be away too long"! and then asked the question. "Would they be okay on their own"? They seemed disappointed at what I had done and replied. They were fine but "what did you have to pack your job in for? surely you could have got a couple of weeks off work if you wanted".

I mumbled in reply. "I was getting rather fed up at work". Knowing me like they did, they realised I had made my mind up and never mentioned it again.

I had lots of friends at work and when I met them a day or so later in the pub, they all thought I was mad for packing my job in and that I had made a terrible mistake. They insisted it was still not too late to go back to work. I knew I was leaving a good job and I enjoyed my work very much, but I had definitely made my mind up, there was no going back. I now felt that I had to get away from Liverpool for a short period of time.

A few day's later when discussing my plans with a close friend Brian Duffy, he suggested that perhaps he could go with me? He was in between jobs at the time. I thought about it for a moment and decided it was a good idea! We would be company for each other. The more we spoke about it, the more excited we became. for the next hour or so we bounced suggestions off each other like a rubber ball. " Both of us are not working, so why not take as much time as we liked and hitch hike across Europe" he said. I thought about it for a minute and replied " Good idea, I'm going to forget about Belgium, if Maria doesn't want anything to do with me anymore, that's okay by me, lets visit our Alec and his wife in Malta instead, that will be a great trip"! Brian without hesitation agreed.

We then thought it would be a good idea to join the Youth Hostel Association and stay at hostels they provided en route.! That evening we decided that is what we would do.

The following day I told my mam and Hughie of my conversation with Brian and what we now intended to do. they seemed much more pleased knowing I would not be alone, they particularly liked the idea of visiting Alec in Malta. I said, "don't write and tell him anything about it mam, I want it to be a surprise".

The next few days were spent arranging our trip. We visited the YHA offices at 93a Scotland Road, seeking information on what we required to become a member, and informing them of our intentions. We were told that to become a member of the association, we would have to pay a membership fee of fifteen shillings and supply a photograph of ourselves. It was as simple as that. We were also advised that before we undertook a trip abroad, we ought to go hosteling in England and Wales in order to find out the customs and traditions of hosteling. We nodded in agreement but had no intentions of doing anything like that whatsoever. We had already made our plans. That same day, we returned with our photographs, paid our subscription fee, and purchased a number of maps of the continent. The next day we returned to collect our identity cards. We were now ready to leave.

That evening we met in the Albion pub with our friends for a final drink not knowing how long we would be away, Hughie and my mam joined us there aswell. We promised to send postcards to the pub from time to time letting them know how we were doing.

Early the next morning dressed in Jeans and tee shirt and carrying a back pack, we walked to Everton Valley and caught a bus to Sparrow Hall on the East lancashire Road.

The East Lancs Road is the main artery out of Liverpool for many vehicles leaving the docks. Within a short period of time we were able to hitch a number of lifts, and late that evening we arrived in London and slept at our first youth hostel, the Inns Of Court Mission in Drury Lane.

The following morning we set off early once again hitch hiking, anxious to reach our next destination which was Dover, from were we took the ferry to France, and spent the next few days at le federation Unie Des Auberges De Jeunesse, 30 Rue Porte Gayole, Boulogne-Sur-Mer, making friends with other back packers and planning our journey.

Brian and I had decided we must visit Paris before heading south, and after spending a few days there seeing the sights, we set off once again staying at various hostel's throughout France. After spending some time in Biarritz we crossed the border to Burgos which at one time was the capital of the Spanish civil war. Having read Ernest Hemingways novel about Spain and being that time of the year, we headed for Pamplona, to take part in the festival of the running of the bulls. The next few weeks was spent wandering around Spain, often sleeping under the stars, before continuing our journey to Monaco and the French riviera to Italy.

Taking lots of photographs en route, we made a point of seeing all the capital cities of each country we visited and if we liked the place we would stay a little longer. We visited many places of interest, living off the land and obtaining information from other back packers on where to find work. We never once had to separate in order to hitch a ride, and If you want to see the world cheaply, I suggest this is the way to do it.

It would take far too long for me to tell the readers all that we did, and perhaps in the future I may do so, but suffice to say we eventually crossed from Reggio Calabra to Messina, and a few days later we took the ferry from Catania to Malta.

By now we had been away from home approximately nine months, and we were both very suntanned. Wearing straw hats to protect us from the sun we could almost be mistaken for some of the locals.

Having reached Valetta and clutching Alec's address in one hand, we asked for directions to his office which I knew was in the G.O.C.'s headquarters. The guards on duty not knowing who we were and perhaps mistaking us for 'special forces soldiers' allowed us in the building. Wandering through the corridors we eventually found somebody to take us to Alec's office. By this time we had confided to our escort who we were and that we wanted it to be a surprise for Alec. The soldier seemed to understand and agreed to go and tell Alec that he was wanted outside. With our hats pulled down over our faces and our clothes covered in sand, you can imagine the shock he got when we eventually identified ourselves. Later when he got over the shock he told us that he thought we were two Maltese fishermen.

We spent the next four weeks with Alec and his family, it was a most enjoyable period. Margaret his wife was a wonderful host and made us very welcome, showing us many parts of the Island and introducing us to all of their friends.

Fortress Malta. With its huge Royal Naval presence. Standing by the side of the statue of Don Quixote on the barracas, it was a lovely view looking down to St Angelo bay and hearing the sound of a bugle played by a seaman, every time a Royal Naval ship entered or left Grand harbour.

Finally we decided we would have to leave all this swimming, sunbathing and eating and start making our way home. After studying the map for some time, we agreed to return home by way of the Adriatic coast.

The day came for us to return home. We took the ferry from Valetta to Sicily our back packs full of food, thanks to Alec and Margaret. We stood on deck waving goodbye to them until finally we could see them no more.

Embarking at Catania we waited at the side of the road until a motorist stopped at our "thumbs up" sign and took us to Messina. Here we caught another ferry for the short crossing to Italy. When you hitch a ride you never know who you are going to meet, or where you are going to end up that day. that's very much the thrill of it. We met some kind and wonderful people, and we hoped in our small way we left a good impression on them.

The next few weeks found us heading north in Italy staying at hostels if we were near one, if not we would wrap ourselves up in our waterproofs and shelter in some barn or other.

Unknown to me Maria had obtained a divorce, I wasn't exactly surprised by this but I wouldn't know anything about it for some time yet!

Brian and I continued our trek north eventually reaching Switzerland, we stayed in YMCA hostels but more often than not we camped out. When you camp out it is most interesting when you wake up the next morning, you feel dirty but Brian and I on this particular occasion were camped by a large lake, I believe it was lake Lucerne. Looking about us we saw that there was nobody near us so we decided to undress and wash all our clothes, it was a beautiful summers day. Having undressed and done all our chores we decided to swim whilst waiting for our clothes to dry, it was absolutely wonderful, we were so clean and our clothes were clean also. We took some photographs and soon afterwards left.

At that time I contemplated looking for a girl I knew who I used to work with at SPD, her name was Dot Lacey and I knew she had obtained a position looking after children in Lucerne, but when you realise just how big Lucerne is and you have no address for her, I decided against it. I know Dot eventually married a Mexican and now lives somewhere in Mexico.

Continuing our hitchhiking, we had now reached Karlsruhe in Germany at that time this was part of the American Zone in Germany and consequently we met some American servicemen there who we became friends with. Many years later one of the servicemen married the sister of Dave Ormesher's wife and today they both live happily in Brisbane Australia.

After several weeks there we once again set of, once again catching lifts.

Leaving our last lift we looked at our surroundings and comparing it with our map found ourselves near the village of Remagen-Am-Rhein which is famous for being the point where the Allies made the first crossing of the Rhine in the last war. (A film was made about it) We ventured into the village looking for somewhere to stay and noticed a guesthouse. We entered to have a glass of beer and enquire if there was any work to be had locally. Being the only two present we were able to talk to the proprietor who informed us that the local "rose farm" usually required labour. Finishing our beer we thanked him and following his directions made our way to the farm. Within a few minutes of leaving the guesthouse we where having discussions with the farmer who asked us could we drive? when we replied yes, he seemed very pleased and asked us to report back to the farmhouse at 8am the following day and we could go with Tony to the fields. When we enquired who Tony was he pointed to a volkswagen van which was used to take the workers to the fields.

We thanked the farmer and promised to return the following morning. Now we required somewhere to sleep so we retraced our footsteps back to the guesthouse to see if they had two beds to let.

Reaching the guesthouse, we ordered another two beers and then engaged the proprietor once more in conversation, thanking him for what he had just done for us (obtaining us employment) we then asked him about accommodation for the next few weeks. He seemed somewhat puzzled and then excused himself for a moment returning soon afterwards accompanied by a woman. Apparently the woman was his wife and they were about to go on holiday to Italy in the next day or so for a few weeks. After some more conversation, it was decided that we could stay there "rent free" provided that we looked after the hotel for them, the hotel would be empty of course but he would leave a key with us. Brian and I were delighted and readily agreed.

So there we were accommodation and work, it worked out very well, each day we would go to work and in the evenings after eating out, we would return to the guesthouse. We could bathe in hot water and shower whenever we wanted to, it was great! We got to know Remagen very well, we visited all the local landmarks and even went inside the quarters of the old bridge that was destroyed in the war, seeing the writings on the wall that the German soldiers had left.

A few weeks later in the hotel. I was having a bath and on hearing some one outside the door thought it was Brian, suddenly the door opened and it was the wife of the proprietor who had just returned from holiday.

So our "rent free" period was now over but who would think that two "Scousers" in the middle of Germany would be given the task of looking after a hotel for a few weeks?, without the owner not knowing anything about us! we could have done anything, but we didn't, it was really nice.

It had been twelve months now since we set off from Liverpool and we decided that it was time to return home. Brian and I had saved some money since we had been working so we both went shopping in Remagen, I eventually bought two ladies watches, one for Maria and one for my mother. Not knowing my changed circumstances in Belgium, we decided to call at Antwerp and see the family.

Setting off from Remagen we said goodbye to all the friends we had made and continued to Belgium arriving at Antwerp a few days later.

Going to Rupel Straat were I last lived with Maria I found other people living there, although Brian and I wrote cards and letters home quite often we were unable to receive any replies. The people now staying there were unable to provide me with any forwarding address of were Maria might live, so I decided to visit my in-laws house instead.

Taking the tram we visited Twee and Neten Straat and rang the bell.

Wim my father in law answered the bell and we were invited in, I could feel things were not the same anymore, I had been away from Belgium for years and since I'd finished work in Liverpool had sent Maria no money! What a dope I'd been. My in-laws were really wonderful people and many years later they spent a number of occasions with me in Liverpool.

They informed me that I was divorced and that Maria was now living in Ostend, They were concerned that I was going to cause trouble and were reluctant to give me her new address. Although I was shocked at the news I half expected something like this to happen, it seemed like the whole world was against me, eventually it was decided that they would contact Maria by telephone and ask wether or not I could see her and my son Jim before returning to England. After about a further two hours talking with them of everything, it was decided that if I returned to their house later that day they would tell me what Maria had decided.

We left the house and Brian and I went visiting the old places I used to know, it felt unreal and I felt choked but somehow for the best. We returned to the house and Wim informed me that Maria had decided that I could visit her and see my son on the way home. Having obtained the address and said our goodbyes to them, we set of to Ostend and eventually England.

Arriving at Ostend and looking at a street map, we eventually found the house, I rang the bell and Maria answered the door, my heart stopped, she still looked as beautiful as ever, I could see that she was nervous to and after inviting us in things became more relaxed. We spoke for ages and I asked her how Jimmy my son was, she replied he was alright and that he was at school. I felt as sick as a pig, I was still very much in love with her and I suspected she was with me to but circumstances prevented us from being together. It was decided that on the way to the ferry we could visit the school and see my son. We hugged each other and the tears were running down both our faces, reluctantly I let go of her and remembered the watch I had bought her, I pulled it from my pocket and gave it to her, then left the house, walking a short distance I looked back and Maria was still at the door, I felt like running back but I didn't.

At the school I introduced myself to the Headmaster who then arranged for Jim to come to his office, it was so heartbreaking talking and hugging my son who I'm sure really didn't know me. After some more hugging and kissing I then made my excuses and left to get the ferry to Dover.

On the ferry I was still very mixed up, I was leaving my loved ones and going back home, it felt very unreal like in a dream, the impulse I had to return to Maria was unbelievable but with Brian with me I overcame them. After a number of hours on the ship we docked at Dover, walking through customs we noticed a lorry who's depot was immediately facing my Mothers house, we ran to speak to the driver but were unfortunately too late. We both stood there as the lorry accelerated past us presumably to Liverpool.

There was no motorways then, so after three or four lifts and a few more hours we eventually arrived back in Liverpool, I said goodbye to Bryan who lived in Kirkby and continued on my way to Everton.

IN LIVERPOOL

Returning home was good I had so much to tell everybody. I gave the watch I had bought to my Mother and said hello to Hughie, after seeing all my mates and going to the pub with Bryan I decided I had to get a job. After a short period of time I obtained a job with Richmond Pork Sausages Ltd, as production and transport manager in Linacre road, Bootle.

I had my own car space painted in the yard and occasionally I could take home some meat pies and sausages.

Things were starting to get back to normal, I was now working and going out most evenings with my friends, although quite often I couldn't help but think of Maria and my son. One day at work I informed the manager's that the vehicles had to be loaded with sausages that evening for the following morning early deliveries, around the country, but I was informed that nobody would work overtime that night because Liverpool was playing at home and everyone was going to the match.

What could I do? I had about four managers willing to work that night and ten vehicles to load. I then decided to jump on a fork lift truck and place a pallet board of sausages on each vehicle ready for loading, this I continued to do until such time as all the vehicles were loaded. Everything went well and we finished loading the lorries. It was not until the following morning at work, when the union representative approached me and accused me of working on a fork lift truck and threatening me with going on strike.

That was it! I turned my back on the union representative and immediately approached the General Manager's office and on entering it, I told him what the union representative had told me. I was most surprised therefore when he smiled slightly and agreed that the union representative was right, he said "You know Jim, you cant drive a fork lift truck unless you have a union card". I was flabbergasted! How were the deliveries going to take place?. I then said, staring straight back at him. "Perhaps he can do my job aswell" and removed my white overall and hat. The General Manager face was dumbstruck, he started to say something but too late, I opened the door and had left his office and soon afterwards was in my car and back home.

Later that same year, Richmond Pork Sausages Ltd, closed their Liverpool depot completely, presumably because of union difficulties.

I had not been to Belgium for three or four years and by now I was courting a girl I had met at the Grafton Ballroom in West Derby road, her name was June who's parents had the "famous" Broadway stores on Stanley Road Bootle. This is were all the seaman from the docks used to come to purchase goods to take back to their own country. It's still the same today a little gem of a shop, with darts and clocks and toys and everything you could not buy anywhere else and to me the prices seem not to have changed. June worked there. I still kept in touch with Marias parents and now and again would send them money for my son.

By now I was working as a salesman for NCR ltd and soon afterwards June and I got married. After about a year working for NCR I was offered a promotion by them but it meant having to move to Manchester. June and I discussed this for quite some time until we finally decided to make the move.

Having moved to Manchester and finally settled in. June then went into hospital and gave birth to our son Jonathan James, he was tremendous and I was absolutely made up, we loved him so much, no more would I make mistakes, this time it was for real. I used to play with him whenever I could, he had blonde hair and deep blue eyes and like every other father I thought he was the best ever.

My Mother and Hughie would sometimes come to stay with us and the job was good to. On weekends I would return to Liverpool to see my parents and then one day I received a letter from Marias parents informing me that she had died. I was so shocked and tears came to my eyes, apparently she had a cut on her leg and it had turned to septicemia of which she died.

My son Jimmy would now be looked after by his Grandparents they told me, I immediately contacted my brother Alec who had now been demobbed, having served nine years in the Army and invited him to come with me to Belgium. He said he would.

He knew Maria very well having come to stay with us on a number of occasions when I lived in Belgium.

We were far too late for the funeral of course but we managed to go to the church yard in Ostend were she was buried. It was a beautiful cemetery and unlike here each grave has a photograph on it of its occupants. It was very moving. After visiting the grave we once again went to her parents in Antwerp to see them and my son. They informed me once again that they intended to look after him. Who could blame them, my son hardly knew me! Alec and I returned to England and continued with our lives.

About this time Everton had won the cup at Wembley and some one had painted a donkey blue and took it into Yates' wine lodge, I remember Hughie and his friends all singing and dancing enjoying the occasion.

One day on visiting my parents, I was sitting down enjoying a cup of tea when there was a knock on the door, on opening the door I was surprised to see a friend of Hughies who worked with him on the docks standing there. He looked very serious faced. After exchanging hello's with each other he informed me that Hughie had had an accident at work and had been taken to the Royal Infirmary. Recovering quickly from the shock I asked him what had happened and he told me that Hughie had been injured by a vehicle reversing at the docks and that he was in a bad way. I asked him in the house to see my Mother but not to mention how badly injured Hughie was, which he did.

Thanking him for the information he left soon afterwards. Comforting my Mother who had now regained some of her composure, I said lets go to the hospital and see him, knowing how tough Hughie is I'm sure he's going to be okay. Donning our coats we set off for the hospital.

After identifying ourselves, we were taken to the doctor who was looking after Hughie.

He advised us that Hughie had received some very serious injuries and we could see him for a very short time but he wouldn't know a great deal more until later. We were then taken to see Hughie who was unconscious and unaware of our presence. Lying there with tubes stuck in his body was heartbreaking. I then realised that he might die but I continued to assure my mam that he was going to be okay.

There was a plain clothes police officer there also who wanted to know what had happened, I spoke to him momentarily.

I didn't know exactly what had happened to Hughie but he had been crushed by a lorry at the docks and as a result it had effected his spine and broke his arm. To see Hughie just laying there was awful but like I said he was tough. All the family went to visit him and slowly he began to get a bit better, and would joke with us and the nurses, but on visiting him you could see he wasn't himself, his body seemed somehow broken.

After several weeks in hospital Hughie began to slowly recover, soon afterwards he was transferred to Southport hospital were he undertook physiotherapy and each day he would go to the gymnasium by wheelchair and get on the bars in the gym and try to walk, it was so distressing seeing him like that, but Hughie was so tough and you could see him struggling so hard to walk. After about twelve months he had improved a lot and my visits to him became less frequent. My brother Alec and I used to take turns in visiting him. He used to be so active, the days of getting in the bag were now over.

Then one day the doctor said he could be released, he would never get any better, in fact he would never be the same again, so consequently he was released from hospital and went straight to LLandudno, to the miners club there with my mother for a short holiday. On my visits to Llandudno to see them I would find him struggling in the garden trying to walk on walking sticks given to him by the hospital with my Mother alongside him.

Soon afterwards they returned home. Now my visits from Manchester were back to a weekly visit, Hughie would still go out on his own but it was quite a struggle for him, bent slightly forward on his walking sticks.

But believe it or not, before long he started to do the queues again, playing his mouth organ. I'm sure people felt sorry for him.

Then one day the telephone rang in Manchester, it was my brother Alec who informed me that Hughie had died! Again I was terribly shocked! Apparently Hughie had been out that day and on returning home had gone into the kitchen and sat down at the kitchen table. My Mother was in the living room and on entering the kitchen saw Hughie sitting there and spoke to him, when he didn't reply she thought he was asleep and on further investigation discovered he was dead!

What a shock for my poor Mother. My poor Mother!

I travelled back to Liverpool, Hughie had been taken to the mortuary and soon afterwards the funeral was arranged. Alec and I did a lot of running about arranging it, the funeral was "over the road" once again at St Georges Church in Heyworth Street and we saw the vicar to arrange the service. We even arranged for Hughie's songs to be played at his funeral. It was so sad. This time we didn't have his body at home, we had it in the funeral director's office in Breck Road and this time I didn't go to see his body like I did when our brother John died.

At the coroners inquest it was decided that Hughie had died as a result of the injuries he received some time ago. Hundreds of people turned up for Hughies funeral and he was interred with his son John at Anfield cemetery. Occasionally Alec and I visit the cemetery to see the grave. I am now retired and once again living in Liverpool. I just thought it would be of interest to "jot down" some of my memories, perhaps you who read this will also agree.

I have tried to communicate the nostalgia that I feel for that period, to those who read these pages. I hope I have been successful.

Much has happened in my life since then, some good , some not so good, but that, as they, say, is another story. But if I had the opportunity of living my life over once again, I wouldn't change one piece of it.

IN LIVERPOOL

FORGOTTEN EMPRESS -
THE TRAGEDY OF THE EMPRESS OF IRELAND
by David Zeni

The fascinating story of the Steamship Empress of Ireland which within two years of the sinking of the Titanic, was also lost at sea and in terms of passenger fatalities was an even greater tragedy.
The event sent shock waves around the world. Just one year later, the loss of the Lusitania completed a sad triangle of maritime disasters, yet whilst these names are well remembered, the fate of the Empress of Ireland remains shrouded in the cloak of history, as impenetrable as the fog that brought about her total loss along with 1012 souls, on 29 May 1914 . £14.50

THETIS - THE ADMIRALTY REGRETS -THE DISASTER IN LIVERPOOL BAY
by C.Warren & J.Benson

The definitive minute by minute account of this terrible tragedy in 1939 when 99 souls lost their lives as HM Submarine Thetis undertook her first and only dive. With new photographs and documents as well as a new foreword by Derek Arnold, a survivors son and a new postscript by maritime historian David Roberts.
Why didn't anyone cut open the submarine? Why was there no urgency in the Admiralty's rescue system? Did the Admiralty really regret?   £14.50

BLUE FUNNEL - VOYAGE EAST
by Award winning author Richard Woodman

What was life aboard a British vessel in the last great days of the Merchant Navy? Blue Funnel - Voyage East takes us in one of the Holt Line's 'China Boats' on a typical trip out of the Mersey, to the Far East and back.
'This is life at sea, warts and all, and a better book because of it'.
~ Sea Breezes   £14.50

HMS THETIS - Secrets and Scandal : Aftermath of a Disaster
by David Roberts
The sinking of Thetis costs 99 men their lives and is still today the worst
submarine disaster in British History. This book
contains interviews with relatives of victims; sons, daughters, brothers,
sisters and those very rare ladies, living widows. Also here are never
before seen documents from the time; Offers of outside
help, Secret navy reports and even descriptions of bodies for identification.
Why did the Official Inquiry blame nobody,
explaining it away as 'an
unfortunate sequence of events'? Why did the civil action on behalf of the
widow's fail? Did the Admiralty cover it up? How
much did Churchill know? How were those left behind treated? A huge
publicly subscribed disaster fund was collected for the relatives. How was
this managed and distributed? Who got what and
why? What ever happened to the money that was left?   £13.50
'a book that shocks ... tells the hidden story of those left behind'
Sea Breezes

CHILDREN OF THE BENARES
- A WAR CRIME AND ITS VICTIMS - Ralph Barker
Foreword by Beth Williams (nee Cummings) - the only Liverpool
Survivor
The true story of the Ellerman and City passenger liner City of Benares
and her carrying a precious cargo - 90 children from the bombed cities of
Britain bound for safe haven away from the war - to Canada.
Four days later, without warning, she was torpedoed and sunk by a
German U-boat in mid - Atlantic. An event that shocked the world in its
brutality, much use of the atrocity was made by the British authorities in
an attempt to persuade the United States into joining the conflict.
However it was not long before the parents of the lost children, who had
entrusted their loved ones to the evacuation scheme, began to suspect
those same authorities of neglect, when they learned that the promised
naval escort for the convoy had abandoned the unarmed ships twenty-one
hours before the U-boat struck!
The Children of the Benares is a gripping story of the disaster itself and
exposes at last what went on behind the scenes at the Ministry of Shipping
and the British Admiralty.
It is a chilling tale of fallibility and human survival. £14.50

THE GOLDEN WRECK - THE TRAGEDY OF THE ROYAL CHARTER by Alexander McKee

The effects of the great hurricane of October 1859 were to shock the nation. 133 ships were sunk, 90 were badly damaged and almost 800 people lost their lives. More than half of those that perished were on one ship, on her way home to Liverpool- *The Royal Charter.*
News of the wreck, off Anglesey, soon spread and the Royal Charter's other cargo, **GOLD**, became the focus of people's attention.
Was all of it ever recovered? If not where did it go? £12.50

THE ALABAMA AFFAIR
by David Hollett

One of the very few books to deal with the Involvement of Britain in the US Civil War. A book that reads like the most exciting of novels - but it remains historical fact.
This book reveals the turmoil and intrigue surrounding a deal involving the British government, the now defunct Merseyside
shipyard of Cammell Laird and a country engaged in civil war, America.
'...a tale of subterfuge, cheating and double dealing that makes today's politicians look like saints.'   Liverpool Daily Post
'Although Britain sympathised with the bid to free the slaves, she also needed the cotton which the slaves produced. This conflict of interest is deeply investigated by the author...'   Sea Breezes.
'...lifts the lid off an unsavoury episode in Britain's maritime history...'
Navy News £12.50

THE LIVERPOOL LIFEBOAT DISASTER
by Jim Sullivan
'A labour of love that deserves to be told a story of astonishing courage, brilliantly researched.'- ALAN BLEASDALE
The little known story of the Liverpool Lifeboat Disaster of 1892 is one of those true stories that has simply been waiting around in history be told. Now at last the waiting is over. Jim Sullivan has painstakingly researched these real life events, which, because of his own family's connection, becomes even more compelling. £10.00

LUSITANIA by Colin Simpson

THE definitive work on the real story surrounding this still mysterious ship.
On the 7th of May 1915 the Cunard vessel Lusitania was torpedoed by a German submarine off the Old Head of Kinsale, Ireland resulting in the loss of the vessel itself and 1,201 men, women and children. It also ultimately brought the United States entry to the First World War. More than eighty years on the story of the Lusitania continues to be shrouded in mystery and suspicion.
What was her real cargo? Why wasn't she protected? Why did she sink so quickly?
Containing rare photographs from Germany and elsewhere; It is a truly intriguing and fascinating tale. £12.50

LIFE AT LAIRDS - MEMORIES OF WORKING SHIPYARD MEN
by David Roberts

'When Cammell Lairds has gone and we are a generation or two down the line who will answer the questions ...What did they do there, ... What was it like? This book answers the questions.'

Sea Breezes

'.. A Piece of Social History ..' Liverpool Echo

Life at Lairds is a book of more than 120 pages about what life was like for the thousands of ordinary people that worked in the world famous Birkenhead shipyard. Contains many rare photographs of Lairds, its' ships and its' surroundings. £10.00

JUST NUISANCE AB - HIS FULL STORY by Terence Sisson

The amazing but true story of the only dog that was officially enlisted into the British Royal Navy, a Great Dane whose name was Nuisance, his official rank and name was AB Just Nuisance. Famed for his preference for the company of navy ratings (he wasn't too keen on Officers) in and around the famous World War II naval base of Simonstown, South Africa, Nuisance helped many a sailor to rejoin his ship after a night on the town.
Today his own statue overlooking the bay off the Cape of Good Hope commemorates AB Just Nuisance. £11.00

CAMMELL LAIRD - THE GOLDEN YEARS - by David Roberts.
Foreword by Frank Field MP
Looks back at the world famous shipyard's history with particular
focus upon the 1960s and 70s when Lairds were engaged in the
building of Polaris Nuclear submarines. A unique look at the history
of this yard that contains many photographs and references.
**'Captures life in the prosperous years of the historic Birkenhead
shipyard' ....** Liverpool Echo
*'Puts into perspective---the strikes ... the Polaris contract ... and those
who worked at the yard'* - Sea Breezes
£10.00

DVD / VIDEO

BLUE FUNNEL -VOYAGES AND VOICES (DVD only)
Vittoria dock In Birkenhead was the home of what was once the
biggest and probably the best General Cargo shipping company in
Britain; Alfred HoIt's... perhaps better known as 'The Blue Funnel
Line' or' the 'China Boats'. Many thousands of people, both
passengers and crews sailed on famous ships like 'Hector'
`Patroclus', 'Laomedon' and many more.
This new film has been compiled with the help of never before
published footage taken all over the world by some of those men who
actually sailed with 'Blueys' on many of their well-known vessels.
Contains some of the sights and sounds of typical Blue Funnel
voyages; leaving the home shores of the UK, sailing through both
the Suez and Panama canals, the legendary gilly gilly man, Hong
Kong, Singapore, Kobe, Tokyo, and other 'exotic' ports.
We also see and hear the thoughts and memories of some of those
who actually sailed with 'Blueys' over their working lives, from Able
Seaman to Captain, Steward to Engineer.
The film is a must for anyone who sailed with 'Blueys' or who sailed
in the merchant navy of old.
£16.95

CAMMELL LAIRD
- OLD SHIPS AND HARDSHIPS
- THE STORY OF A SHIPYARD.
(DVD ONLY)

After an extensive search for moving footage of this world famous shipyard at work a film of the history of this shipyard has at last been compiled. How Cammell Laird served the nation through two World Wars, building world famous vessels like the Rodney, Hood, Mauritania, Ark Royal, Windsor Castle and many more, up to the tragic day in 1993 when Lairds was shut down.
The story of the yard is also told through the voices of the men who worked at Lairds; Welders, cranedrivers, electricians and plumbers, they tell of the hardships of building ships in all weathers and the lighter moments that came from some of the 'characters' of the yard.
£16.95

VIDEOS

'ALL IN A DAY'S WORK'
VOLUME 1 & VOLUME II
- A LOOK AT WORKING LIVES ON THE RIVER
MERSEY - VIDEO ONLY

Just when you might have thought that the River Mersey was dead and buried the biggest surprise of all comes along. There is life in the old dog yet! The River Mersey Is alive and well. Liverpool, Birkenhead, Tramnere, Eastham and Runcorn are still places that enjoy marine traffic and employ people working on the river. There are interviews with River Pilots, shipbuilders,
shiprepairers,
tugmen and dredgermen that show that the age-old crafts and seamanship itself are still as strong as they ever were.
There is also archive footage of working life on the river. Volume II features Rock Boats, Mersey Ferries, the Bunker boats & crews on the Mersey, the Vessel Tracking System for river traffic,
new vessels on the river, lockmasters and much more. £14.95

Available direct from:-
Avid Publications, Garth Boulevard,
Hr. Bebington, Wirral,
Merseyside, CH63 5LS.
Tel / Fax : 0151 645 2047

e-mail: info@avidpublications.co.uk

Look at the books and dvds /videos on
www.avidpublications.co.uk